Another one
for Kay

WINTER BROTHERS

Books by Ivan Doig

This House of Sky
Winter Brothers
The Sea Runners
English Creek
Dancing at the Rascal Fair

Koot
(The Fish Eagle)

WINTER BROTHERS

A Season at the Edge of America

By Ivan Doig

A Harvest/HBJ Book
Harcourt Brace Jovanovich, Publishers
San Diego   New York   London

The author and the publisher wish to thank the following for their permission to quote material: Institute for the Arts, Rice University, for the lines from Bill Reid on pages 32, 46, and 184 of *Indian Art of the Northwest Coast: A Dialogue on Craftsmanship and Aesthetics*, by Bill Holm and Bill Reid (Houston, Texas: Institute for the Arts, Rice University, 1975; distributed by the University of Washington Press, Seattle); McGraw-Hill Book Company for an excerpt from the diary of Patience Loader as quoted in *The Gathering of Zion* by Wallace Stegner, copyright © 1964 by Wallace Stegner; The New York Times for lines from "Times of the Males," by Wright Morris, *The New York Times Book Review*, January 1, 1979, © 1979 by the New York Times Company. The photograph of James G. Swan and Johnny Kit Elswa was provided by the University of Washington Library, Special Collections. The four Haidah Indian designs, by James G. Swan, are reproduced from the Smithsonian Institution collections through the courtesy of the New York Public Library.

Library of Congress Cataloging in Publication Data

Doig, Ivan.
Winter brothers.
Based on the journals of James Gilchrist Swan.
1. Swan, James Gilchrist. 2. Washington (State)—History—To 1889. 3. Makah Indians.
4. Pioneers—Washington (State)—Biography.
5. Indianists—Washington (State)—Biography.
I. Swan, James Gilchrist. II. Title.
F891.S972D64   979.7'03'0924   [B]   80-7933
ISBN 0-15-697215-8   (Harvest/HBJ : pbk.)

F G H I J

HBJ

THIS ONE IS FOR THE MISSOULA GANG,
WHEN WE OWNED THE WEST.

Bill Bevis	Bill Farr	Steve Krauzer
Juliette Crump	Bud Guthrie	Norman Maclean
M. C. Crump	Carol Guthrie	Bob Reid
Sarah Crump	Duane Hampton	Gayle Reid
Jim Crumley	Dick Hugo	Annick Smith
Madeline DeFrees	Ripley Schemm	Ross Toole
Rick DeMarinis	Dorothy Johnson	Jim Welch
Carol Doig	Margaret Kingsland	Lois Welch
Dave Emmons	Bill Kittredge	

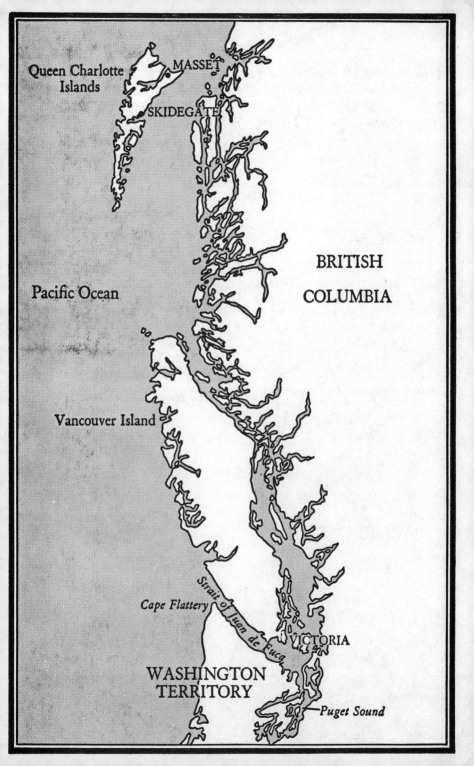

Queen Charlotte
Islands

MASSET

SKIDEGATE

Pacific Ocean

BRITISH

COLUMBIA

Vancouver Island

Cape Flattery

Strait of Juan de Fuca

VICTORIA

WASHINGTON
TERRITORY

Puget Sound

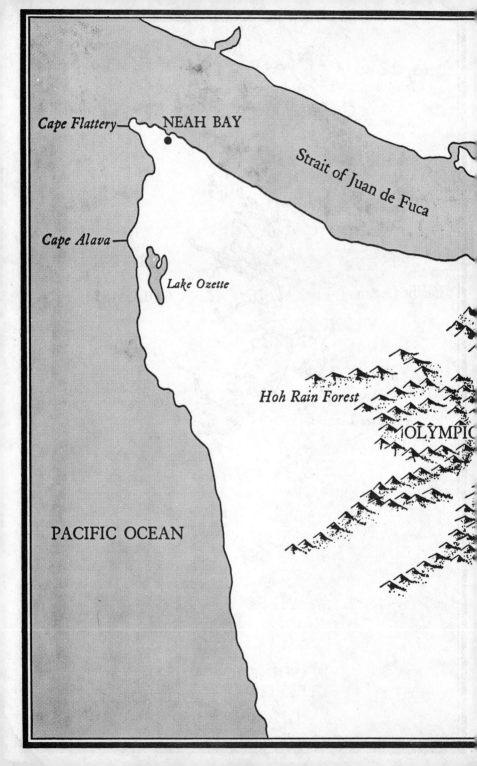

Cape Flattery
NEAH BAY
Strait of Juan de Fuca

Cape Alava

Lake Ozette

Hoh Rain Forest

OLYMPIC

PACIFIC OCEAN

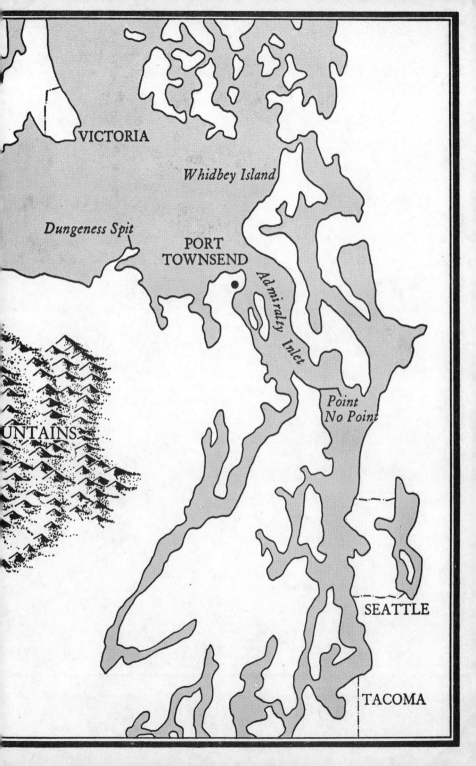

The Boston Bird

HOOYEH
(The Crow)

DAY ONE

His name was James Gilchrist Swan, and I have felt my pull toward him ever since some forgotten frontier pursuit or another landed me into the coastal region of history where he presides, meticulous as a usurer's clerk, diarying and diarying that life of his, four generations and seemingly as many light-years from my own. You have met him yourself in some other form—the remembered neighbor or family member, full of years while you just had begun to grow into them, who had been in a war or to a far place and could confide to you how such vanished matters were. The tale-bringer sent to each of us by the past.

That day, whenever it was, when I made the side trip into archival box after box of Swan's diaries and began to realize that they held four full decades of his life and at least 2,500,000 handwritten words. And what life, what sketching words. *This morning we discovered a large wolf in the brook dead from the effects of some strychnine we had put out. It was a she wolf very large and evidently had five whelps. Maggs and myself skinned her and I boiled the head to get the skull. . . . Mr. Fitzgerald of Sequim Prairie better known as "Skip," walked off the wharf near the Custom House last night and broke his neck. The night was very dark and he mistook the way. . . . Jimmy had the night mare last night and made a great howling. This morning he told me that the memelose were after him and made him crazy. I told him the memelose were dead squid which he ate for supper very heartily. . . . Mr Tucker very ill with his eye, his face is badly swelled. This evening got Kichook's Cowitchan squaw to milk her breast into a cup, and I then bathed Mr Tucker's eye with it....*

I recall that soon I gave up jotting notes and simply thumbed and read. At closing hour, Swan got up from the research table with me. I would write of him sometime, I had decided. Do a magazine piece or two, for I was in the business then of making those smooth packets of a few thousand words. Just use this queer indefatigable diarist Swan some rapid way as a figurine of the Pacific Northwest past.

Swan refused figurinehood, and *rapid* was the one word that never visited his pencils and pens. When, eight, ten years ago, I took a segment of his frontier life and tried to lop it into magazine-article length, loose ends hung everywhere. As well write about Samuel Pepys only what he did during office hours at the British admiralty. A later try, I set out carefully to summarize Swan—oyster entrepreneur, schoolteacher, railroad speculator, amateur ethnologist, lawyer, judge, homesteader, linguist, ship's outfitter, explorer, customs collector, author, small-town bureaucrat, artist, clerk—and surrendered in dizziness, none of the spectrum having shown his true and lasting occupation: diarist. This, I at last told myself, wants more time than I ever can grant it.

Until now. Here is the winter that will be the season of Swan. Rather, of Swan and me and those constant diaries. Day by day, a logbook of what is uppermost in any of the three of us.

It is a venture that I have mulled these past years of my becoming less headlong and more aware that I dwell in a community of time as well as of people. That I should know more than I do about this other mysterious citizenship, how far it goes, where it touches.

And the twin whys: why it has me invest my life in one place instead of another, and why for me that place happens to be western. More and more it seems to me that the westernness of my existence in this land is some consequence having to do with that community of time, one of the terms of my particular citizenship in it. America began as West, the direction off the ends of the docks of Europe. Then the firstcomers from the East of this continent to its West, advance parties of the American quest for place (position, too, maybe, but that is a pilgrimage that interests me less), imprinted our many contour lines of frontier. And next, it still is happening, the spread of national civilization absorbed those lines. Except that markings, streaks and whorls of the West and the past are left in some of us.

Because, then, of this western pattern so stubbornly within my life I am interested in Swan as a westcomer, and stayer. Early, among the very earliest, in stepping the paths of impulse that pull across America's girth of plains and over its continental summit and at last reluctantly nip off at the surf from the Pacific, Swan has gone before me through this matter of siting oneself specifically *here: West.*

The companion I feel an urgency to spend this winter with, meet day by day on the broad seasonal ground of time, here along the continental edge that drew us both.

If Swan attracts me in the way that any oracle among the coastal Indians of the Pacific Northwest inevitably attracted him —that here flashes the bard of a vivid tribe, worth all amount of attention—it is the diaries which throw his particular needle-sharp glints.

The diaries dazzle and dazzle me, first simply by their total and variety: Out of their gray archival boxes at the University of Washington library, they could be the secondhand wares of an eccentric stationer dreamed up by Charles Dickens. Some are mere notebooks with cheap marbled covers, and occasionally even a school exercise book sidles into the collection, but most are formal annual volumes (*for the purpose of registering events of past, present, and future occurrence,* announces the opening page of the 1860 version) and a good number of them display deft clasps to snug themselves closed from outsiders' eyes. It exaggerates marginally to say no two Swan diaries look closer alike than cousins, but I haven't yet turned up three of any single kind. Black-covered and green, tan and faded maroon, what they do present in common is that nearly all are small enough to fit into the palm of a hand, or a busy pocket. Those that won't are actual ledgers, such as the aristocrat of the congregation, 1866, some nine inches wide and twelve high, weighing four and a quarter pounds and displaying an elaborately hinged and embossed spine and a cover panel of leather into the middle of which has been tooled in rich half-inch letters **J. G. Swan.** I can scarcely wait for 1866—lay it open to the first of its 380 lordly pages, and handwriting neat as small embroidery instantly begins to recite: *Diary and private journal of James G. Swan, being a continuation of daily record commencing July 1862 at the Makah Indian Agency Neah Bay, Washington Territory*—but what browsing I have done into any of the diaries has been seductive. Opening the pages of Swan's years is like entering a room filled with jugglers and tumblers and swallowers of flame, performance crowding performance. *Went to see Capt John this morning, found him better. All the Indians except his squaws and children have left the lodge. John is alone in one corner, surrounded by a mat screen. He tells me that the small pox will collect in his head and when it leaves him it will come out of the top of his head like a puff of smoke. To prevent it spreading he has a large hole left open in the roof directly over his head, through which the sickness is expected to escape. . . . Last evening when the gentlemen from the Cutter were here, Capt Williams asked me for a drink of water. I handed him a dipper full from my pail, and he found a live toad in it which I had dipped up from the brook. . . . Bricktop the blacksmith and some other roughs got on a spree & took Hernandez the loony shoemaker to Hunt's Hotel and made him treat. John Cornish was there and stripped himself to his drawers to fight. . . .* Swan records the weather morning-afternoon-night; notes down when salmonberry has popped into spring bloom, when autumn's geese begin to aim past to the southern horizon; logs all ships that sail past his eyes and on along the Strait of Juan de Fuca or Puget Sound; remarks his off days (*Severe attack of neuralgia today Dr. Minn tried to cure it injecting morphine or something of the sort under the skin on my left cheek—This checked the pain but made me feel dizzy & sick at the stomach—the remedy was worse than the disease*) and the other coastal days that

shone as doubloon-bright as the most exhilarating hours anywhere; keeps account of letters written and received, and books
borrowed and lent, and of his exceedingly ramshackle finances.
His jottings overflow the day-by-day pages onto the inside covers of the diaries: mailing addresses of relatives in his native
New England, Indian words and their definitions, sketches. On
one back page *a little Indian girl on the wharf at Seattle*, the
child prettily prone on the planks as she directs a tiny fishing
stick-and-string to the water and a level stare at the pencilman
creating her. Elsewhere the unmistakable pyramidal outline of
Mount Baker, dominant peak of the Strait country; how many
thousand times Swan saw its wide white cone. On an inside
cover inspiration of one more sort, a pasted-in clipping of a
poem by John Greenleaf Whittier: *Though dim as yet in tint and
line / We trace Thy picture's wise design / And thank Thee that
our age supplies / The dark relief of sacrifice / Thy will be done!*

Terrific as the various expended diary energy is, page upon
page and volume after volume, the simple stubborn dailiness of
Swan's achievement seems to me even more dazing. It compares,
say, to that of a carpenter whanging an hour's hammerstrokes
on the same framework each morning for forty years, or a monk
or nun spending that span of time tending the same vineyard. Or
to put it more closely, a penman who a page or so a day writes
out a manuscript the equivalent length of five copies of *War and
Peace*, accomplishing the masterwork in frontier town and Indian village and sometimes no community at all.

For example, this: *This is the 18th day since Swell was shot
and there is no offensive smell from the corpse. It may be accounted for in this manner. He was shot through the body &
afterwards washed in the breakers—consequently all the blood
in him must have run out. He was then rolled up tight in 2 new
blankets and put into a new box nailed up strong.*

Swell was a chieftain of the Makah tribe of Cape Flattery,
that westmost prow of this coast. He also was Swan's best-
regarded friend among the coastal tribes of Washington Territory, a man Swan had voyaged with, learned legends from. The

diary pages show them steadily swapping favors: now Swell detailing for Swan the Makahs' skill at hunting whales, now Swan painting for Swell in red and black *his name and a horse on his canoe sail. Swell said he always went faster in his canoe than the other Indians . . . like a horse, so he wanted to have one painted. . . .* On yet another diary end-page there is the roughed outline of a galloping horse and above it in block letters the name *SWELL,* with five-pointed stars fore and aft. If Swan carried out the design, Swell sailed under the gaudiest canvas in the North Pacific.

I know the beach at Crescent Bay where Swell's life was snapped off. Across on the Canadian shore of the Strait of Juan de Fuca the lights of modern Victoria now spread as white embers atop the burn-dark rim of coastline, and west from the city occasional lighthouses make blinks against the black as the Strait seeks toward the Pacific. But on Swell's final winter night in 1861 only a beach campfire at Crescent on our southern shore flashed bright enough to attract the eye, and Swell misread the marker of flame as an encampment of traveling members of his own tribe. Instead, he stepped from his canoe to find that the overnighters were from a nearby village of Elwha Indians, among them chanced to be a particular rival of Swell, and his bullet spun the young Makah dead into the cold quick surf.

The killing was less casual than the downtown deaths my morning newspaper brings me three or four times a week—the Elwhas and the Makahs at least had the excuse of lifetimes of quarrel—or those I might go see in aftermath, eligible as I am for all manner of intrusion because of being a writer, were I to accompany the Seattle homicide squad. James G. Swan did go hurrying to be beside Swell's corpse, and there the first of our differences is marked.

A morning soon after learning of Swell's death Swan strolled into the Elwha village. *Charley, the murderer, then got up and made a speech. He said that he shot Swell for two reasons, one of which was, that the Mackahs had killed two of the Elwha's a few months previous, and they were determined to kill a Mac-kah chief to pay for it. And the other reason was, that Swell had taken his squaw away, and would not return either the woman or the fifty blankets he had paid for her.*

Swan was not swerved. *I could not help feeling while standing up alongside this murderer . . . that I would gladly give a pull at the rope that should hang him. . . .* The day's chastisement was administered with vocal cords rather than hemp, however. *My object was not to punish or kill Indians, but to recover property.* Swan haggled out of Charley the potware Swell had been carrying as cargo for a trader, several blankets, and a dozen yards of calico, and *as I had no authority to make them disgorge any other plunder* called it sufficient.

Swan next carried the matter of Swell's death to the federal Indian agent for Washington Territory. Met inconclusion there. Sent a seething letter to the newspaper in the territorial capital of Olympia . . . *an Indian peaceably passing on his way home in his canoe, laden with white men's goods . . . foully murdered . . . too good an Indian and too valuable a man . . . to have his murder go unavenged . . . agents of our munificent government have not the means at their disposal to defray the expenses of going to arrest the murderer. . . .* And at last canoed once more along the Strait to accompany Swell, still nailed up strong, to burial at the Makah village of Neah Bay.

At Neah, Swell's brother Peter *came and wished me to go with him and select a suitable spot to bury Swell. . . .*

I did as he desired—marked out the spot and dug out the first sand.

And this further: Peter *also brought up the large Tomanawas boards*—the Makahs' cedar tableaus of magic which would stand as the grave's monument—*of Swell's for me to paint anew. . . .*

There, then, is Swan, or at least a shinnying start on him. A penman from Boston asked to trace afresh the sacred designs of a murdered Northwest chieftain. I can think of few circumstances less likely, unless they are my own. The onlooker who has set himself this winter's appointment back into the last century and across geography to the Olympic Peninsula and elsewhere along the coastal tracery of Puget Sound and the Strait of Juan de Fuca, and indeed into the life of a person born ten dozen years before him.

DAY TWO

... Capt John was here today, Swan writes from a century ago, *and I related to him a dream I had last night, in which I saw several Indians I formerly knew who are dead. John said it was a sign the "memelose" or dead people are my friends and I would soon see that they would do something to show their friendship....*

Fifteen past nine. Out in the dark the Sound wind visits favorite trees, is shaken off, hankers along the valley in stubborn search. The gusting started up hours ago, during the gray fade of daylight that is December evening, and by now seems paced to try to last the night. Until the wind arrives with dusk, these past days have been at rest: sunless but silent and dry. The neighborhood's lion-colored cat, inspector general of such weather, all morning tucked himself atop the board fence outside the north window as I began to read Swan. Out of his furry doze each several minutes a sharp cat ear would twitch, give the air a tan flick just to be certain it still could. Then the self-hug into snooze again.

The breakers, now Swan the third day after his dream, *tore up the beach and rooted out immense numbers of clams which were thrown up by the surf. I gathered a few buckets full and soon the squaws and Indians came flocking up like so many gulls and gathered at least fifty bushels....*

Nine-nineteen. I see, by leaning to hear into the wind, that the night-black window which faces west off the end of my desk collects the half of me above the desktop and its spread sheaf of copied diary pages into quiet of my own.

Nine-twenty. *Capt John told me,* this the morning following the beach bonanza, *that the cause of the great quantity of clams*

*on the beach yesterday was the dead people I dreamed about the
other night and they put the clams there to show their friendship....*

Nine twenty-one. Last night at this time, winter began. I noticed the numbered throb of the moment—the arrival of season
at precisely 21:21 hours of December 21—which took us
through solstice as if we, too, the wind and I and the fencetop
cat and yes, Swan and the restless memories of departed Makahs,
were being delivered by a special surf. The lot of us, now aus-
piciously into the coastal time of beginnings. Perhaps I need a
Captain John to pronounce full meaning from that.

No, better. I am going to have Swan's measuring sentences,
winterlong.

DAY THREE

A phrase recalled this morning from John McNulty when he
wrote of having journeyed to his ancestors' Ireland: that he had
gone "back where I had never been."

Our perimeters are strange, unexpectedly full of flex when we
touch against them just right. A winter such as this of mine—or
any season, of a half-hour's length or a year's, spent in hearing
some venturer whose lifespan began long before our own—I
think must be a kind of border crossing allowed us by time:
special temporary passage permitted us if we seek out the right
company for it, guides such as Swan willing to lead us back
where we have never been.

So Swan on one side of the century-line, myself on the other.
Bearded watchful men both, edge-walkers of the continent, more
interested in one another's company than the rest of the world is
interested in ours, but how deeply alike and different? That is
one of the matters Swan is to tell me, these journal days when I
stretch across to his footings of time.

James G. Swan had hastened west in the same scurry as many

thousands of other mid-nineteenth-century Americans. Their word isn't much known today, but at the time they were called *Argonauts*, the seekers drawn to the finds of gold in California streambeds as if they had glimpsed wisps of the glittering fleece that lured Jason and his Greeks. Like Jason's, the journey for many of them was by ship, the very impatience for wealth to come evidently weighting the sailing vessels to slowness. Swan stepped aboard the *Rob Roy* in Boston harbor in late January of 1850 and climbed off at San Francisco a half-year later.

What exact cache of promises and excuses this man of New England left behind him can't be known in detail, but they likely amounted to considerable. Something of the bulk and awkwardness of my own, I suppose, when I veered from Montana ranching to college and a typewriter. Swan was thirty-two years old when he set foot on the Pacific Coast. By the time of his birth in 1818—Turgenev's year, Karl Marx's year—in the north-of-Boston village of Medford, the Swan family name already had been transplanted from Yorkshire to Massachusetts for eighteen decades, evidently the devout achieving sort of New England clan which began to count itself gentry from the moment the Indians could be elbowed out of sight into the forest. (Swan himself was known to mention the family point of pride that his great-grandfather had been a landowner *on the N.W. side of Bunker Hill*, the Revolutionary War battleground.) Merchants, doctors, educators, lawyers populate the erect generations. Swan's own older brothers stayed standard, Samuel as physician, Benjamin a minister.

But not James. He evidently reached down the excuse that occasional seafarers had cropped up in the family—his own father, said to have been lost in a gale while captaining a brig back from Africa in 1823; a legendarily adventurous uncle who had sailed in an early fur-trading vessel to the Pacific Northwest —and in his midteens started in on the try of a waterfront life in Boston.

Dallying around the docks, first as a clerk with a shipping firm and eventually as a merchandiser of ships' supplies, must have suited the young Swan comfortably enough. With forests of sail sweeping back and forth before his eyes and the new steam vessels shuddering to life around him, this adventurer of the waterfront shows no sign that he made any ocean voyage of his own until he was twenty-three. Then he embarked on a Boston-to-Liverpool jaunt with a chore or two of his employer's business attached and seems to have been content to do it just the once.

That once to Britain, however, jarred Swan's writing hand into motion, and by my terms the wan sheaf of paper that has survived comes as ancient and entrancing and intriguingly hued as a cave painting. The thirty brownish tatty-edged long manuscript pages are by a decade the earliest of all Swan's surviving paperwork, and must be a version he copied from a pocket notebook—it would have been the start of that habit, too—as soon as he returned to America. Any comparable paperwork having to do with my family would be drily governmental, in the Scottish archives, and likely would show sundry Doigs irretrievably in arrears on croft taxes or enlisting one of our number to die an infantry death in Madras or the Crimea. A bonus of archival magic, it is for me, that the pages of Swan's life from his own hand begin here on the second of March 1841 and recite the two months in which he sailed the Atlantic and rambled interestedly around Britain.

The wilderness of waters which surround us on his crossing; the storm which tossed a fellow passenger beneath the table and his breakfast after him, *his head was covered with a shower of fried eggs which looked for all the world like doubloons stuck in his hair*; arrival to Liverpool and St. Patrick's Day, *the Irish have been walking in procession the whole day . . . all rigged out with green sashes and sprigs of shamrock, a species of weed similar to the chick weed.* Weather, conveyance, schedule, meals, roadside fields, birds of those fields, even Swan's morning disposition: *I was very stupid today,* the sixteenth of March, *from the want of sleep last night and for the first time since I left home I felt really homesick & would have been glad to have been home but as soon as I walked out I felt much relieved & hope to get my thoughts on a business train after a good nights rest.* All, all come on report at the nib of his pen. So, too, the social impress of Britain of Dickens's time. Liverpool astounds and horrifies this Bostonian with the hurly-burly of its streets: *female scavengers . . . go round with baskets and collect all the manure & offal in the city which they put in heaps & offer then for sale. Their heaps are bought by the gardeners for a few pence to enrich the garden beds—It struck me as the filthiest work I had ever seen a woman engaged in & more especially as they used nothing but their hands to work with.* Then the proverbial fishwives, *a queer lot of beings & probably the lowest of the human race.* Quickly the unsurprising exclamation: *Liverpool is a shocking dirty place & I am sick enough of it.* But Edinburgh is beguiling, *the streets are laid out with a good deal of taste,* and the trip southward a lark: *In the carriage with me were a party of Irish Gentlemen & Ladies. . . . They all took me for a Scotchman & as I had just left Scotland I could talk to them finely.* London proves to be downright wondrous, *Walked two hours this morning in one direction & every step of the way the street was crowded with people & vehicles.* His young American eyes have not seen the like except possibly on a Boston market day when a drawbridge over the Charles River would hold up traffic, *the crowd then is just the same as the streets are here all the time from sunrise to sunset.* He glimpses the young queen, Victoria, trundling out of the Buckingham Palace grounds on her way to church: *had a good sight of her face as she was looking out the carriage window she had on a little blue silk bonnet.* He is drawn back and back to the stupendous dome of St. Paul's, even though the Easter service there seems to him *mumbled over in a very bad manner.* Tours the new museum of wax figures *shown by an old French woman & her son*—the Tussauds—*who are making a deal of money out of this affair.* Rides the night mail train from London back to Liverpool: *they go with the greatest velocity sometimes 50 miles an hour*—about as fast as you could travel on the planet at the time—*only stopping to get water.*

Swan-among-the-Britons arrives at the last line of his journey having viewed *a great deal to admire & much to censure,* and that already is the exact Swan style I have begun to find amid his accumulating day-by-day pages on my desk, here at our shared ledge of the American landscape: banquet of details, ready snifters of opinion.

Something else of moment happened to Swan that year of 1841. He married rather above himself. Matilda Loring, of a prominent Boston printing and publishing family, a small, neatly built woman with a firm line of jaw, became his bride on the twenty-sixth of October.

Of the courtship and its aftermath Swan's archival heap of paper is all too conspicuously silent. But from the circumstances, this reads as one of those marriages in which it is unclear whether the wife chided because the husband took on the world's whiskey as a personal challenge or the husband fled into the bottle because the wife was a shrike. What is plain enough even in the thumbing scan of his life I have been doing these first days is that Swan continued to court the bottle long after, in the eighth year of marriage to Matilda, he pointed himself west across America.

I hunger to have overheard just how he said that pivoting decision. Swan and Matilda were living apart by the year 1849 —he in a Boston boardinghouse handy to his waterfront life; she in Chelsea with the two children of the divided household, four-year-old Ellen and seven-year-old Charles—and did Swan simply come onto the porch one day and offer, *Matilda, I have been thinking I will go to California?*

The many weeks to round Cape Horn in 1850, the long climbing voyage along the Pacific shores, arrival: then Swan, to judge by his readiest recollection, was like a good many of us ever since in not quite knowing what to make of California. Dozens, scores of deserted ships clogged the San Francisco harbor he sailed into, a fleet of *Marie Celeste*s left ghostly by crews which had swarmed to the goldstrikes.

Swan, too, completed the pilgrimage up the Sacramento to the mining camps, but only as a purser on a river steamer. I find that he hesitated in that job, and at a maritime firm's dockside office in San Francisco, for only a matter of weeks, then signed onto a schooner bound for Hawaii to take aboard a cargo of potatoes.

Why Swan so promptly went sailing off for spuds is not at all clear to me, but his ear must have heard sweet somethings out there in the Pacific. The abrupt jaunt into the ocean does seem to have been instructive. (A proclamation from this period of his life: *I never yet found that information was useless to any one.*) He managed to linger at Lahaina on the Isle of Maui for twenty-five days, and one of his rare surviving letters to Matilda gives the islands and islanders a dozen pages of the same blunderbuss observation Liverpool and London had received: *on great occasions or when the white men will pay the expenses they get up a feast called a Lu wow. . . . This Lu wow consists of a series of Baked dishes such as Dogs Hogs Turkeys fowls fish Fruits and Greens. . . . Their native dances being prohibited are only given by stealth or by express invitation of the whites. They are called Hoolah hoolah. I was desirous of seeing one. . . . The natives all call themselves mickonaree or missionary which is the term they use to express their ideas of christianity . . . there are but very few really sincere & devout persons among them, and are mostly like one I saw in Mr. Bolles store, who was cutting up some capers, when Mr B remarked, I thought you was a missionary Yes said the fellow pointing to his mouth "me mickonary here, all rest no mickonary."*

Back from that sudden Hawaiian sojourn, Swan at once settled again into a dockside way of life in San Francisco, again as a clerk for a ship-outfitting firm, through the rest of 1850, and through 1851, and through most of 1852. Evidently he found life sufficiently interesting by just being away from Massachusetts and alongside the rougher torrent of California waterfront traffic. His routine indeed seems to have been all but identical to the career left behind him in Boston except that he could do it at about half speed and without regard for hometown opinion: laxities which have been high among the rewards of the West ever since there was an America.

Then, late in 1852, down from the Oregon country to San Francisco arrived Charles J. W. Russell.

A self-described oyster entrepreneur, this visitor from the shaggy North was better portrayed by Swan as *possessing a good deal of the romancing spirit of the Baron Munchausen.* Russell had materialized in Oregon Territory in dream of some real estate scheme at the mouth of the Columbia River, found that he was a number of generations ahead of his time with that notion, and instead ended up at Shoalwater Bay, some few miles north of the Columbia, where he began dispatching shiploads of oysters to San Francisco. Even at the distance of 130 years the gent has a sheen. Russell in his swanky spielster's way invited Swan to the oystering enterprise, and Swan seems to have accepted as rapidly as he could get the words out of his mouth.

I have prowled the Washington coastline where Swan plopped ashore at the end of 1852, and a misted, spongy, oozeful kind of place it is. On the western rim of bay what appears from a distance to be a line of white-gabled houses proves to be the foaming surf of the Pacific. The salt water reaches hungrily in through this entrance, and in a momentous splatter of inlets and fingers, the bay lying stretched from north to south for twenty-five miles and nearly ten across its greatest width, mingles with the inflow of half a dozen sizable rivers and who knows how many creeks and seeps. This mix yields a maximum of tan marshes and gray muddy tideflats, twenty-seven of these Shoalwater sloughs having been granted names by mapmakers and almost as many more not thought worth the effort. Yet around its eastern extent the squishy bay surprises a visitor with sudden firm timber-topped cliffs about a hundred feet high. *Banks of a sandy clay,* Swan once categorized them, *intermingled with strata of shells and remains of ancient forest-trees that for ages have been buried.*

All in all, a vast estuarine pudding in a clay bowl. One of the few ascertainable advances since Swan's time has been the amendment of the big shallow bay's name from Shoalwater to the less embarrassing Willapa.

When Swan showed up here, more than likely shaking the rain off his hat brim, Shoalwater Bay's sum of civilization totted up as a few huts, a temporary crew of sawyers cutting pilings, a shifting population of members of the Chinook and Chehalis tribes, and fourteen white "residents" who pottered away at oystering or homesteading. Fourteen kinds of Swan, it could be pertinently said. The flotsam group of whites hired the Indians to do the bulk of the oyster harvesting; the Indians held their own leisured ebb-and-flow view of life. Put at its more generous, this colony on the eastern shore of Shoalwater Bay in the early 1850s—Bruceport, it was dubbed, in memory of the schooner *Robert Bruce* which caught fire and burned to a hulk there— amounted more to an episode of prolonged beachcombing than a serious effort at enterprise. And Swan, stretching ever more distance between himself and those 220 years of New England rectitude in his family line, Swan fit with the idling oysterers like a pinky in an opera glove.

Much of the lulling appeal of that beachside life, as Swan recounts it, was simply the stomach's common sense. The bay in those days set a kind of floating feast, offering as it did clams, crabs, shrimp, mussels, sand lobster, salmon, sturgeon, trout, turbot, sole, flounder, and, of course, oysters. The facet of Swan that was an interested and inventive cook—his victuals often make a sudden savory appearance in his pages; among the Indian delicacies he tried and liked are seal liver and cold raccoon —couldn't help prizing this easy bounty. Just once in these plump years did Swan undergo a hungry time, and that was during one hectic onset of winter spent under a shared roof with an old whaling captain named Purrington. *The captain was famous for cooking every thing that had ever lived. We had eaten of young eagles, hawks, owls, lynx, beaver, seal, otter, gulls, pelican, and, finally wound up with crow; and the crow was the worst of the lot. The captain once tried to bake a skunk, but not having properly cleaned it, it smelt so unsavory when the bake-kettle was opened that he was forced to throw skunk and kettle into the river, which he did with a sigh, remarking what a pity it was that it smelled so strong, when it was baked so nice and brown.*

While Swan carried on his love affair with Shoalwater's food and leisure, he likely flirted often enough with alcohol as well. The bayside residents, white and native, emerge out of his words and those of others as a boozy bunch who did as much roistering as oystering. One Fourth of July, to take the prime frolicsome example, after orations and eating and a *feu-de-joie by the guns and rifles of the whole company*, the Shoalwater patriots stumbled onto the inspiration *to close the performances for the day by going on top of the cliff opposite, and make a tremendous big blaze*. They found a colossal hollow cedar stump, filled it to the brim with dry spruce limbs, touched the pyre off. *It made the best bonfire I ever saw*, Swan recollected with considerable understatement, *and after burning all night and part of the next day, finally set fire to the forest, which continued to burn for several months, till the winter rains finally extinguished it.*

A jolly conflagration of four or five months' duration couldn't have been entirely usual, but much other unsober behavior was. And when Swan remarked of one of his Shoalwater compatriots that *like all the rest of the frontier people, he was fond of Old Rye*, the unwritten admission is there that also among those frontier people was numbered James G. Swan.

In the spring of 1853 when the region north of the Columbia River was hived off from Oregon to become Washington Territory, several of the Shoalwater oysterboys had been inspired to file for land claims. Swan selected a site at the mouth of what is now the Bone River (the Querquelin, it was called by the Indians: Mouse River) on the bay's northeastern shore. Reasoning that the absence of a wife by some three thousand miles didn't really unhinge the marital status all that much, he claimed 160 acres for himself and a second 160 for Matilda.

A half-mile manor of frontier conjured from ink. *I was perfectly delighted with the place*, Swan enthuses in one breath, and notes in the next that the unwooded portion stood overgrown with nettles and ferns three feet high. In that divided comment he sounds precisely like my kin who grew up on our pair of Doig homesteads south of Helena, entranced to the end of their lives with memory of the blue-timbered glory of the Big Belt mountains and still furious with the impossible winter snows as well.

Swan and the convivial Captain Purrington eventually set about building a cabin on the new riverside estate. Their cabin work went at a creep, or something less. You can all but see the pair of them, midmorning upon midmorning, sighing regret at the blisters on their hands and settling onto a handy log for the captain to recite another sea story. With winter stalking in fast, they at last cobbled together a shack from the split cedar boards of an abandoned Indian lodge, and Swan inventively masoned a huge fireplace out of clay blocks cut from a nearby cliff. The first real storm of winter made mud of his handiwork, *sluiced a couple of bushels of coals and ashes into the middle of the room* and very nearly set the abode ablaze. Not long after, Swan catches a schooner back to San Francisco, to clerk under a dry roof until spring.

Fresh dollars in his pocket, he is on display again at Shoalwater at the start of summer 1854. For the first of numerous times in his life Swan now wangles a brief, modest niche in the federal payroll. He was appointed assistant customs collector *for that portion of the coast north of the Columbia, including Shoalwater Bay and Gray's Harbor to Cape Flattery; the duties of the office being to report all vessels arriving at or departing from Shoal-water Bay, and to keep a diligent watch on the coast to see that none of the Russian or Hudson Bay Companies' vessels came around either for smuggling or trading with the Indians.*

Since this comprised an all-but-empty stretch of shore, with only the lackadaisical oysterers at Shoalwater, a handful of stump farmers and sawmillers up around Grays Harbor, and the tiny tribal settlements at a few river mouths, Swan's precinct seems to have been spectacularly free of major smuggling prospects. The only time he is on record as having had to exert himself was when the Indians, as a joke, lured him several days up the coast to check on a vessel which turned out to be a U.S. Geological Survey steamship. Swan being Swan, he did not much mind the futile jaunt. *So far as related to smuggling, I had walked sixty miles up the beach for no purpose, but I did not regret having started, as I had seen a line of coast which few, if any white men had been over before.*

Months slid past, years began to go. Yet not nearly all of Swan's time at Shoalwater could have been spent promenading the coast or aiming himself into the bottom of a bottle. He has left us a frontier view greatly wider and deeper than that. The maraud of a smallpox outbreak at Shoalwater which merely made the white men ill but slaughtered the Chinooks and Chehalis. The pride of place when selecting a homestead site. The casual reach of distance as Swan strolled sixty miles of wild coast to gaze upon an innocent steamship. These carry a sense of this rough margin of the west as true as a thumb testing the teeth of a ripsaw. And all of them derive from Swan as serious and published author, in a work I have been quoting from ever since he squished ashore at Shoalwater. (If Swan was diarying regularly in these years, and I judge he was not, although he mentions having written and lost a collection of notes about the Indians, the volumes never have come to sight.) *The Northwest Coast*, he titled the book, then thought he had better elucidate: *Or Three Years' Residence in Washington Territory*.

This coastal drifter, then, this dabbling man born two decades or so before my own great-grandfather, spent part of his life at the enterprise I do, shaping words into print. Whether the fact nudges Swan closer into resemblance of me or me to Swan I am not ready to say, but certainly it fetches both of us into the same cottage industry at least some hours of the week. I imagine that Swan, like me, when he held pen in hand for another chapter of *Northwest Coast* or, as later, to begin an article for a frontier newspaper, had his times of wishing he had chosen some sounder cottage job, such as lacemaking or raising chinchillas. I imagine as well that in the next minute or so he was knuckle-deep into the words again. Cottagers have to be like that.

Harper & Brothers brought out *Northwest Coast* in 1857, and with its lore of baked skunks and patriotic pyromania the tome stands as a jaunty grandfather of us all who face west above our typewriters. But more than that. This book of Swan's time at Shoalwater conveys, as he would in the diary pages for all the length of his life, his rare knack of looking at the coastal Indians as flesh and blood rather than the frontier's tribal rubble.

He does not go all the way, sometimes dwelling overmuch on the simplicities of the bay's natives, while he and the other oysterboys were not exactly an advanced institute themselves. Oftener than not, however, his remarks carry uncommon sympathy and insight about the Chinooks and Chehalis:

The Indians can see but little or no difference between their system of Tomanawos and our own views as taught them. For instance, the talipus, or fox, is their emblem of the creative power; the swispee, or duck, that of wisdom. And they say that the Boston people, or Americans, have for their Tomanawos the wheark, or eagle and that the King George, or English people, have a lion for their Tomanawos.

Or again: *One day, while being more than usually inquisitive, old Suis . . . after trying to make me understand that the names I was asking about had no meaning, at last said, "Why, you white people have names like ours; some mean something, and others mean nothing. I know your name, Swan, is like our word Cocumb, and means a big bird; and Mr. Lake's name is for water, like Shoalwater Bay. But what does Mr. Russell's or Baldt's, or Champ's or Hillyer's, or Sweeney's, or Weldon's name mean?"*

I told her I did not know. "Well," she replied, "so it is with us. We don't know what those names you have asked mean; all we know is that they were the names of our ancestors—elip tillicums, or first people."

Thoughtful jots about first people, and the tamanoas of whites. The time of comradeship with Swell and the honor to repaint his funeral boards lay not so far ahead from such lines.

With Swan you never know where a competence is going to lead, if indeed it ever ambles anywhere. It is his skill with the native lore and languages which now transports him for a while out of the Pacific Northwest. In the mid-1850s, territorial officials of Oregon and Washington began to summon the Northwest tribes into treaty councils. These worked out as was usual in our continental history: The Indians got a chance for soulful rhetoric, and the whites got the land. When this ritualistic process of dispossession reached southwesternmost Washington with a treaty parley at a site on the Chehalis River in February 1855, Swan inevitably was on hand, having been invited by Territorial Governor Isaac I. Stevens to come over from the coast and interpret. Swan's service lasted beyond the riverbank oratory. When Stevens later was elected territorial delegate to Congress, Swan the scholarly frontiersman was enlisted as his secretary.

First his follow of Charles J. W. Munchausen-Russell up to Shoalwater, now this traipse back around the continent behind a political patron. Moves of this sort cause me to think Swan must have been something like a jack in life's deck, not a man of an instinct quite to be king. A bit of a courtier, say.

In any case, the Swan trajectory now loops from the frontier Washington to the governmental Washington. But only until Stevens's term in Congress concludes. Swan then swerves like an oiled windvane to the Pacific Northwest again.

Not again to Shoalwater and the oystering life, however. On some amalgam of advice from Stevens that the community might be a comer and his own none-too-well-formed notion that he maybe would set up a supply station for whaling ships, Swan decides this time his site will be the customs port for Washington Territory, an aspiring frontier village called Port Townsend.

The location was, and is, one of the most intriguing on this continent. The Strait of Juan de Fuca swings broadly in from the Pacific, a fat fjord between the Olympic Mountains of Washington and the lower peaks of British Columbia's Vancouver Island, until at last, after a hundred miles and precisely at the brink of land which holds Port Townsend, the span of water turns southward in a long, sinuous stretch like an arm delving to the very bottom of a barrel. The topmost portion is Admiralty Inlet; the rest of the thrusting arm of channel is Puget Sound. I live at its elbow. This small valley which holds my house is one of the wrinkles in the Sound's tremendous timber-green sleeves.

So it is that there is a route I walk regularly, a few hundred strides along this suburban valley, to the bluff above my house for a studying look northwestward, to where the Sound bends off toward the Strait. Around that horizon, at six on the morning of

February 13, 1859, Swan awakes aboard the schooner *Dash-away* to find the ship passing the lighthouse at Dungeness Spit, coming on the wind into these waters where he will spend the rest of his years.

DAY FOUR

Sour ink today, Swan's and mine both. Again I am alone in the house, a week now, and the fact echoes. The cottony moodless weather which arrived yesterday does not help. No winter I have spent in the Pacific Northwest—this will make an even dozen—ever has been as grayly bland and excitementless as the season's reputation. ("Oh, *Seattle*," anyone from elsewhere will begin, and one of the next three words is "rain.") There can be winter weeks here when the Pacific repeatedly tries to throw itself into the air and out across the continent, an exhilarating traffic of swooping storms. Other durations when the days arrive open-skied and glittering, the mountains of the Olympic and Cascade ranges a spill of rough white gems along two entire horizons. All else quiet, this modest valley invites wind, the flow of air habiting to the southwesterly mood of winter and arriving into this green vee like rainflow to a stream bed. Oceanburst or brave thin days of sun or spurting breeze, Northwest winter I enjoy as restless, startful; except that this gray first of morning, it has followed me onto dead center.

To work, the reliable season of the alone. To Swan, that other winterer. As I have told, by the time Swan spoke good-bye to Matilda and the East in the first month of 1850 there were two children of the divided household: Ellen, four, and Charles, seven. In that moment Swan jettisoned them. Left daughter and son to Matilda and her lineal Boston colony as part of his passage price, which he seems to have been little enough agonized about assuming, for his leaving of New England.

At about the age of Charles, I was jettisoned myself, by the death of my mother. Following my father up and down our

Montana ranching valley I began to learn that a sundered family can heal strongly across the break. If, that is, the remaining parent possesses the strength of stubbornness, and I think it can be granted that Matilda likely had her share of that. Hard witness that I am today, then, I am able to wish for Charles and Ellen only that they could have come argonauting with Swan. To reverse him in the imagination from stepping aboard the ship to San Francisco is merely to see him spending his time on the Boston waterfront, or any other waterfront, in preference to twiddling under the family roof. To transfer the roof with him, Swan and Matilda and the children all staunchly mutual new citizens of the Pacific shore, is to find the family settling to the grooved routines of a city neighborhood again; likely in Portland, with its New England affiliations. But could the Swan youngsters have grown up at their father's inquisitive side here along this new coast in the life he led, absorbing the Indian languages and lore as he did, poking along the shore with him into the bays he appraised like a portraitist, stooping as he did to the frontier's odd bouquets of salal and kinnickinnick and yarrow and skunk cabbage, what western venturers that daughter and that son might have been.

Come they did not, of course; could not except as I would reinvent their lives; and but for Swan's scanty visits back to Boston heard their father's voice only from across the continent, by the paper echo of mail, for the next half-century.

Evening, last inches of the leaden day. Ellen and Charles missed sprigs of knowledge indeed when their father left them to Boston. From Swell's tribe, the Makahs, Swan noted down that their version of the sun arrived robustly each morning by thrusting away the stars with his head and trampling night underfoot. Rainbows, they considered, had claws at either end to seize the unwary. Comets and meteors were the luminous souls of dead chiefs. As for the mysterious northern lights that sometimes webbed the sky beyond the Strait, Swell explained them astutely to Swan:

Under that star, many snow's sail from here in a canoe, live a race of little men, very strong, who are dressed in skins. They look like Indians, but they are not taller than half the length of my paddle. They can dive down into the sea and catch a seal or a fish with their hands. Their country is very cold, and they live on the ice where they build great fires, and that light is the fires of those little people....

Swell as tutor about Eskimo life puts light on something else as well. Along the wilderness that was the North Pacific coastland, more than five hundred miles of broken shore from Neah Bay even to southernmost Alaska and greater distances beyond that to the people of the ice, ideas of that sort must have traveled like thistledown on puffs of breeze: canoeing tribe in wary touch with canoeing tribe, a seed of story deposited, to be borne along by the next barter-trip southward. By the time the Makahs received the story of the miniature ice-men of the north, lore had been nurtured into legend. I recognize such wafts of alchemy, for I live with them as well. A morning in the nineteen-twenties a dozen riders are returning to their home ranches after a weekend rodeo. Whenever the horses' hoofs strike the dryness of a Montana country road, dust drifts up until from a distance the group looks like men of smoke. Most of the journey, however, cuts across open sageland, and the slap of the gray tassels of brush against leather chaps competes with their talk of the rodeo broncs. Unexpectedly the loose troop reins to a halt. Across a stretch of pasture they have always ridden through, a fresh barbed-wire fence glints. The owner of the land emerges from a nearby cabin to explain that he intends to plow the ground, that they can no longer go across the field-to-be. A rider with a notch-scar in the center of his chin—he was my father—grins down at the man and says in his style of half-joke, half-declaration: "We never saw any place yet we couldn't go." Turning his horse to the fence, he touches spur to flank, and mount and man pass through the air above the blades of wire. One after another the others soar after him, like boys on great birds of sorrel, roan, dapple gray.

The story and its impromptu anthem of the West's last horseback generation have come down to me, on embellishing lips, very much as legends of the Eskimos must have arrived south to Swell. "The same winds blow spring on all men's dreams," I read once from a folklorist. Whether there were a dozen rodeoers or just four; whether they all lofted themselves in the barbed-wire steeplechase or just the rider with that starred chin: in the tale as it has whiffed to me, they are twelve and they soar.

DAY FIVE

Christmas.
Carol steps from the airport ramp at 6:03 P.M., five lofted hours from New Jersey. Swan in his lifetime managed to go from one coast of America to the other, and back, a half-dozen times. In the fourteen years of our marriage Carol and I have crisscrossed the continent on family visits or business so many times we have lost count.

The retributive pun I have been saving for days—"Hey, I've heard of you. The Christmas Carol, right?"—draws her groan and grin. We hold each other, amid the community of hugs of families reuniting. The New Jersey report is good; her parents are in health, and chipper.

Our car enters the freeway aqueduct of headlights streaming north to the city. We are to stop for Christmas dinner at the home of friends. On the table we can predict will be sauerkraut from her Baltimore, pecan pie from his Texas. Christmas Day of 1861 on the Strait, I read in the pages this morning, Swan set to work at this business of holiday dinner with similar seriousness. Duck stew and roast goose he produced for his guests, a pair of other batching pioneers, then brought out his gamble of the day. That autumn when a Makah canoeman had presented him a chunk of whale meat, Swan thoughtfully boiled it and chopped it, plopped in apples, raisins, wild cranberries, currants, brown sugar, salt, cloves, nutmeg, allspice, cinnamon, and a quart of rum, then crocked the works in a stone jar. These months later he cautiously offers to his guests slivers of the baked result. Lifts a forkful himself, chews appraisingly for a moment. The eyes of the holiday trio light in elation, and they hurry on to further helpings of the whalemince pie.

DAYS SIX, SEVEN, EIGHT, NINE, TEN

I have begun to follow Swan exactly year by year through his long muster of diaries. His own brevets of identification still are on them—a small paper label on each cover where the title of a book would appear, the year inked there in his slanting hand—and upon opening the earliest diary, 1859, I found that it advertises itself as *Marsh's Metallic Memorandum Book WITH METALLIC PENCIL The writing of which is as permanent as when written with ink,* a claim I could now tell Swan is not nearly true. Luckily his experiment with Marsh's wan stylus ended when Swan ran out of pages in the memo book on the last day of August and switched to a plain tan pocket notebook and an ordinary pencil of blessed black clarity. But it is back in those dimmest of pages, early 1859, that Swan's daily words of his Pacific Northwest life commence: the twenty-ninth of January, when he embarked at San Francisco *on board ship Dashaway Capt J M Hill ... bound for Pt Townsend, W.T.*

When the *Dashaway* hove into Port Townsend on a morning in mid-February, a few weeks past Swan's forty-first birthday, almost precisely at the midpoint of his life, the diary shows that Swan at once ruddered himself as many directions as there were routes of water spoking out from the little frontier port. The editor of the San Francisco *Evening Bulletin* had agreed to buy from him a series of articles about Washington Territory; what San Francisco didn't take, Swan could readily place in one or another of the weekly papers in the fledgling port towns of Puget Sound; and there still hovered that proclaimed notion of his *to examine certain harbors, with a view of ascertaining the best locality for a whaling station.* Whenever a ride could be hitched by schooner, steamboat, or canoe, then off Swan would jaunt along the Strait or into the serpentine length of Puget Sound, up amid the San Juan archipelago or across Admiralty Inlet to long-cliffed Whidbey Island. His wake of ink shows him voyaging in and out of Port Townsend, his purported new site of enterprise, eight times in the first six months.

Inside all that motion, however, a pattern is shaping. Time upon time Swan's loops of travel happen to stretch westward the same distance, like the whorls of a topographic map compressing at an abrupt face of landscape.

March seventeenth: *... came to anchor in Neah Bay & after dinner went ashore to Mr Webster's house where I passed the night.*

June fourth, fifth, and sixth, again at Neah Bay.

September fourteenth, *Left Port Townsend at 5 PM in Swells canoe ... for Neah Bay.* Nine days, he stays this time.

October ninth, back at Neah Bay. Length of stay: fifty-five days.

At that time Neah Bay had its place as the geographical pinpoint on the American map that, say, Alaska's Point Barrow holds today: a final tribal outpost before the north margins of the planet take over entirely. The crescent eye of bay and its namesake village peek out between headlands at the entrance to the Strait of Juan de Fuca. The site nicks into the top—that is, the north-facing shore—of the coastal prow of rock which was dubbed Cape Flattery by Captain James Cook on his 1788 voyage, when a deceptive indent of the shoreline "flattered us with hopes of finding a harbour there." It vouches about the stormy remoteness of Cape Flattery that along its coastline the luck of even the incomparable Cook was nil; two and a half explorations around the world by sail, but here not only was he misled about a harbor prospect, Cook missed as well in the gray drifts of weather his chance to discover the dozen-mile-wide entrance to the Strait of Juan de Fuca and all the shoreline of Puget Sound beyond.

Cape Flattery's resident sailors, the several hundred Makah

tribal members at Neah Bay and four smaller villages dotted
west and south along the peninsula, deservedly would have
guffawed at seamanship of such low order. Out on their promontory into the Pacific which Swan began to share from them in
1859 and I now try to share from him, the Makahs casually
launched away in canoes to hunt creatures ranging in size and
threat from sea otters to gray whales. In land terms that would
be spaniels to dinosaurs. A prodigious seagoing people, these,
and small wonder that from here on, in steady diary and occasional newsprint, the Makahs come off Swan's pages like people
flinging open a door.

*. . . The Makahs are fond of music . . . and, as many of the
men have made voyages to San Francisco on lumber vessels,
they have learned a number of popular tunes. . . . I was astonished, on entering a lodge one day, to hear a party singing "Oh
Susannah" and "Old Folks at Home," accompanied by an ac-
cordion. . . .*

*The Makahs, in common with all the coast tribes, hold slaves.
. . . In former times, it is said, that slaves were treated very
harshly. . . . On the death of a chief, his favorite slaves were
killed and buried with him. . . . Latterly, this custom seems to
have been abandoned, and their present condition is a mild kind
of servitude. . . .*

*This morning some squaws were swimming in the brook at
high tide and sporting about as if it was midsummer. I don't
think these people are as sensitive to pain as whites. They cut
themselves on all occasions without seeming to mind it at all.
And go into water at times when a white man would be chilled
to death. . . .*

*At daybreak this morning I was awakened by children singing
and on getting up I found it proceeded from twelve girls who
were going in a sort of procession with Sustaies, who has had
her months' turns commence . . . for the first time. She had a
blue blanket over her head and the party went a short distance
up the beach where she was washed and then covered with a*

white blanket and the procession started for home. They came out twice afterward and had two more washes....

The festivals are but few, and are confined to the ta-ma-na-was ceremonies, which usually take place during the winter months; to certain "medicine" performances ... and the pot-lat-ches, or distributions of presents, which are made at all seasons of the year. The pot-lat-ches occur whenever an Indian has acquired enough property in blankets, beads, guns, brass kettles, tin pans, and other objects of Indian wealth, to make a present to a large number of the tribe; for the more an Indian can give away, the greater his standing with the others....

Blankets are the principal item of wealth, and the value of anything is fixed by the number of blankets it is worth. In the early days of the Hudson's Bay Company, and until within the past ten years, a blanket was considered equal in trade to five dollars; but since so many different traders have settled on the Sound, with such a variety of qualities and prices, the Indian in naming the number of blankets he expects to receive ... will state what kind he demands. Thus, if the price is to be twenty blankets, he will say, "how many large blue ones," which are the most costly, "how many red, and how many white ones?" ...

They believe that, originally, mankind were animals, and that the present race were formed by a series of transformations. The Mackah tribe were a hybrid race, half-dog and half-Indian—the progeny of a white dog and the daughter of a great chief or necromancer, who lived on Vancouver Island, nearly opposite Neah Bay. His chief being angry with his daughter, sent her and her seven progeny to Cape Flattery, where a magician turned them into human beings, and the present race of Mackahs are their descendants....

More than legend linked the Makahs and their Vancouver Island neighbors, the Nootkans. The tribes shared that brilliant skill, their seagoing hunting of whales, which sets them apart in the history of this coast.

From what Swan could judge, the Makahs by the late 1850s

were not as headlong avid about whale hunting as they had been in their past. *Whether the whales were more numerous, or that the Indians, being now able to procure other food from the whites, have become indifferent to the pursuit, I cannot say. . . .* Yet when Swell in the autumn of 1859 recited off for Swan the year's toll of whales, the kills added up to seven, which seems not too lackadaisical a tally. Fully practiced or not, the ocean abilities of the Makahs were so evident that Swan set down his estimation of the tribe in the most exalted terms a Massachusetts man could think of. *They are, in fact, to the Indian population what the inhabitants of Nantucket are to the people of the Atlantic Coast.*

As Swan discerned, when whales plowed north past Cape Flattery in their spring migrations, the Makahs would push out to hunt the sea behemoths with methods and tools they had honed to stiletto keenness. Their canoes were swift high-prowed blades of cedar which carried crews of eight: helmsman, six paddlers, harpooner. This last performed as the gladiator, the one who triggered death for the whale; stood above the cruising creature with a harpoon eighteen feet long, twice the length of a modern javelin, made of two pieces of yew scarfed together with splicing bark, and lunged it home. The wooden shaft detached when the whale was struck and left embedded in the flesh a harpoon point of sharpened copper or iron, barbed with spikes of elk or deer horn so that it would claw within the whale's body the way a fishhook snags itself with wicked irreversible angle inside a trout's mouth. Trollers of leviathan, were these Makahs.

Roped to the harpoon point with a cord of whale sinew was a buoy-like float made by skinning a seal and turning the pelt with the fur in, as when a sweater is pulled wrongside out. *Then the apertures of the head, feet and tail are tied up airtight,* Swan narrated, *and the skin inflated like a bladder. When further harpoons were hurled into the body of the whale, it is not unusual for from thirty to forty of these buoys to be made fast to the whale, which, of course, cannot sink, and is easily despatched by their spears and lances.*

Dispatched and towed ashore, the whale begins to become bill of fare. *All hands swarm around the carcass with their knives, and in a very short time the blubber is stripped off in blocks about two feet square. The portion of blubber forming a saddle, taken from between the head and dorsal fin, is esteemed the most choice, and is always the property of the person who first strikes the whale. The saddle is termed* u-butsk. *It is placed across a pole supported by two stout posts. At each end of the pole are hung the harpoons and lines with which the whale was killed. Next to the blubber at each end are the whale's eyes; eagle's feathers are stuck in a row along the top, a bunch of feathers at each end, and the whole covered with spots and patches of down . . . The* u-butsk *remains in a conspicuous part of the lodge until it is considered ripe enough to eat, when a feast is held, and the whole devoured or carried away by the guests. . . .*

Swan would, and did, journey almost anywhere with the coastal Indians in their canoes, but I do not discover in his diary pages or other writings that he ever went whaling with the Makahs. My guess is that he lost any such appetite early on, the time he was idling along in a canoe full of Makahs paddling for Port Townsend when a whale innocently broached beside them in the Strait. Swan emerged from the resulting commotion enormously grateful that no harpooning equipment happened to be aboard and the Indians had to forfeit their excited plan of pursuing the whale to the water-end of the earth or to his death, whichever arrived first.

Swan's eyewitness knowledge of the Makahs' soldiery of the sea, their whale hunts, then stops at the shoreline, and my questions go unmet. Whether the seabirds shadowed the canoes in white and gray gliding flocks as the whale-men stroked out from Cape Flattery into the Pacific. Whether there hung—I cannot see how else it could have been—an audible silence of held breaths before the first paddler behind the harpooner judged the distance to the whale and cried: *Now throw!* Whether the crew shouted a united great cry when the harpoon blade snagged home, a chorus of conquest. And whether some tincture of apprehension mixed with whatever exaltation they clamored, for success meant this: their canoe lashed behind the harpooned whale: a seagoing cart harnessed to a creature several times the size of a bull elephant and dying angry.

Yet if he did not go see whales stabbed, not a lot else of Makah life escaped Swan's attention. What a listener he must have been, the rarest kind who aims his ears as if being paid by the word. Whatever the majority of the Makahs thought of their white newcomer—and just as surely as his constant mention of some of them is testimony that they were attracted to him in friendship or something very close to it, there would have been those who suspected Swan, supposed him silly or perhaps even vaguely dangerous—a great number of the tribal members did talk with him, allowed him to rove along on the rim of their Neah Bay life. Even yet in his words their personalities breathe hotly to me. Swell, of course, with his knack for fact and his easy competence. His brother Peter, a brawler and restless under the cleft of the white men's growing power over the natives. The obliging Captain John, something of a tribal bard, who *drew on the first page of this book one of the skookums who cause the lightning by running out its tongue.* (Swan in turn later sketched Captain John into the front of a diary—an oval ocher face, low broad-lipped mouth, dark quarter circle eyebrows of surprising delicacy, amused eyes. Swan estimated him as *without exception the biggest coward in the tribe and at the same time the biggest braggadacio, but he is shrewd and smart and accomplishes by finesse . . . as much as some of the others do by their physical prowess.*) The exuberant Billy Barlow, who escorted Swan duck hunting and *wanted me to shoot everything I saw from a crow to an old woman who was at work on the prairie.* Tsowiskay, *an inveterate old savage* implacable against white men; on his death a rarely harsh Swan raps out that *the old fellow is no loss and his death did not affect the other Indians (except his own family) any more than if a dog had died.* Colchote, a war chief who recited his skirmishes with other coastal tribes as if from a list in hand.

And the one of them all I would give most to have stood beside Swan and heard, an ancient woman, one of Colchote's slaves, from Nootka Sound on Vancouver Island, who recounted for Swan the explorers she had seen arrive from the sea. *She said she remembered when Meares brought a lot of Chinamen to Nootka, and built a schooner:* 1788, more than seventy years before. And Vancouver, *whom she called Macowber:* 1792. And *she saw the massacre on board Astor's ship, the* Tonquin, *and spoke of Mr. McKay, the purser, who it was supposed blew the ship up:* 1811, the year before Swan was born.

Two sudden and vital friendships make themselves known here in Swan's notations of his first visits to Neah Bay. The earliest, and the one that would last for decades, took hold with the single resident of Neah Bay who was not a Makah: the white man Henry Webster, owner of a trading post at the eastern headland of the bay. It is enough to say of him now that Webster assays as a bleak-faced, obstinate frontier entrepreneur who did not get along with Indians notably well. In these beginning months of Swan's acquaintanceship with him a clash occurred in which, after an argument of some nature, five Indians pummeled Webster with rocks, dragged him along the beach, and threatened to kill him. Another instance Swan reports to the diary page: *The Indians talk very saucy today about shooting Webster.* Neither the battering nor the threats at all dissuaded Webster from staying on at his trading post, or indeed from patiently pulling political strings for a couple of years until he won appointment as the first federal agent for the new Makah Reservation. Swan had that tendency to lean on men chestier than himself—Russell, Isaac I. Stevens—and Webster amply seems to have been of the type. (He also, Swan noted promptly and gladly, was a man who knew how to fill a table. *The old adage that "God sends meat and the devil sends cooks" does not apply to my friend Webster's culinary department. Epicurus himself would have rejoiced over the nice and palatable dishes of fresh codfish tongues, fried; fresh halibut fins, broiled; fresh salmon, baked; together with side dishes of sea eggs, deep sea oysters and brook trout; with puddings made of the luscious salal and other rich berries of the season, winding up with cranberry tarts and pies; the whole the product of the ocean and land in the immediate vicinity of the house.)*

The other immediate friend, supple and deft as Webster was granitic, of course was Swell. Rapidly in the diaries it becomes evident how valued a companion the young Makah chieftain proved to be. The pages of Swan's eight weeks at Neah Bay in late 1859 bustle with the forming connection: *Went to Swell's house and made a sketch of some Tomanawos boards. . . . Swell told about their land, that they were not satisfied with the way the treaty was written. . . . Went to Swell's house. He says that the past year there were 30 canoes engaged in the whale fishery 8 men to each canoe but they have not all been out this past year. . . . Swell says that there are in the Makah tribe 220 men 300 women 200 children 100 slaves. . . . Made sketch of Swell. . . . Swell started for Dungeness this morning. Saluted him with the swivel—1 gun. . . . Swell brought down 50 bushels of potatoes from Dungeness. . . . Swell's name Wha-laltl Asabuy. . . . Made a carving today of the Ha hake to ak or the animal that makes the lightning . . . I cut it on a piece of sandstone from the cliff & intend giving it to Swell. . . .*

Elsewhere Swan testifies of Swell's intelligence, of his knack for leadership, his prowess as a canoeman; I could almost say, reading not very deep between the lines, his alacrity to meet and learn about the white way of life that had come calling at Cape Flattery. Swell was a stag of a man, his name among the whites deriving from his posh sartorial preference: he sat resplendent *in a new suit of Boston clothes* when Swan made his first canoe trip to Neah Bay with him in mid-September of 1859. *Swell has been among the white men as sailor and pilot,* Swan recorded, and *was the person who assisted in rescuing Capt. Weldon and the crew of the Swiss Boy, which was wrecked in Nittinat Sound in early 1859. He saved them from bondage, and landed them safe among their friends. . . . He is still quite a young man, but if he lives, he is destined to be a man of importance among his own and neighboring tribes.*

They are, then, a set of mutually interested men. The Makah

canoeman who has adventured aboard steamships and schooners; the Boston ship's chandler who has adapted to cedar canoe. A young chieftain who knows the politics of his tribe and is attuning to some of the white version; a middle-aging white man with keenest interest in the coastal Indian cultures. At first they can only have been curiosities, griffin met with centaur, to one another; then, as Swan's diary agenda shows, exchangers of lore; then, from every evidence of the aftermath of Swell's slaying, friends. Such a growth of regard sometimes will happen when two people are cupped together in a single happenchance season of closeness—aboard a fishing boat, in a line cabin of a cattle ranch, at a military outpost; in this instance, at an outpost of another sort, the frontier pinnacle that was Neah Bay. Swan was able to know the Makah chieftain for about a year and a half before the life was blasted from Swell in the breakers at Crescent Bay. By that late winter night, the two of them had entered what I would phrase a kind of adopted kinship, stronger than differences of blood can ever be. Winter brothers, perhaps call them.

But Swan. What besides tireless ears did a domestic fugitive from Massachusetts have to offer Swell and the other Makahs? That answer too puts itself together from these diary entries, in the remark of a sketch here, a carved gift there; clearest of all in the laconic and intriguing entry for an October day in 1859 that Swan had gone down to a sandstone cliff along the Neah Bay beach and carved a swan into the rockface.

Artistry. Right there, in the fact that virtually the only skill of hand lacking in Swan was the ability to clutch a dollar, was his ticket into the Makah community. Draw, cut stone, invent patterns of paint, produce creatures from within the covers of his books: he could perform a range of tasks admired by a tribe in love with ornament. What was more, not much daunted Swan: *Went to Billy Balch's house and finished the Thunder bird. This was the hardest sketch I ever undertook. The lodge was dark and the board covered with smoke & grease and hid by boxes & baskets of food. The Indians removed these & washed the board*

*with urine & then the only way I could decypher the painting
was to mark round the drawing with a red crayon....*

In fire and reek, as the storymasters of sagas would have said,
and Swan blithely tracing. The Makahs met him at least halfway
in rampant enthusiasm for picturizing, as Swan noted some
years later when he wrote at length about his role as a frontier
ambassador of art. *I have painted various devices for these Indians and have decorated their ta-ma-na-was masks; and in every
instance I was simply required to paint something the Indians
had never seen before. One Indian selected from a pictorial
newspaper a cut of a Chinese dragon, and another chose a
double-headed eagle, from a picture of an Austrian coat-of-
arms. Both these I grouped with drawings of crabs, faces of
men, and various devices, endeavoring to make the whole look
like Indian work; and I was very successful in giving the most
entire satisfaction, so much so that they bestowed upon me the
name of Cha-tic, intimating that I was as great an artist as the
Cha-tic of Clyoquot* (a tribe living north of the Makahs, on the
coast of Vancouver Island).

So, no small gifts these—twin-headed eagles, dragons from
beyond the rim of the Pacific, new flaunts of paint, a stone swan
set afloat through time—to a people as vivid and showy as the
Makahs.

Whale hunters, coastal annalists, slaveholders, art fanciers,
the Makahs also were a people who chafed more than a little
under the pale regime of frontier bureaucrats wanting to refash-
ion the tribe's life. Swan is once more at Neah Bay—his sixth
stint there so far—when in the autumn of 1861 the Makahs,
after six actionless months by the territorial officials, decide to
exact their price for the death of Swell.

Once resolved upon, their vengeance on the Elwhas begins to
be brewed, savored. Conference, more conference, the Elwha
village sketched on the sand, a plan of attack argued out. As
Swan watches and jots, Neah Bay's largest canoes are worked
up into fighting trim; the outsides blackened, interiors daubed a
fresh red. Lord Nelson, with his blood-colored battle decks,

would have nodded approval. Bow and stern of each canoe are embellished with green spruce limbs. Onto long poles are lashed faggots of pitchy wood to torch the hapless Elwhas' lodges. Guns, knives, spears, clubs, arrows, bows are hefted judiciously, made ready.

At last, the nineteenth of September of 1861, two hundred and two days after Swell's death, the war party mills together in final encouragement on the Neah Bay beach. Some speeches, a few dances, and they leap to their decorated canoes and head east the sixty miles to deliver holocaust to the Elwhas.

Twelve canoes, with eighty warriors, they aim up the Strait past Swan like a volley of arrows on the water. His account of the scene was published in a territorial newspaper, and so has been primped and extended beyond the usual:

I stood on top of the rocks at Webster's point and saw them pass. . . . Their green headdresses, black faces and brown arms, flashing paddles and beautiful canoes, urged to their utmost speed, presented a scene at once novel and interesting. I watched until a projecting point hid them from view.

Then the waiting, the war spirit still boiling in the Makah village. *Women and children, seated on the tops of their houses, were beating the roofs with sticks and uttering the most piercing shrieks I ever heard. Every day at sunrise and sunset they performed these savage matins and vespers. . . .*

On the third day the canoes flash back into sight, the crews announcing themselves across the water by exuberant musket shots and songs of victory. The war, however, turns out to have been considerably less than total. *The avenging Makahs landed on the beach opposite the monument of Swell . . . and forming into a line came up the beach in single file with old Cowbetsi, their great war chief, at their head. A short distance behind him came a savage holding with both hands a bloody head that had been severed from the body of an unfortunate Elwha. Two or three Indians followed this and then another grim trophy, held in the same manner as the first.*

Swan learned that the war party had lucked upon the hapless pair of Elwhas hunting seals at Crescent Bay, the precise site of

Swell's murder. When blood was most ready to answer blood, the two were simply targets of opportunity. Having shot and beheaded them, the Makahs noted the alarms being shrieked by several Elwha women who had watched the ambush from a distance, held a rapid council, and decided revenge had been sufficiently done.

In all of this Swan takes greatest interest, so much so that he makes the mistake of spectating too close to the song circle which has formed around the severed heads. *After they had finished their war song, I heard my name called, and thinking I was in the way of some of their operations was about moving off, when I was again summoned in a manner that left no doubt in my mind but that I was wanted.*

The Makahs gesture Swan into the circle, beside the heads. Cowbetsi and an Indian who is to interpret to Swan face him.

Cowbetsi orates to Swan that they killed the Elwhas because the territorial Indian agent did not settle the matter of Swell's murder. A line of fact indisputable.

Swan responds gingerly that the Indian agent at the time has been removed from office, *consequently he could not come as he had promised, but that he had not lied for I knew that he fully intended to have done just what he had promised to do; that Mr. Simmons was a friend of Swell's and they all knew*—a careful veer here—*I was a friend also.*

"Yes," said Cowbetsi, "we know you are our friend, and we are friends of yours."

Swan emits a degree of relief *when I was assured of the fact; but I thought that their friendship was of the kind that might induce them, should I give offence, to stick my head on top of a pole for a memento.* . . . He stands stock silent through a victory dance performed while four Makahs point guns at the heads and his general vicinity, and does not give offense. Only the two trophy skulls of the Elwhas go up on poles above Neah Bay like queer jack-o'-lanterns.

Swan by this time has written his way, in years and fractions of years, through four diaries—black, tan, black and tan again

—and been back and forth between Neah Bay and Port Town-send until he seems more a citizen of midwater than of either community. Early in the diary of his fourth year on the Strait, the brown pocket volume for 1862, a different rhythm begins to rise out to me. Swan is at Neah Bay with the hope now, through Webster's doggedly achieved new position as agent in charge of the Reservation, of staying on for some steady span of time, and a beat of hour comfortably nudging hour, of settledness, sets in.

Wind NW fresh, the seventeenth of March. *Caught a large male skunk. Finished the Tomanawas stone for John. Sundown, sch* Alert *off San Juan harbor trying to beat out. A ship and two barks also working out slowly. A year ago, the salmonberry & other shrubs were in blossom. Now no signs of vegetation are visible. Peter came up today and I cut out a coat for him out of some blue flannel he had.*

Wind SE rain all day, the twentieth of March. *Ship* Wm Stur-gis *from Pt Townsend hove to this forenoon & landed Charly Howard, who came down as pilot. Howard brought letters & papers. . . . Caught another skunk . . . measured 28 inches from nose to tip of his tail.*

Wind SE very light, the twenty-first of March, *Foggy with constant rain. Brook very high. Peter came up today and told me that he had made up his mind to buy Totatelum, Colchote's daughter, but he did not wish either white men or Indians to know it except myself. He wishes to make the girl a present and will bring it up to me and wishes me to give it to Totatelum . . . I am curious to see the result of this courtship.*

Light airs from SE, the twenty-second of March, *with calms and thick fog. Walked down to Neeah to see Totatelum and announce to her Peter's desire. She was somewhat surprised and said she would think about the matter. . . . Old Sally, the para-lyzed woman, died last night and the Indians buried her by caving in the bank of sand under which she has been lying since they turned her out of the lodges. They are cruel wretches to the poor and sick.*

Calm, cloudy & some fog, the twenty-third of March. *Carried*

Peter's present—calico, needles, thread, and two bars of soap—
down to Totatelum, who received it very modestly....

Wind SE Morning cloudy and showery, PM calm, the twenty-
seventh of March. *John said that the people in Victoria told him
that Queen Victoria had ordered a very hot summer to make up
for the cold winter. Caught another skunk—8.*

Day and day and day the diaries say it now. Swan's life is
patterning itself to this frontier coast. Tomorrow, then, to the
first of the coastal sites where Swan's paths and mine braid
together. To Dungeness.

DAY ELEVEN

Above the two of us the eagle glides a complete slow circle, as if
studying from the corner of his eye our surprising plaid skins.
Near enough he floats, perhaps a hundred fifty feet over Carol in
her jacket of gray and yellow and black, me in my red and
black, that we easily can see the scalloped pattern of feathers at
the ends of his wings, the snowiness of head and tail that marks
him as a bald.

One more silent exact noose of patrol, then the dark flier flaps
off southwest across the bay. *The Boston bird*, Swan says the
coastal Indians began to call the eagle after arrival of the earliest
American trading ships, pale New Englanders aboard them with
the glittering wide-winged image on their coins. Under this
taloned hunter's glide now a fleet of swimming ducks crash-dives
in fear, but they are not the target of the moment. When the
eagle scrapes into the water, it is a fish that lofts away to doom.

We stand atop Dungeness Spit's rough spine of driftwood to
watch the bald eagle and his meal vanish into the shore trees.
From up here, all its bowed length into the Strait of Juan de
Fuca—seven miles—Dungeness prickles into view like a gigantic hedgerow somehow weired atop the water. Age-gray drift
logs tumble across each other to the height of a Dutch dike,
fresher logs perpetually angle ashore, yellow and tattered from

grinding across the gravel beach, to pile in turn onto the long heap. The rarity of Dungeness in all the dozen thousand miles of America's coastal edge speaks itself even in the flat intonings of scientists: *longest natural sandspit in the United States; driest point on the West Coast north of San Diego.* A thin hook of desert snagging the water, within walk of glaciered mountains and cool fir forests.

Swan, as said, voyaged by here for the first time on a February morning of 1859, inbound for Port Townsend and his resumed western life. With his feathered name and that migratory nature he was something of a Boston bird himself, testing new waters, fresh paths of glide. For the several years after his arrival to the Strait, Swan shows up time upon time at this sandy breakwater, usually portaging across the base of the Spit as the most direct canoe route between Port Townsend and the Makah settlement at Neah Bay. If he happened to journey by ship, the route cut close past the site of the lighthouse which rises like a white candle at the far end of the Spit . . . *A keeper's house and fine brick tower 92 feet high,* he recorded in that year of 1859, *in which is placed a stationary light of the order of Fresnel.*

The Dungeness light tower is now white-painted concrete, and not so lofty, that original beacon having proved to be so eminent that it blinked futilely above the fogs that drift on the face of the Strait. Until a few years ago a Fresnel lantern still was in use, not the one Swan describes but an 1897 version, an exquisite six-sided set of glass bull's-eyes which flung a beam of brightness eighteen miles.

Once Carol and I had the experience of being drawn the full length of the Spit, through the exact blackest center of night, by the focused blaze out of that elegant box of glass. I was to write a magazine article about the Coast Guard families stationed there at the remote end of the Spit's ribbon of sand, and Carol to shoot photographs for illustration. We arrived here to Dungeness about an hour before a November midnight and met a specter.

The bosun's mate in charge at the lighthouse had phoned that he would drive in to meet us on the coastal bluff overlooking the

Spit. He wavered now out of the blackness like a drunken genie, clasping a hand to half of his forehead and announcing thickly that we had to hurry to keep the tide.

Wait a minute, we said. What exactly had gone wrong with his head?

Groggy but full of duty, he recited that when he judged the time had come to drive in above the tide, he traveled fast. Racing through a bank of spume, his four-wheel-drive vehicle bounded over a log the way a foxhunter's horse takes a hedge, and when man and machine plunged to sand again, his forehead clouted the windshield.

With woozy determination our would-be chauffeur repeated that we would lose the tide if we did not hurry. I looked at Carol, some decision happened between us, and we clambered into the four-wheel-drive.

Headlights feeling out the thin route between driftwood debris and crashing waves, our Coast Guardsman ducked us through cloud upon cloud of spume sailing thigh-deep on the beach. That spindrift journey was like being seated in a small plane slicing among puffy overcast. From that night I have the sense of what the early pilots must have felt, Saint-Exupéry's blinded men aloft with the night mail above Patagonia, avid for "even the flicker of an inn lamp." We had our ray of light, leading us with tireless reliable winks, but even it could not see into our foaming route for us.

At last at the lighthouse, with the engine cut, no next encounter between four-wheel-drive and fat driftlog having been ordained, the Fresnel lens wheeling its spokes of light above our heads: we breathed out and climbed down to the Dungeness sand for our weekend stay.

Two moments stand in my memory from that next day at the tip of Dungeness Spit. The first was seeing the lens itself, coming onto the fact of its art here on a scanty ledge of sand and upcast wood. What I had expected perhaps was something like a titanic spotlight, some modern metallic capsule of unfathomable power: not a seventy-five-year-old concoction of magnifying prisms, worked by the French artisans to angles as precise and acute as those of cut-glass goblets, which employed a single thousand-watt bulb and stretched its glow across nearly twenty miles. The magnifying power from this small cabinet of glass was as pleasantly astounding as Swell's explanation of the aurora borealis glinting up from Eskimo campfires.

The second memory is of the mustached bosun's mate himself. With what pride he showed off his domain of Dungeness, not only the artful glass casing at the top of the lighthouse but the radio beacon apparatus and the foghorn and even the flagpole with a red storm-warning flag bucking madly at the top. "The wind wears out about ten flags a winter," he said to impress us, and did.

Lighthouse life dimmed a bit when he escorted us in to talk with his wife and the wife of the young petty officer on duty with him. Both proved to be edgy about the strand-of-sand way of existence. Mrs. Bosun's Mate calculated to when their oldest child would start school, which would loft the family away to land duty: "I WANT to move inland." Until that could happen she was forbidding the children to leave the fenced yard around the quarters because they might injure themselves in the driftwood. The petty officer's recent bride, dwelling in the building attached to the base of the lighthouse tower itself, was disconcerted to have in her living room one huge round wall which emitted a night-long beamish hum.

The bosun's mate heard them out, evidently not for the first time, then led the pair of us off to see any further feature of lighthouse keeping he could think of. The day, blown pure by last night's wind, had its own magnifying clarity. Mountains rose in white shards far north along the Canadian coastline. Mount Baker lorded over the glinting horizon of the Cascades to our east, highest ice-flame among dozens of ice-flames, while the Olympic range crowded full the sky south and west of us. Dungeness seemed more astounding than ever, a gift of promontory grafted carefully amid the mountains and strait.

The knot on his forehead barely visible beneath his cap bill, hands fisted for warmth into his jacket pockets, the bosun's mate looked around at this ice-and-water rim of the Pacific Northwest in a quick expert glance, then turned to us.

"I'm a shallow water sailor," he announced as if introducing himself. "A true coastie."

The Dungeness light has blinked through a number of hundreds of nights since then, and today in bright sun Carol and I casually prowl the inside shore of the Spit, around to where smaller Graveyard Spit veers off from Dungeness. In outline from the air Dungeness and Graveyard together look like a long wishbone, Graveyard poking shoreward from near the end of Dungeness like the briefer prong of the forked pieces. Out there now just beyond where they join, the lighthouse and outbuildings sit in silhouette against Mount Baker, a white peg and white boxes beside that tremendous tent of mountain.

I am watching for snowy owls. This is a year in their cycle of migration which brings them far south from the Arctic, and we once sighted one here, a wraith of white against the gray driftwood. Pleased with ourselves, we returned to Seattle to discover that another snowy had taken up a roost on a television antenna above a midcity restaurant and half the population had been out to see him. No owl today, nor the blue herons who often stilt along Graveyard Spit.

We stay with the inside shore, the one facing Graveyard. The wild-fowl side, commissary for migrating ducks and brant, as the outward shore is the lagoon for seals who pop up and disappear as abruptly as periscopes. Today's find presents itself here on the interior water: a half-dozen eider ducks making their *kor-r-r, kor-r-r* chuckles to each other, then, as if having discussed to agreement, all diving at once.

An edge of ice whitens the shoreline, a first for all the times— fifty? seventy-five?—we have come here. Full-dress winter greeted Swan once, in January of 1880: *We arrived in Dungeness harbor at 10 AM and found three feet of snow had fallen during the night. Everything was covered with a white mantle, our boat's deck was loaded with snow and the light house tower on its north east side had a thick coating from the base to the lantern. Fog signal house and all the other outbuildings were covered, and the whole scenery of Dungeness Spit and bluff was the most like an Eastern winter of any I have seen in this country.* This afternoon, mountains stand in all directions with the clear loveliness Swan observed during one of his early visits— *unobscured by mist or clouds their snowy peaks shone most gloriously....* Across the Strait at Vancouver Island, where we can see in miniature detail the tallest downtown buildings of twenty-mile-distant Victoria, Swan had marveled at the endless timber *level as a field of wheat, following the undulation of the ground with a regular growth most wonderful for such a dense forest.*

How cold the day, but how little wind, not always the case in this restless spot. Swan on an excursion past the Spit on a day in May of 1862:

Stopped for the night at the light house where Mr Blake, the keeper treated me very politely to a supper & a share of his bed. Next morning: *Left the light house at 3:15 A.M., calm. Passed round the spit where a breeze sprung up which freshened into a squall wth rain. A tremendous surf was breaking on the beach & we for a time were in great peril. But finally we managed to get ashore at Point Angeles where we found shelter....*

Dark settles early, the sun spinning southwest into the Olympic Mountains instead of dropping near the end of the Strait as it does in summer. We leave the Spit before dusk, heading back to Seattle to spend New Year's Eve in our traditional geographically diverse game of penny-ante poker. Baltimore—"Ballumer," she says it—will play her challenging, by-God-you're-not-going-to-get-away-with-it style. Texas, behind a cigar which would credit J. P. Morgan, contents himself until a strong hand, when he raises and reraises relentlessly. Carol— New Jersey—is the steadiest of the bunch, and wins regularly from the rest of us. By way of Montana—me—comes an uncharacteristically fevered kind of style which can swathe through the game, devastating everybody else for three or four hands in a row, or obliterating my own stake.

Swan would approve the pastime, if not our particular card-table temperaments. He once passed up a chance to visit with the lightkeeper at Dungeness because he and the others *concluded to remain on board, devoting our energies to the successful performance of a game of seven-up, or all-four, or old sledge, as that wonderful combination of cards is variously termed.*

DAY TWELVE

The new year.
On Sunday, January 1, 1860, his first New Year's Day on the coast of the Strait of Juan de Fuca, Swan creased open a new tan pocket diary and inscribed on its first page:

May it be not only the commencement of the week, the month and the year, but the commencement of a new Era in my life, and may good resolve result in good action.

DAY THIRTEEN

Today Mr Brooks, William Ingraham & myself finished setting the posts for the main building of the school house and when we had all ready which was at noon, I told Capt John to call the Indians. Some twenty-five or thirty came out and when Mr Brooks was ready I told John who then gave the word and the sticks were lifted into their places and the whole of the sills for the main building fastened together in about an hour. I told John that when the buildings were done Mr Webster would give them a treat to pay for the good feelings evinced on this occasion. They have been opposed to having the building erected back of their lodges and I have had a deal of explanation to make, to do away with the superstitious prejudices of the old men. But by the exercise of a great deal of patience I have succeeded in inspiring them with a confidence in me, which makes them believe not only what I tell them is true, but what we are doing is for their good.

The noontime came on the fifteenth of October 1862, and the exertions which overtopped the cedar longhouses of the Makahs with the framework of a schoolhouse lofted more good for James G. Swan than he let his pen admit.

Precisely when his mind had become set on securing the job as teacher at Neah Bay, there is no direct evidence. But hints murmur up from the diary pages. Likely as early as those first visits to Cape Flattery in 1859 Swan divined that Henry Webster would try for the appointment as Indian agent when the Makah Reservation came into being. Even more likely is that Webster, noticing Swan's knack of getting along with the Indians, advised or asked him to seek a Reservation job.

Those discernments and Swan's rummaging curiosity about Makah tribal life were the pulls to Neah Bay. The push was that Port Townsend had not worked out well for Swan, and a fundamental reason seems to have been whiskey.

Once I happened across the lines of a diarying compatriot of Swan's, a Scot named Melrose who also had alit to the Pacific Northwest—to Victoria, north on the Canadian coast of the Strait—early in the 1850s. The alcoholic atmosphere of this frontier enthused Melrose to near rapture. "It would almost take a line of packet ships," he wrote cheerily, "running regularly between here and San Francisco to supply this isle with grog, so great a thirst prevails among its inhabitants." Melrose took care to note down how far his companions in thirst overcame their parching: whether each had become one-quarter drunk, one-half drunk, three-quarters drunk, or wholly drunk. Every so often the Melrose diary presents the forthright wavery notation: "author whole D."

Swan, I hardly need say, was not a man to record himself as whole D or any other degree of it. But that he was tussling with the temptation of the bottle is plain enough in his own diary even so.

Joined the Dashaway Club of Port Townsend—a group who

took a pledge of abstinence and whom one unsympathetic editor dubbed a claque of "high-toned drunkards."

Cut my lip with a brush hook this evening in Gerrishes store in a scuffle with Maj. Van Bokkelin—Van Bokkelin was one of Swan's closest friends and a pillar of community respect, and a scuffle hardly thinkable of a sober Swan.

Days later, *Made a pledge . . . not to drink any more liquor for two years from this date*, the ninth of December 1860.

That pact may have been as much with Webster, gatekeeper to future employment at the Makah Reservation, as with himself. Whether or not, most of the next twenty-one months until Webster finally was able to pluck the appointment as Indian agent found Swan odd-jobbing in sobriety at Neah Bay. (And quartering at the Baadah Point trading post with Webster and whoever else happened to be on hand, in what seems to have been a peppery household: *During the evening a skunk came into the kitchen to eat swill. Mr Webster fired at him with his pistol, cutting some of his hair off with the ball. The skunk made his escape but filled the house with his stench.*) Some months more had to pass before Webster could enroll Swan on the Makah Reservation payroll as teacher, but then, the first of July of 1862, at last Swan having secured position and salary, immediate dignification sets in. Three and a half years of jotted doings in pocket notebooks leave off and the first of Swan's ledger diaries, the pages long and officious and the handwriting scrupulously clear and margined, ensues.

What is recorded for the first year and more has nothing to do with education, except that over this course of time Swan's classroom ever so slowly gets carpentered to completion. Instead Swan spent the time lending a hand in the sundry chores of the little Neah Bay work force, especially the labors of the Reservation's farmer, Maggs, earnest bearer of agriculture to damp Cape Flattery.

"Making the earth say beans instead of grass," Thoreau teased himself about his garden at Walden. At Neah Bay, the official notion was that the brush-tufted coastal soil ought to orate potatoes.

We plow the land twice, Swan recorded, *harrow it twice, then plow in the potatoes and harrow the whole over again. . . . If what we plant grows as thrifty as the wild raspberry, currant, gooseberry and elder and nettles, cow parsnip and other rubbish grew we shall have a famous crop.* A kind of Hibernian woefulness moans through this idea of remaking such a people of the sea as the Makahs into potato farmers. I think of the "potato Protestants" of Connaught in the Irish famine, forced to barter their religion for the meals of survival. (Credit Swan with grave doubts about persuading the Makahs to trade canoe for plow: *Indians cannot live on potatoes alone, any more than the white man; they require animal food, and prefer the products of the ocean to the farina of the land. It will take many years, and cost the Government large sums of money to induce these savages to abandon their old habits of life and acquire new ones. . . . I think they should be encouraged in their fisheries. . . .*) The Makahs, however, with an oceanful of seafood at their front doors, were not at the edge of desperation and so managed to make the best of the potato policy. As democratic eaters they blithely demanded their spud allotments whenever a harvest was produced. But as uninspired agriculturalists they conspicuously left most of the plowing and other field labor to Maggs and Swan.

Through 1862 and most of 1863, Swan dabbles as extra muscle in the potato field. Gleans lore from the Makahs. (Captain John is an ever-ready, if problematical, fund of it: *John as a general thing is a great liar, but he is well informed on all historical matters. . . .*) Does sketchwork. Keeps the diary constant. And otherwise disposes of days until the carpenter hired by Webster at last whams the final nail into his schoolhouse.

Webster himself is absent from Neah Bay much of the time now that he has Swan and the others in place there, so Swan fairly often discovers himself standing in as arbiter among the Indians. *Peter came in this evening and had a long talk with me relative to his conduct since he came back from California. He promised to do better and said he hoped I would be friendly to him. I told him I always had been his best friend and was now, but his actions had displeased me and in particular the fact that he had not paid a debt he owed in Port Townsend to Sheehan the tinsmith. . . .* And sometimes the tumbleweed white population as well. *Capt Melvin arrived in the schooner* Elisabeth. *He had been down on a trading voyage and had been trading whiskey among the Nittinat Indians in the vicinity of Barclay Sound . . . he assured me positively that he had not nor would he sell any liquor near the reserve. He however inadvertently showed me his account book and I saw that he had with his potatoes one barrel 33 gallons whiskey . . . I advised him to keep away from where I was for so soon as I had proof of his selling whiskey so sure would I complain of him.*

This Neah Bay Swan, if you look steadily at him for a moment, is a greatly more interesting and instructive fellow than the Shoalwater oysterer/loiterer first met on this frontier coast. He has shown himself to be a chap who likes to hear a story and to take a drink, not absolutely in that order; reveals a remarkable fast knack for friendships, among whites and Indians both; is as exact a diarist as ever filled a page and as steadily curious as a question mark; contrives not to stay in the slog of any job very long (although we shall have to see about this forthcoming profession in the Cape Flattery schoolhouse); can drily characterize—*I thought that their friendship was of the kind that might induce them, should I give offence, to stick my head on top of a pole for a memento*—or get a bit preachy—*I told Peter I always had been his best friend and was now, but—;* long since has unwifed and defamilied himself yet maintains week by week steady correspondence with Matilda, Ellen, and Charles; hardly ever meets a meal he doesn't like or a coastal scene he doesn't hanker to sketch; muses occasionally, observes always.

And is about to offer more instruction yet. Mid-November of 1863, the potato harvest in, the schoolhouse at last roofed and windowed, *I painted the alphabet on the blocks Mr. Phillips made for me and tomorrow I intend to commence teaching.*

DAY FOURTEEN

Neah Bay pedagogy gets off to a stuttery start. The first morning, the seventeenth of November of 1863, a single student showed up; Captain John's ten-year-old nephew, Jimmy Claplanhoo. Swan chose a bit of guile. *This evening I got out the magic lantern and gave Jimmy an exhibition of it as a reward. . . .* Within a few days four more Makah children edged into the schoolroom and were treated to Swan's picture show. By the end of the first week, *Twenty children present today   exercised them on the alphabet and then gave them a pan full of boiled potatoes.*

Success in the schoolroom, discord in the world. Something here sets Swan unusually to brooding about the Civil War and its politics: *I do not believe in the principles of the Republican party as enunciated by Greely, Sumner, Phillips, Beecher . . . but I do believe that the country is in real danger and I believe at such times it is the duty of every true man to stand by his Government (no matter what the party) in saving this country and ourselves from ruin.*

That out of his system, Swan goes on to record that the Indians' dogs killed two skunks in the lumber pile.

He next has to take three days out to supervise the digging of the schoolhouse cellar, introducing the Makah laborers to the wheelbarrow, which they think a hilarious machine. Then a drain to carry the runoff from the schoolhouse roof needs to be finished. Jimmy Claplanhoo comes down with a cough so severe that Swan worries the ailment may be consumption. The Makahs put on a raucous tamanoas ceremony to boost Jimmy's health, just as a gale rips across Neah Bay. Crows tip over Swan's rain gauge. He sets to work on them with shotgun and strychnine. Makahs from the village of Waatch arrive for Swan to dispense potatoes to. One of the Makah men brings his two-year-old son to school to learn the alphabet and creates uproar by spanking the tot for not mastering it. A number of the Indians embark on a drinking spree which gets rougher as it progresses day by day. There are knife wounds and one combatant smashes three canoes with a stone before other partyers knock him out with a brick.

At risk here was more than a few cedar hulls. *This drunken frolic shows how easily these people can be excited to deeds of violence,* Swan's pen scolds. *We are powerless under the present circumstances either to prevent these drunken scraps or protect ourselves in case of an attack. But I have not the least apprehension of any difficulty if liquor is kept from them.*

Now Swan catches cold; *I have not felt so sick for a year certainly.* Jimmy Claplanhoo's health mends and he arrives back at school. The agency's winter larder begins to be questionable: *Sometimes we are very short of provisions and have to depend on our beef barrel, then again the Indians will bring in such quantities of fish and game that there is a surfeit.* The agency cattle start dying. Cold, damp weather holds and holds. On December 16 *the most remarkable fall of rain I have ever known,* gurgling to the top of his rain gauges twice, a total of nearly seven inches. A number of the Indians begin another knockabout drinking party. One participant this time is blasted in the arm with a dragoon pistol and another asks to borrow a shovel from Swan. *He went to where old Flattery Jack Sixey's father had been buried and dug up one of his arm bones which was taken and bound on as splints to the arm of Sixey. The Indians believing that the bone from the father's arm would cure.*

A weakened bull from the staggering agency herd has to be put in the basement of the schoolhouse for shelter. He takes out a window on his way in. Another party of Makahs from Waatch troops in to purchase a bride: *They came in the house and rigged themselves up with masks and feathers and all went to Whattie's house to make their trade.*

Five weeks since Jimmy Claplanhoo inaugurated the schoolhouse, Webster at last sails into the bay with some supplies, and an audible sigh lifts from the ledger pages as Swan turns his pen toward the coming of Christmas and the making of a plum pudding.

DAY FIFTEEN

The strop of this weather on the days, each one brought identically keen, tingling. Rainless hours after rainless hours glimmering past, it has dawned on me how extraordinary is this dry cold time, as if I were living in the Montana Rockies again but without the clouting mountain-hurled wind. There is a bright becalmed feel, a kind of disbelief the winter has about itself. Other years, by now I might have shrugged almost without noticing into our regional cloak of rain and cloud, the season's garment of interesting texture and of patterned pleasant sound as well. "Rain again," a friend growls. "Right," I say and smile absently, listening for the *boommm* and *whoommm* of foghorns out in the murk of Puget Sound. But through yesterday morning the temperature hung below freezing for four days and nights in a row, the longest skein of its kind I can remember here at the rim of the Sound. I bury our kitchen vegetable scraps directly into my garden patch each evening as immediate compost and the shovel brings up six-inch clods of frozen soil, like lowest-grade coal.

But what speaks the weather even clearer is today's renewed presence of birds. This morning kindled into warmer sun than we have had and already, Carol minutes gone up the hill to teach her first class of the day, just to be out in the fresh mildness I have walked to the top of the valley. Clouds were lined low across the southern reach of the Olympics while clear weather held the northern end, the Strait country. The view west from me was bannered in five blues: the water of Puget Sound in two shades, azure nearest me, a more delicately inked hue farther out; the foreshore of the Olympic Peninsula in its heavy forested tint; the mountains behind their blue dust of distance; the clear cornflower sky. Such mornings shrug away time. Vessels on the Sound—freighter, tug harnessed to barge, second freighter, the ivory arrow that is the Edmonds-to-Kingston ferry —seemed pinned in place, and I had to watch intently before my eyes could begin to catch the simultaneous motion of them all, inching on the water. Then as I turned home, the flurry. Robins in fluster at the mouth of the valley, abruptly dotting suburban fir trees and frost-stiff lawns. Motion doublequick, headlong. Airful of flying bodies, a vigor in orbit around fixed beauty of Sound and mountains.

Soon after, a jay cry, like rods of some terrible substance being briskly rasped against each other. Then framed in the desk-end window, popping from place to place along the bank beneath the valley slope's evergreens, a tiny brown flying mouse which proved to be a wren.

These past iced days I have tried to picture this valley's birds, up somewhere in innermost branches, fluffed with dismay and wondering why the hell they didn't wing south with their saner cousins. I live in this suburb for its privacy, the way it empties itself during the workday—people evaporated off to office, school, supermarket—and delivers the valley to me and the birds and any backyard cats. I suppose I could get by without the cats, or trade them for other interesting wanderers, maybe coyotes or foxes, but a birdless world, the air permanently fallow, is unthinkable. To be without birds would be to suffer a kind of color blindness, a glaucoma gauzing over one of the planet's special brightnesses. Bushtits must bounce again out there on the thin ends of birch branches like monks riding bell ropes. A fretful nest-building robin—we always have one or two nattering in the trees at either end of the house—must gather and gather dry spears of grass until the beakful bristles out like tomcat whiskers. Towhees, chickadees, flickers, juncoes. (All the creatures of this planet that do not know they have splendid names.) Occasional flashing hummingbirds; seasonal grosbeaks who arrive in the driveway and, masked like society burglars, munch on seeds amid the gravel. Besides Carol and the pulse of words across paper there exist few everyday necessaries in my life, but birds are among them.

And Swan, with his name which the Indian woman at Shoalwater had said is *like our word Cocumb, a big bird:* depend on it, birds perpetually aviate across his horizons. Time upon time I marker incidents of birds in his pages. *This forenoon,* the tenth of July of 1865 at Neah Bay, *I saw a kingfisher fluttering in the brook and supposed he had a trout which he could not swallow. On going to him I found he had driven his bill into an old rotten stick with such force as to bury it clear up to his eyes . . . hard and fast. I took him with the stick to the house and called Jones & Phillips to see the curiosity. It was with difficulty that his bill was pulled out again.* Two years previous, in the same week of July: *I discovered a dead Albatross on the beach yesterday which had a large dogfish which it had swallowed partially but it was too large, and while the fish's head rested in the bird's stomach, its tail was out of its mouth. Consequently the bird was soon suffocated. . . . I never met with a similar instance of voracity.* And the twelfth of February of 1863: *Quite a number of crows have been washed ashore dead. They have a rookery at Waadah Island and probably the stormy wind that has prevailed for several days with the thick snow blinded them and they fell into the water. . . .* Catastrophe of that sort marauds here as well, although fortunately not in bunches. This house I live in sits as a glass crag in the birds' midst. Swan once tells of a canoe crew of Makahs stopping for the night at the cabin of an Olympic Peninsula settler; of how they swung the canoe mast wrong while stowing it and crashed an end through the hard-bought one window of the homestead cabin; of the settler's highest fury, as if they had shattered a diamond. This suburban house of mine glints with fourteen windows; wobbly mastbearers could pass none of my walls without creating crystal. Badger-like, I hunch in here at the typing desk and watch helplessly as this building with windows to every direction and inclination imposes itself athwart the birds' paths and every so often will kill one of them. Grosbeaks have been the most frequent victims of headlong smash against a window. During one of their migrations, twice in two days I found corpses, flat on their backs and feet curled in a final surprised clutch, below the north window.

One bird outside these transparent walls is invincible: the

Stellar's jay. Jays attack their way through life like cynical con-
nivers in a royal court. A Stellar's will alight on the garden dirt,
cock his head in disdain, scream twice, burst off into the hemlock and set the lower branches dancing, almost before its blue
sheen has blazed on my retina. What a vacancy a jay leaves in
the air. The Makahs explained to Swan that the blue jay was the
mother of a rascally Indian named Kwahtie. *She had asked him
to fetch some water, saying that she wished he would hurry,
because she felt as if she were turning into a bird. Kwahtie
ignored her and went on making the arrow he was at work on.
While she was talking she turned into a blue jay and flew into a
bush. Kwahtie tried to shoot her, but his arrow passed behind
her neck, glancing over the top of her head, ruffling up the
feathers, as they have always remained in the head of the blue
jay.* It sounds to me as good an explanation as any for this
sharp-hooded brigand.

And then the most arresting of Swan's notations, the one that
halts me in dismay: *During the spring, when the flowers are in
bloom and the humming birds are plenty, the boys take a stick
smeared with the slime from snails, and place it among a cluster
of flowers . . . if a humming bird applies his tongue to it he is
glued fast. They will then tie a piece of thread to its feet and
holding the other end let the birds fly, their humming being
considered quite an amusement.*

That scene is doubly unsettling to me. The doom of the hummingbirds, and the knowledge that had I been one of the Makah
boys I would have had my own captive bird whirring like a toy
on the end of a tether.

DAY SIXTEEN

Swan as disclosed by the few, damnably few, photos of him. In a
portrait studio at age sixty-five, he sits wearing a small round-
crowned hat, brim serenely without crimp, and has trimmed his
snug white beard, toyed a chain and fob into precise place above

the middle button of his vest, and primped a little show of handkerchief at the breast pocket of his jacket. His right hand, holding wire-rim reading glasses, rests amid books and sheafed paper atop a tablecloth so Victorianly brocaded that it looks as if it would stand in place without the table beneath it. Just slightly he faces to the left of the camera, the photographer's experience evidently having been that dignity is an oblique matter. Angled as Swan is, a white wedge of collar stands out sharply between his high-cut vest and his left jawline. This stiff bright fence of fabric at his neck and the dark orb of hat exactly flat across his head make the portrayed figure startlingly like a priest of the era, probably shyly sidled in to pose while home on leave from some far missionary billet or another.

Five years later in a crowd scene at Port Townsend, his beard is fuller and he sports a derby with the brim making a dapper little swoop to his brow. Here he looks somehow . . . elfin; somehow not quite of the same world as the foursquare town-folk all around him.

Another shot, when I judge him to be perhaps fifty. Hatless this time, and his hairline arcing fairly far back. A comb has done careful work and scissors have tidied around ears and back of neck. White, or more likely gray, is wisping into the beard only at either side of his chin. According to what one writer of regional history has remarked the dark cheek portions of beard and Swan's hair were brown, but I have no word yet from any contemporary of his on that. One surprise: the corners of his eyes are touched with only a few brief lines. I conclude that dry Montana of this century, which early engraved a web of lines on the upper face of my father and grandmother and made a no-ticeable start on me, is more erosive than Swan's maritime frontier of a hundred years ago.

Next, Swan older again, and in high regalia. He wears a fez and a broad sash, evidently trigged up for a convention of the Order of Red Man, one of the several Port Townsend lodges he belonged to. As a frontier pasha Swan looks spendidly silly, and there may be a hint held in around his lips that he more than suspects it. The new feature here, fez and sash aside, is the clear profile of Swan's nose. For most of us the nose looms as an open hinge in the center of the face, shaped to no discernible purpose except revenge on us by forgotten ancestors. But Swan came off rather well, a straight unfleshy version proportioned comfortably between the wide set of his eyes and the emphasis of his barbered heard. A restrained Boston nose.

A smatter of other scenes exists—one I particularly grin over, Swan at ease in his Port Townsend office with a deluge of Indian regalia covering every wall and shelf around him; the place looked as this writing room of mine is beginning to with the copied heaps of Swan's paperwork stacked around—but they do not offer further detail. Except one final pose, unquestionably snapped the same day in the studio as the priestly portrait. This time Swan perches on a queer chair-sized square of small notched logs, evidently the photographer's notion of a rural setting, and with casual care is holding a large canoe paddle slantwise across his body. If a flash flood should sweep through the studio he will be ready atop his small square floe. He has company in this photo, a blocky and strong-faced young Haida Indian named Johnny Kit Elswa. Wearing a suit jacket which his chest and shoulders threaten to explode, Johnny Kit Elswa stolidly stands just apart from Swan, also grips a paddle, and a fistful of arrows and a small bow as well.

Both men, one of Massachusetts and the other of the wild native coast of the North Pacific, are stiffly tethered by their stares to the camera's lens. But precisely between them breaks out a vertical riot of animated faces: a ceremonial Indian carving roughly the length and shape of the canoe paddles, agog every six inches with some fantastic woodfaced creature or another popping its eyes in the direction of the camera. Giddy, droll, mischievous, outright heehawing, the carvings are an acrobatic ladder of forest imps. In this company the humans seem dry solemn stuff indeed.

Swan, then, in the entirety of his gallery of likeness. Slightly narrow-shouldered, with a tendency to build a bit at the waistline. Surprisingly long-armed: a 32½-inch sleeve when he orders a coat from Boston. An average chest: 37 inches, on that same garment. He is perhaps five feet eight inches in height and not heavily built: *Batsie took me across the Waatch Creek on his shoulders,* the diary discloses. Say, at his best-fed, perhaps 160 pounds. All in all a shape which could be pared and stretched a bit into my own, I notice. But his beard, with its regular, combed smoothness, is nothing like my copper-wire version. My bet is that he grew it aboard the *Rob Roy,* coming west to California in 1850: new life, new face. In the ceremonial pictures in his later years he seems to have begun shaving his cheeks along the top of his beard, declaring a definite border such as where a department-store Santa's whiskers begin. Which leads to the thought that, like me, he may have been a touch overproud of a firm face of beard. A sack of hair from ear to ear may be less enhancing than we imagine.

Not an elaborate man, but with a small dressy touch now and again. A ring with a stone there on the ring finger of the left hand; that chain and fob. A favorite white meerschaum pipe. A pocket watch which he tries, with no great success, to keep accurate with the precision clock of the Port Townsend jeweler. Average vanities aside, Swan impresses as tidy; deft enough within his radius of interests; indeed, even painstaking about any matter he thinks sufficient to warrant it, such as presenting his face for the world to see. And yet in every pose more distance to him than merely the span from the camera's lens. An inward man, a winterer within himself as well as his far-frontier surroundings.

As I have fingered through the photographs Swan has seemed more than half familiar to me, the kind of visage seen from the tail of the eye and not quite willing to register. The tiny jungled planet that is the human head can be mysterious this way. Forest of hair and that sometime cultivation of beard, plain of brow, the twin seas of eyes, wrinkled country of memory and cunning and wonder and who knows what all: you can look on constellations of heads all day long without fully seeing any single orb. (Unless you sense reason for comparison. I am interested that Swan seems never to have gone bald at the north polar region where I have, but his forehead began to extend into the farthest tundra country.) At last the exact resemblance clicks. Swan looks more than a little like the history book portraits of the steel king of the nineteenth century, Andrew Carnegie. Similar wide clear brow, same trim half-face of beard more white than gray, with downward arc of mouth in it.

Between brow and beard, however, exactly there across the eyes and cheekbones, entire difference arrives. Even at his most carefully benign, Carnegie's scrutiny lances off the page at you as that of a man gauging just how far you can be tantalized with the gift of a public library. Swan blinks the middle-distance gaze of a fellow who would be in that Carnegie library thumbing through the collected works of John Greenleaf Whittier all the afternoon.

DAY SEVENTEEN

Neah Bay, mid-January 1864: a week of Swan's winter.

Sunday. *Russian Jim came in this evening and requested me to intercede with his squaw who has recently left him and try and induce her to return. Jim told me that when any one came to my door at night I should always ask "Who is there" for the Skookums sometimes came to peoples doors and did mischief. I told him I was not afraid of the powers of the air at all. He said I had a skookum tumtum*—a strong heart.

Monday. *This is my birth day 46 years old. Cleaned up the school house today, piled the lumber, and placed things in order. I shall be glad when the building is completed for the constant interruption I have and the various duties I am called on to perform prevent my giving that attention to the children I wish to. I have no time that I can call my own or in which I am not liable to interruptions except evenings and then I am generally* alone but I can find but little time to write for my sight is getting too poor to attempt writing much except by daylight.

The Indians think I have a skookum tumtum to live alone in this great house. I do not suppose one of them would dare sleep here alone for anything they are so afraid of spirits. I think the spirits of the earth are more to be feared, both spirituous liquors and evil prowling Indians but I don't apprehend any dangers or alarms from any source and thus far never have been more peacefully situated.

Tuesday. Today took an inventory of Government property for Mr Webster. Billy Balch came in this evening and gave me a very lucid explanation why the spirits of the dead did not molest me. He says that it is because we have a cellar to the house and a floor over it, but in Indian houses there is nothing but the bare ground or sand. That when any of the Indians are alone in a great house and make a fire and cook, that the memelose or dead come up through the earth and eat food and kill the Indian, but he thinks they can't come up through our floor altho as he says he would be afraid to try to sleep alone here for there might be some knot hole or crack in the floor through which they could come.

Billy also related an interesting tradition. He says that . . . at not a very remote period the water flowed from Neeah Bay through the Waatch prairie, and Cape Flattery was an island. That the water receded and left Neeah Bay dry for four days and became very warm. It then rose again without any swell or waves and submerged the whole of the cape and in fact the whole country except the mountains. . . . As the water rose those who had canoes put their effects into them and floated off with the current which set strong to the north. Some drifted one way and some another and when the waters again resumed their accustomed level a portion of the tribe found themselves beyond Nootka where their descendants now reside and are known by the same name as the Makahs. . . .

There is no doubt in my mind of the truth of this tradition.

The Waatch prairie shows conclusively that the waters of the ocean once flowed through it, and as this whole country shows marked evidences of volcanic influences there is every reason to believe that there was a crust which made the waters to rise and recede as the Indian stated.

Wednesday. *Very heavy surf during the night and this morning, showing there must have been strong winds outside the cape recently. . . . At 8 PM Jackson & Bob came to the door and informed me that a vessel had run on the rocks on the north end of Waadda Island. I went out on the beach and saw a light in that direction, but after watching it some time I concluded it was as likely to be a vessel at anchor in the harbor as one on the rocks. The Indians refused to go off to ascertain, as the wind was blowing too strong, so I came back to the house and after going up to my room in the upper part of the turret, where I had a better chance to judge I concluded from the appearance of the light that it was the US Rev Cutter Joe Lane . . . expected here with Mr Smith the keeper of Tatooche Light.*

Thursday. *My surmise last evening proved correct, it was the cutter Joe Lane which arrived. Mr Webster came down and breakfasted with me and then went on board the cutter in a canoe with five Indians who afterward conveyed him to Baadah.*

Yowarthl brought one cord oven wood today. Paid him 12 buckets of potatoes.

Went to Baadah this PM Mr Webster gave me a letter to send to the Cutter, which I sent by Hopestubbe & Yachah, who carried it and delivered it safe. Wrote this evening. . . .

Friday. *7:30 AM The Cutter got under way and stood out of the bay bound to Barclay Sound in search of Bark Narramissic, said to be lost or missing. . . .*

Saturday. *Went to Baadah to pay off Indians. Peter says that a short time since a Quillehuyte Indian named Towallanhoo came across by way of the Hoko river and from thence down on foot to Baadah where he arrived at night and reconnoitered Mr Webster's premises and then passed on to Waatch. This may account for the Indians asking me if I was not afraid to be alone in this great house and also the reason why Russian Jim cautioned me not to open my door to any one without enquiring who was there, for the Indians say that the Quillehuytes have threatened to come here and attack the whites. This may or may not be true and may be only some scheme of these people to do mischief and charge it on the Quillehuytes.*

DAY EIGHTEEN

Swan's day-upon-day sluice of diary words: why?

Was the diarying habit something which surfaced out of instinct, the unslakable one that murmurs in some of us that our way to put a mark on the world is not with sword or tool, but pen? Or did contents mean more to him than the doing of it—the diary a way to touch out into life as it flowed past him and skim the most interesting as an elixir? Either way Swan clearly was not using his pen nib merely to pass the time. So much interested him, inside the covers of books and wherever else his glance fell along this coastline, that boredom seldom seems to have found him. I do accept that the brown-inked words helped to keep straight in memory what he was seeing or being told; Swan possessed a granny's passion for gossip, and a broker's fixity on exact sums and issues. But passions and fixities do not commonly last for forty years and two and a half million words by hand. Any of us serve summer terms as diarists, generally at some moonstruck time of our lives. Somewhere in the tumble of family items in a closet of this room is interred, deservedly, the five-year diary I began in my final year of high school. I lasted at the routine a few months and am now told nothing by it but a recitation of football and basketball scores and journeys between my boarding place in town and the family's sheep ranch. That dry stick of a youngster tracing such items into my life, I

can scarcely recognize. Almost twenty years passed before I
undertook a diary again—oddly, the occasion was the same as
that earliest eddy of Swan's torrent of paper, a time spent in
Britain—and even yet I dodge behind the constant excuse that a
page should be a hireling, not the field boss, to evade for days,
weeks, at a time. This journal of winter, ninety days of exception, I face down into regularly because it must be kept, as a
ship's log must. To navigate by; know the headway. But Swan's
diary plainly masters him. Pulls his hand down onto each day's
page like a coaxing lover. How far beyond the surface of the
paper he ever can be coaxed is yet to be seen. Swan's days and
the land and people of them get scrupulous report; less so his
own interior. Unlike that other tireless clerk, Pepys of plague-
time London, Swan does not confess himself every second sen-
tence, gaily jot down whom he last tumbled to bed with and is
eyeing next nor repent every hangover nor retaste every jeal-
ousy. Much more assessor than confessor, is Swan. Yet, yet, his
words do configure, make enough significant silhouette that I
stare hard for the rest. No, the Swan style of diary-keeping—this
dialogue of a man with his days—is not merely maintenance but
more like architecture, the careful ungiddy construction of
something grand as it is odd. Swan works at these pages of his as
steadily, incessantly, as a man building a castle out of pebbles.

Castling his own life, I suppose, while I have the luck to look
on in curiosity.

DAY NINETEEN

In continental outline the United States rides the map as a gal-
leon carpentered together from the woodyard's leftover slabs:
plankish bowsprit ascending at northernmost Maine, line of keel
cobbled along Gulf shores and southwest border (Florida the
Armada-surplus anchor chain hung fat with seaweed), the surprising long clean amidship straightness of the 49th parallel
across upper Midwest and West. This patchwork ship of states

is, by chance, prowing eastward. Or as I prefer to think of it, forecastle and bow are awallow in the Atlantic while great lifting tides gather beneath our Pacific portion of the craft.

Trace to the last of this land vessel at the westernmost reach of the state of Washington, to the final briefest tacked-on deck-line of peninsula. There is Cape Flattery, where the Makahs of James G. Swan's years lived and where I am traveling today.

Towns thin down abruptly along this farthest-west promontory. In the sixty-five-mile stretch beyond Port Angeles only three—Clallam Bay; within sight of there, Sekiu; then after fifteen final miles of dodgy road, Neah Bay—and each one tightly hugs some cove in the northern shoreline of the Olympic Peninsula, as if grateful to have been rolled ashore out of the cold wallowing waters of the Strait.

The tiny communities exist on logging and seasonal salmon fishing and, as such places do, produce ample vacant time for their citizens to eye one another. The man beside me this morning at the Sekiu café counter was working his way through hash browns, sunnyside eggs, toast, sausage, coffee, and vehemence.

"That kid," he grumped across the room to the waitress, "that kid never did make much of a showing for himself around here. Glad to see him gone." An instant later, of someone else: "Never liked that lamebrained SOB anyway." As fork and tongue flashed, a close contest whether his meal or the local population would be chomped fine first.

At Neah Bay, now at midmorning, I am the one looked at, for my red beard and black watch cap. The Makahs of Neah Bay have been studying odd white faces in their streets for the past two hundred years. One story suggests that an early Russian sailing vessel smashed ashore at Cape Flattery and Swan believed that those survivors and probably other voyagers had left their genetic calling cards. (Some Makahs, he noted, *have black hair; very dark brown eyes, almost black; high cheek-bones, and dark copper-colored skin; others have reddish hair, and a few, particularly among the children, light flaxen locks. . . .*) It is definite that Spanish mariners arrived in the late eighteenth century to build a small clay-brick fort, which seems to have lasted about as long as it took them to stack it together. Every so often Swan and a few interested Indians would poke around in the Spanish shards, and the midden would stir up righteousness in him: *How different our position from theirs. They came to conquer. We are here to render benefit.*

After a hundred and twenty years as a reservation people under United States governance the Makahs might care to argue that point of benefit. Neah Bay meets the visitor as a splatter of weather-whipped houses, despite its age a tentative town seemingly pinned into place by the heavy government buildings at its corners: Bureau of Indian Affairs offices, Coast Guard enclave, Air Force base on the opposite neck of the peninsula. One building stands out alone in grace, a high-roofed museum built by the tribal council to display the finds from an archaeological dig southward along the coast at Cape Alava. Despite the museum's brave thrust and the bulky federal presence, the forested hills which crowd the bay seem simply to be waiting until the right moonless night to take back the townsite.

I have brought with me the copied portions of Swan's diaries where he writes of Cape Flattery's place in the tribal geography of the North Pacific. Remoteness and the empty expanses of Strait and ocean ought to insulate such a site, but that was not the case at all when Swan lived among the Neah Bay villagers in the early 1860s. He discovered them carrying on a complicated war of nerves, and occasionally biceps, which would do credit to any adventurous modern nation. South, north and east, the Makahs looked from their pinnacle of land toward some tribal neighbor they were at issue with.

The slowest-simmering of these rivalries extended southward, about a half-day's canoe journey down the coast to the territory of the Quillayute tribe. The Makahs suspected the Quillayutes of having massacred one of their whaling crews which had been blown downcoast by storm. Time and again this dark tale reached Swan at Neah Bay, occasionally with the added note that the murdered canoemen had been glimpsed as owls *with shells hanging from their bills similar to those worn by Makahs in their noses.*

Suspicion of the Quillayutes remained a matter of muttering, however. With the Elwhas, east along the strait, the galling issue was their killing of Swell, and it rankled hard and often. (Nor does it seem to have been assuaged by the harvest of those two Elwha heads at Crescent Bay.) In Swan's diary months Neah Bay jousts repeatedly with Elwha over the dead young chieftain. Early on, Swan and a Makah canoe crew returning from Port Townsend brought back with them an Elwha chief who wanted to talk peace. The Elwha breakfasted with Swell's brother Peter, *everyone seemed to be pleasant and friendly* but the point was sledged home to the Elwhas: *It is generally understood that if they will kill Charlie entire peace will be restored.*

Weeks later, other Elwhas showed up to parley some more, to no further result. Months later, a Makah elder abruptly announced that he was going to set fire to Swell's burial monument because the white men had not arranged vengeance for his murder.

Of a sudden, inspiration evidently lit by that torching speech, the Makahs now scored a move: *Today Peter stole a squaw from Capt. Jack, one of the Clallam Indians who was here on a visit. The squaw was part Elwha and Peter took her as a hostage to enforce pay from the Elwhas for robbing and killing a year and a half ago.*

The ransom fell through, one of the Makah tribal elders allowed the woman to escape. *Peter came to me today with a very heavy heart in consequence of the squaw having absconded.*

Just then the attention of the Makahs pivoted abruptly northward, across the Strait, which customarily was the worst direction to have to expect trouble from; the northern Indians beyond Vancouver Island were numerous and powerful canoepeople with a history of raiding almost casually down onto the smaller tribes of the Strait and Sound. The north could mean the Tsimshians and the Tlingits, and most dread of all, the Haidas of the Queen Charlotte Islands, almost to Alaska. Swan once had watched a canoe party of Haidas depart Port Townsend under the uneasy jeers of the local Clallams and Chimakums. For farewell, a Haida woman ripped a handful of grass and blew the shreds in the face of a Chimakum chieftain. That, she said: that is how easily our warriors could kill you.

This once, however, the threat did not loom from the far-north marauders, but from a nearer and smaller tribe, the Arhosetts on the west side of Vancouver Island. A Makah and an Arhosett chief had wrangled about some trading goods: *Sah tay hub getting angry because the Arhosett Indian would not agree to his terms, stabbed him with his knife.*

Here was a bladed version of Swell's death, with the Makahs this time on the delivering end, and Swan records Neah Bay's jitters about the Arhosetts voyaging down on them in revenge: *a whooping and yelling all night occasionally firing off guns to show their bravery. No enemy however appeared.*

Tension now on two fronts, and during a potlatch at Neah Bay a number of tribesmen from the outlying smaller Makah villages declared they wanted peace at least with the Elwhas. *But Peter said that he would never be satisfied until he received pay in some shape for the murder of his brother....*

Next, however, intelligence reached the Makahs and of course Swan's pen that the Arhosetts were having their own problems of pride. *This forenoon Frank told me that he had just received news from his father, old Cedakanim of Clyoquot. It appears that the Arhosett Indians have been trying to induce the Clyo-quots to join them in an attack on the Makahs.... They offered 100 blankets and 20 Makah women as slaves provided they could catch them. Cedakanim and the other Clyoquot chief re-jected this offer and demanded a steamboat, a sawmill and a barrel of gold. This difference of opinion came near resulting in a fight but at length old Cedakanim told them he would not fight the Makahs nor did he want any pay from the Arhosetts as he was much richer than they and to prove this he ordered 100 pieces of blubber to be given them.... This, said Frank, made the Arho-setts so ashamed that the sweat ran out of their faces....*

Perhaps deciding that it would be easier to negotiate with enemies than allies of Cedakanim's sort, the Arhosetts held back to see what might be forthcoming from Neah Bay. Agent

Webster suggested to the Makahs that they offer the Arhosetts a peace settlement of, say, twenty blankets; the U.S. government would provide half the total.

Given the prospect of getting out of a possible war at the cost of only ten blankets of their own, the dramatic Makahs took the chance to preen a bit, find out just how much pride had been sweated out of the Arhosetts. Swan was nominated the Neah Bay plenipotentiary *to go over to the Arhosetts and find out if they are willing to settle the affair by a payment to them of blankets, and if so the Arhosetts were to be invited to come over and get them, but we were not to carry anything at first to them but merely to find out the state of their feelings.*

As it turned out, the luckless Arhosetts did not even have the face-saving moment of receiving an envoy from the Makahs. Swan peremptorily sent word to them through Cedakanim, the Clyoquot chief who had faced them down with his wealth of blubber, and eventually two abashed Arhosetts arrived at Neah Bay to say they would settle for the blankets.

Peace ensued for two weeks, until the Elwhas protested that a cousin of Peter had wounded with a knife the brother of Swell's killer, Charlie. Peter responded that he was sorry. Sorry that Charlie's brother only had been wounded instead of killed, *for he would do it himself if he could get a chance.*

Peter being Peter, the chance was got. This culminating entry by Swan:

Tried to get Indians to go to Pt. Angeles for Mr. Webster but all are afraid as Peter on his trip down killed an Indian at Crescent Bay. The Indian was an Elwha and some years ago killed Dukwitsa's father. Peter obtained a bottle and a half of whiskey from a white man at Crescent Bay and while under its influence was instigated by Dukwitsa to kill the Elwha which he did by stabbing him. Peter told me that after he had stabbed the man several times he broke the blade of the knife off in the man's body.

As might be expected, that stabbing invited battle. As might not be expected, the skirmish lines shaped themselves not be-

tween the Makahs and the Elwhas, but the Makahs and the
United States. These years at Cape Flattery had been passing
with remarkable tranquility between the natives and the white
newcomers, as Swan was quite thankfully aware: *I have been
reading this evening the report of the Comr. of Indian Affairs
and it seems singular to be able to sit here in peace and quiet on
this the most remote frontier of the United States and read of
the hostilities among the tribes between this Territory and the
Eastern settlements.* Peter's knife punctured that state of affairs.
Swan's daily narrative begins to show move, countermove,
counter-countermove:

*Mr. Webster arrested Peter this evening and took him on
board the sch. A. J.* Westen *to be taken to Steilacoom,* the
territorial army headquarters.

*. . . A canoe with a party of Indians followed the schooner
and this evening it was reported that they had rescued Peter and
conveyed him to Kiddekubbut. I think this report doubtful.* But
later *ascertained it was true . . . Old Capt. John and 16 others
came this forenoon to make me a prisoner and keep me as long
as Mr. Webster keeps Peter but when they found that Peter had
escaped they came to tell me not to be afraid. I said I was not
afraid of any of them and gave them a long lecture. John said I
had a skookum tumtum.*

. . . The steamer Cyrus Walker *with a detachment of 33
soldiers under Lieut. Kestler arrived at Neah Bay about midnight of Tuesday. . . . The steamer with Mr. Webster on board
proceeded to Kiddekubbut and succeeded in arresting 14
Indians:* Peter and thirteen others.

Peter now vanishes from the Neah Bay chronicle, to Swan's
considerable relief. *I have tried for the past three years to make
Mr. Webster believe what a bad fellow Peter is,* the diary splut-
ters in farewell to the Makah warlock.

A fiery enough record, these few years of Makah bravado and
occasional bloodshed as chronicled by Swan. Yet while this se-
quence of ruckus was occurring out on the poop deck of the

continent at Cape Flattery, the United States of America and the Confederate States of America were inventing modern mass war at Antietam and Chancellorsville and Gettysburg. If it is a question as to which civilization in those years was more casual with life, the Makahs don't begin to compete with the Civil War's creeks and bayous of blood. Nor has their martial inventiveness kept pace with our own. Driving here from Seattle this morning, I stopped at the west end of the highway bridge which sweeps across Hood Canal on barge-sized concrete pontoons and looked along the channel to where a military base is being built for nuclear-missile-bearing Trident submarines. The killing capacity of Swan's tetchy Makahs compares to that of a Trident as a jackknife to bubonic plague.

Some hours in Neah Bay fitting its geography onto Swan's era—a breakwater, built in the name of World War II security, now stretches from the west headland of the bay to Waadah Island; the Bureau of Indian Affairs buildings top the eastern point where Webster's trading post stood—and I turn toward the ocean.

Cape Flattery is, as I have said, as far west as you can step on the mainland forty-eight states of America. But along the Cape's Pacific extremity there are thrusts of cliff actually out above the ocean; ultimate sharp points of landscape as if a new compass heading had been devised for here, west of west.

From a logging road I climb down the forest trail to the tip of the Cape's longest finger of headland. At the trailhead the Makah Tribal Council has nailed up alarming signs . . . *Rugged High Cliffs . . . Extremely Dangerous Area . . . enter at own risk*. The final brink of the trail lives up to them by simply snapping off into midair.

There, some eighty or hundred feet above the Pacific, rides an oceanlooker's perch, an oval of white hardpack clay about twenty feet wide and twice as long. A clawnail hardness for this last talon of cliff.

I have clambered up all the great capes of this Northwest

coast: Cape Disappointment at the mouth of the Columbia, to step to the Pacific horizon as Lewis and Clark did; Oregon's Cape Falcon with its howling fluency of wind, and south of it Cape Meares and Cape Lookout, and south from them Cape Foulweather and Cape Perpetua and Cape Blanco. But none of those, none, proffers the pinnacle-loneliness of this tip of Cape Flattery. Behind, on all sides, the continent shears away, dangles me to air and the rocky water below. "Those whales," a Makah tribesman has told me of the spring migrating pattern past this spot: "Sometimes they come right in under the cliffs. They scrape those barnacles off themselves on the rocks."

Surf pounds underfoot with surprisingly little noise but wind makes up for it. I crouch carefully, not to be puffed off the continent, and peer out the half-mile or so to Tatoosh, the lighthouse island here at the entrance to the Strait of Juan de Fuca. *While at Tatooche*, Swan entered in his diary on July 18, 1864, *I counted 18 vessels in sight.*

Now machines instead of humans operate the Tatoosh light, visitors are none, and the tiny white cluster of lighthouse, residential quarters, water tower, and a collapsing shed give off visual echoes of emptiness. Tatoosh simply rests out there like a fat stepping-stone off the end of the continent. The next foothold beyond it is Asia.

In the 1860s the Makah tribesmen told Swan that below these cliffs, in hours of calm water, they sometimes hunted seals. Caves drill back in very far at the base of the cliffs and so a Makah would approach by canoe, swim or wade in with a lighted torch and a knife, and stalk back along the tunneled floor until he came onto drowsing seals. The blaze of the torch confused the animals, and the hunter took the chance of their confusion to stab them.

There was risk, Swan noted. *Occasionally the torch will go out, and leave the cavern in profoundest darkness.*

Profoundest darkness, and naked knife-bearing men who would wade into it. Even if you do not know that story, to stand atop this last rough end of the continent is to have it come to mind: what the dwellers of this coast could do before they found other, easier routes.

DAY TWENTY

Cape Flattery must have stood the neck hair on Swan a few times, too. This morning I find that in one of the several articles he wrote about the Makahs he listed in firm schoolteacherly style the superstitions of the tribe, then let burst from him this uncommonly uneasy language:

The grandeur of the scenery about Cape Flattery, and the strange contortions and fantastic shapes into which its cliffs have been thrown by some former convulsion of nature, or worn and abraded by the ceaseless surge of the waves; the wild and varied sounds which fill the air, from the dash of water into the caverns and fissures of the rocks, mingled with the living cries of innumerable fowl . . . all combined, present an accumulation of sights and sounds sufficient to fill a less superstitious beholder than the Indian with mysterious awe.

Yesterday's weather faded and faded, had gone into gray by sundown. This morning is delivering sleet, blanking the coastline of the Strait down to a few hundred yards of mingled sky and water and rock. A worker from a construction crew stepped from the room next to mine and squinted into the icy mush. He shook his head and declared: "I need this like I need another armpit."

The feel of Cape Flattery as an everlasting precipice of existence is strong as I repeat routes of Swan's here. When he established himself in the schoolhouse at Neah Bay in 1863, ready to reason the peninsular natives into the white culture's version of education, he made himself in that moment the westernmost frontiersman in the continental United States. Jones, the Reservation farmer at the moment, moved briefly into the schoolhouse with Swan while his own quarters were being built, but it was Swan who nestled for good into the room atop the school's tall square tower, a mile or so beyond that shared magpies'-nest household at Webster's.

Out here on his pinnacle of the coast, he becomes now the Pacific Republic of Swan, newly independent. Population: one; Caucasian and male. Resources: ink, books, and an occasional newspaper off a passing ship. Languages: Bostonian, Chinook, Makah. Politics: Lincoln Republican, solder-the-Union-back-together-with-bayonet-steel. Industry: very light, allotted mainly to educational manufacture. Foodstuffs: an exuberant variety ranging from halibut-head chowder to something termed beef hash à la Makah. Flag: a river of words against a backdrop of black fir forest.

Delightfully situated as he now was, *with windows facing the north, west, and east, and a glass door opening south,* in a matter of months after the move to his schoolhouse aerie came news from across the continent which reminded Swan how far he had flung himself. On the tenth of February 1864:

. . . letter from my brother Benj L Swan stating that on Sunday Nov 29 my mother died aged 84 years 7 mos & 27 days and that on Wednesday Dec 2d my dear wife Matilda W Swan died of consumption.

The double deaths staggered Swan for days. As I read the lines, the same scimitar of bay before me as Swan stared to during the writing of them, his distress and realization thud and thud like a slow surf:

nearly paralyzed with grief

had fondly thought that I might once again go home and be joined with my dear wife and children, but it was ordered otherwise

aching, breaking heart

but little sleep last night went to bed at two and got up at six

Severe pain in my teeth today. Sick in body and mind.

DAY TWENTY-ONE

Sick in body and mind, and of all air and earth that touch the two. Any of us who have been hit with such news of death know Swan's disorder, and its remedy: routine. After some days of remorseful entries, undoubtedly whetted sharper by the memory of that permanent good-bye to Matilda in 1850, Swan turns to schoolroom worries again. *Today, the fifteenth of February 1864, quite a number of children were in attendance but David and some others came in about trade which I do not desire and frightened the children away. . . . I have been to Baadah every Saturday at Mr Webster's request to issue goods to Indians in payment for work done on the reservation. This has caused the others to think I am the trader and they continually come to me to sell oil, skins and blankets much to my annoyance.*

Annoyance is a broad step up from misery, and as the months of 1864 pass, Swan's words brighten, the classroom perplexity (*slow work teaching these Indians. They appear intelligent enough in most respects but appear to take but little interest in learning the alphabet*) giving way to the glint of the Makahs themselves.

Julia and another squaw came up today, the tenth of April, and stated that the Hosett Indians had discovered that Kayattie one of the old men . . . had caused the late spell of bad weather which has kept the Indians from fishing or whaling. A Squaw and a boy had overheard him at his incantations and had reported to the others, whereupon the whole village turned out and proceeded to Kayatties lodge and told him if he did not immediately stop and make fair weather they would hang him. Kayattie promised to do so. John who told me the story very gravely added his belief that now we should have fine weather. I told him it was all cultus talk, but he said no, that the Indians in former times were capable of making it rain or blow when they pleased. There was one of the Kwillehuytes who made bad weather . . . during the halibut season and the Kwillehuytes hung him, and immediately the weather became fine.

Billy Balch, Kyallanhoo & the others who have been absent since Tuesday returned this forenoon, the tenth of June. They were blown off out of sight of land for one day, and afterwards made land at Oquiet, and remained till this morning. There was a large crowd of their friends and relatives collected together this morning thinking they were lost, and some of the squaws seemed sorry that they did not have a chance to howl.

The Indians told me this morning, the thirtieth of July, that Hadassub one of the best and quietest Indians in the tribe died suddenly last night at Kiddekubbut. I went down after breakfast on foot to the village and learned that he died of apoplexy. He had been very well all day and had joined in the dance at a potlatch given by Chekotte at Peter's house, and in the evening had taken part in a wrestling match and afterward partaken freely of rice and molasses. He had not eaten any molasses for a long time as it did not agree with him but on this occasion thought he would eat some. . . . The Indians always attribute an unusual death to the operation of some bad Tomanawas, and as there is a party of Quinaults here I did not know but they might charge it upon them. I explained . . . the natural causes that would most likely have produced his death and strongly urged them in future not to bury any one until they had tried every means of testing animation.

In the autumn, Swan about to mark his first year in the classroom, school woes return to his daily pages.

For one thing, he has worked out the appalling calculation that to keep the drafty schoolhouse warm through the year will require 100 cords of wood—that is, a woodpile four feet high, four feet wide, and eight hundred feet long, every sliver of it needing to be wheedled from the Makahs by barter of buckets of potatoes.

For another, *the attendance at School has been very meagre . . . and this afternoon, the tenth of November, I sent for Youaitl (Old Doctor) and had a long talk with him on the matter.*

I told him that the Government at Washington had been at great expense to have this school house built, and now I wanted the children to come and be taught, and wanted him to let his second son Kachim come and board with me and be one of a class with Jimmy. . . . That if a few of the boys took an interest to learn others would be induced to come, and finally all the children could be taught. I also told him that the old men were dying off and these boys would shortly take their places, and if they would come and learn now they could be useful when they grew up, and could better adapt themselves to the white mens customs, than the old men who were so prejudiced against the whites.

Old Doctor said my talk was "all good," "all good," and he would send the boy and talk to the other Indians . . .

Two days later Swan has in residence with him at the schoolhouse Kachim, Jimmy, and five other boys. They spend the day toiling on the alphabet and amuse themselves in the evening, and that night's diary page exults that *Today has been the first time that it has seemed like a regular school.*

Soon after this triumph of regularity, Swan wakes a little past five in the morning to a houseful of smoke. *I found George in the kitchen with a big fire in the stove . . . and a pot of potatoes on cooking and the smoke just pouring out into the room. As it created an atmosphere like that which he has been accustomed to in the Indian lodge, he thought it was all right and that he was doing finely.* Swan opened the damper and commended the young chef *for his zeal but told him he need not get up another morning till day light.*

George's breakfast pall seems to hang on and on in the diary pages, clouding the earlier sanguine estimations of the schoolboys' new diligence . . . *the principal inducement at present is the novelty of the thing and the plenty of food I give them to eat. They can be influenced by their stomachs much sooner than their brains. . . .*

After more than a year of the effort to hold classes and compel attendance, two notations even more glum. The twenty-seventh of December 1864:

My whole time is constantly occupied from early in the morning till ten and often eleven oclock at night without an hour that I can call my own. Cooking, looking after the house, attending the sick, prescribing medicines and trying to teach, and the results are far from being in proportion to the great care and anxiety I feel.

The next day: John had a talk last evening in Russian Jims lodge about the school . . . and among others who spoke Jim said that he did not want his boy to learn to read and write for it would be of no use to him, he could not get anything by it, but if he learned to kill whales and catch halibut he would have plenty of things. . . . This attempt to form a school is the most unsatisfactory thing I have ever tried.

DAY TWENTY-TWO

This morning, nagged by a murmur of memory, I finally retraced the entry, Swan's diary words of this exact date, one hundred thirty-nine years ago. The eleventh of January 1860. *Cloudy and calm. This is my birth day 42 years old. I trust that the remainder of my life may be passed more profitably than it has so far. Self investigation is good for birth days.*

Tonight, after another coastal day back and forth between Swan's words and the actuality of Cape Flattery: "Some men and women are never part of the time they were born into," Carol's voice read to me as I hunched in the phone booth at Clallam Bay, "and walk the streets or highways of their generations as strangers. . . . Reinforces our diminishing conviction that there is something special in American earth, in American experience and in the harrowing terms of American survival. Where there is no longer a house of sky . . ."

The words clatter back and forth between my ears. *Never part of the time they were born into . . . walk their generations as strangers . . .* The sort of thing I might write about Swan, restless in

Boston, studious on the frontier. Instead, in the pages of the
New York Times Book Review it has been written of me.

DAY TWENTY-THREE

From places here at the outer corner of the Strait it can be seen
clearest how abruptly close the Olympic range of mountains
stands to this coastline: like gorgeously caped elephants about
to go wading. Along much of the Peninsula south of the logging
town of Forks, for instance, peaks of 4,000 to 7,000 feet rise
within thirty-five miles of the Pacific shore, rather as if the
Rockies were to begin at Philadelphia, or the Sierra Nevada just
beyond the east alleys of Oakland.

There is a kind of stolen thrill, something unearned and simply granted, about the presence of the Olympics. The state of
Washington makes its margin with the Pacific as if the region
west of the Cascade Mountains had all been dropped heavily
against the ocean, causing wild splatters of both land and water:
the islands of Puget Sound and the San Juan group, streaky
inlets everywhere, stretched stripes of peninsula such as Dungeness and Long Beach, the eighty-mile fjord called Hood Canal,
and a webwork of more than forty sizable rivers emptying to the
coast. Amid this welter the Olympic Mountains stand in calm
tall files, their even timbered slopes like black-green fur to shed
the wet. The region's history itself seems to step back and mar-
vel at these shoreline mountains. The coastal Indians appear not
to have troubled to travel much in them. Why wrestle forest
when the sea is an open larder? White frontier-probing too went
into an unusual and welcome slowdown when it reached the
Olympics. Although the range sits only some sixty miles wide
and fifty long, not until 1889 did a six-man expedition spon-
sored by a Seattle newspaper traipse entirely across it and leave
some of the loveliest peaks of America with the curious legacy
of being named for editors. Thereafter its terrific shaggy abun-

dance of timber saved the range; giant fir and cedar and spruce rose so mighty along its shorelines and foothills that the heart of the Olympics was not logged before National Park status came in the 1930s.

Good fortune for the northwest earth that was, for where the early loggers did begin whacks into the Olympic Peninsula forest, some of them butchered the country: you can see it yet in places beside the highway, obliteration where the ancient stumps lie about like knuckle bones after cannibals had done with them. Those cut-out-and-get-out loggers had some excuse, not understanding or having to care that felling the timber that denuded the slope that lost the silt that clogged the stream would smother salmon runs and other interties of nature, and figuring anyway that the trees and salmon and all else would last forever, but we know by now that America's forevers tend to be briefer than the original estimates.

What remains still original, the Olympic peaks, rise to me when I climb to the rim of our valley as the great Sawtooth Range and other sharp horizons gnashed up to the west of my family's Montana grassland. They were my first shore, those rough snow-topped headlands which stop the flow of plains in the Montana I was born to, and later, when I went back to write about that rock-tipped land, I began at last to savvy the geography as a vast archipelago of mountains and to remember how, like people in fast outriggers, we traveled in pickups and trucks the valleys between the high islanded clusters. Now it is Townsend, Buckhorn, the Needles, Constance, Jupiter, the Brothers, two dozen Olympic peaks alive in jagged white rhythm like lightning laid lengthwise, that make the uneven but steady skyline. From the instant I saw them a dozen years ago I have felt exhilaration from these mountains like a gust down from their glaciers. If they did not exist, I think I would not live here; would need to be within sight of some other craggy western horizon. As it is, over the years I have hiked into all the main valleys of the Olympics except a few of the southernmost, and go time upon time upon time to places along the Sound and Strait where I know favorite views of peaks.

And today I have spent hours studying the Olympics rather than Swan's past. I don't much mind; Swan undoubtedly did the same. I find him writing once for the San Francisco newspaper, *The great Sierra of the Olympic range appear to come down quite to the water's edge, and present a wild forbidding aspect.* Other times, I come across him tallying into the diaries a morning when the Olympics happened to be spectacularly sunlit. But I do not find him ever exploring into the so-near fortress of peaks. Enough of Boston evidently remained in Swan that he would admire mountains with his eyes rather than his feet.

DAY TWENTY-FOUR

The Pacific's sounds climb into the forest to meet us, minutes before Alava Island stands through the firs as a mesa in the ocean. Alava, first and biggest and namesake of Cape Alava's strewn collection of seastacks, reefs, isles, boulders. Of this pepper-spill on the coast's map which a despairing cartographer simply summed as The Flattery Rocks.

The rhythmic pound of tidal surge underscores the reputation that, all the fifteen miles down from Cape Flattery to here, and south from Alava for thirty miles more, this coast constantly dodges and tumbles. Boulder formations and landforms sprawl random and ajut as vast weapon heads. Drift logs lodge high on the beach like colossal ax-hafts tossed on a forgotten armory shelf. Each cape and bluff seems braced, banked for the turns of winter storm that flow in from the southwest. While Swan lived at Neah Bay, itself an outpost of the back of beyond, the tiny community here was considered the truly remote settlement of the Makahs. *Hosett,* it was called then.

Carol and I arrive the one easy way, overland from the east, and the route has become more "over" than I am happy with. Nearly the entire trail, three and a third miles from Lake Ozette to Cape Alava, has been built up into a boardwalk of cedar slabs, the size of stair steps and nailed onto hefty stringers.

Wonk wonk wonk wonk wonk wonk, our boots constantly re-
sound on the cedar, *wonk wonk wonk wonk wonk wonk.*
The boardwalk's height from the forest floor puts my head at an
elevation of seven feet or so, and I feel like a Zulu clogging
along in a Dutchman's shoes.

"Just like Asbury Park," Carol offers in joke as we wonk
along. But this is not the New Jersey shore at the bounds of
boardwalk, but a weave of coastal forest, and because the cedar
walkway perpetually stays damp enough to be slick, my eyes are
pulled down to it too often from their pleasure of sorting the
wealth of green: salal, cedar, hemlock, huckleberry, deer fern,
an occasional powerful Douglas fir.

We alight onto the beach at Cape Alava amid a spring noon
which has somehow drifted loose into mid-January. No wind at
all, rare for this restless coast, and a surprise warmth in the air
that denies knowing anything whatsoever about this morning's
winter chill.

As we stride north the mile or so to the archaeological dig, we
find that winter storms have made the Alava beach a stew of
kelp, rockweed, sea cucumbers and sundry unidentifiables. One
ingredient is an ugly rotting bulb which we agree must be the
ocean version of turnip. Gulls, turnstones, and sanderlings patrol scrupulously along the tideline, while cormorants idly crowd
the offshore rocks. Crows swagger now and again among the
seaweed, right to ocean's edge. Some evolutionary instant from
now the first one will swash in to join the gulls amid the surf and
make the species seagoing.

The archaeological site has grown to resemble a tiny silver-
strike town. Board houses and sheds dribble along the hillside,
and then the laid-open ground where the excavation is under-
way. A difference is that the digging here represents the most
delicate of mining, done painstakingly within two-meter squares
of soil at a time. Five buried longhouses have been discovered
on the site, and the contents of the three opened to date have
sifted out as a kind of archaeological miracle. The scholarly
guess is that the Makah residents of some five hundred years ago
felled too much of the forest on the bluff above, probably to feed

their fires; the defoliated slope gave way and an avalanche of heavy clay soil sealed everything below it as instantly and tightly as if in a flood of molten glass. Washington State University archaeologists and their student teams have been sieving the past here for ten years, and the trove of artifacts is to go on display in the museum the Makahs are building at Neah Bay.

The diggers are proud of the site. The young woman from a Colorado university who shows us around says it is known as one of the ten most important digs being done in the world. She tells us, too, details unearthed since our other visits here: that shells of some sixty kinds of shellfish have been found in the longhouses, testimony to the prowess of the Hosett Makahs in trading very far up and down this coast, and that belongings of a head man of a longhouse were uncovered in one building's northeast corner, the farthest from the prevailing weather and therefore the snuggest.

The dig deserves honor as a North Pacific Pompeii, an invaluable pouch of the Makah past. Yet I find as ever that I am stirred less by the treasure pit than by something almost invisible among the Alava tidal rocks. At low tide, if you know where to gaze amid the dark stone humps, a canoeway slowly comes to sight, a thin lane long ago wrested clear of boulders by the Makahs so they would have a channel into the Pacific for their fragile wooden hulls.

This dragway is the single most audacious sight I know on this planet. Musclemade, elemental, ancient, leading only toward ocean and the brink of horizon: it extends like a rope bridge into black space. Mountain climbers, undersea explorers, any others I can think of who might match the Makahs for daring are able to mark their calendar of adventure as they choose, select where and when they will duel nature. But this handwrought crevasse through the beach rocks was the Makahs' path to livelihood, their casual alley, and out along it with their canoes of poise and their sensations cleansed by rituals slid generations of Hosett whalers, lifting away into the glittering Pacific.

The archaeology student mentioned Swan as we toured the

dig, saying that a good deal of what is known about the Makahs' whaling implements was learned from the descriptions he wrote. The words of his that interest me today, however, begin in his diary on July 22 of 1864, when he *commenced a trip for Hosett and the lake said by the Indians to be back from Hosett village.* As we retrace our steps inland to Lake Ozette we will be on Swan's route, and the Makahs of the time assured him that he was the first white man ever to see Lake Ozette.

That may have been native blarney, but the known history of the Alava coast testifies for it. In the journals of the seagoing explorers I have found no record of longboats rowing in to reconnoiter this unnerving rock-snaggled stretch of shore. In July of 1785 at the mouth of the Hoh River, twenty-five miles south of here, the Spaniard Bodega y Quadra did send in from his schooner a boat crew of seven men to fill water casks. The waiting Indians killed five, and two drowned in terror in the surf.

The Lake Ozette corner of the Peninsula was to remain undisturbed until white settlers arrived to its shores—inland from Alava, along the trail Swan walked thirty years earlier—in the 1890s. Their homesteads never really burgeoned and the lake even now remains remote, lightly peopled. Carol and I once hiked in to the southern end of Lake Ozette by a little-used trail to camp overnight. The solitude was total except for hummingbirds buzzing my red and black shirt.

Now, with a last memorizing look toward the beach and the Makah canoeway, to Ozette again. Swan's exploration on that day in 1864 we begin to duplicate with eerie exactness. *The trail commences a short distance south of the village and runs up to the top of the hill or bluff which is rather steep and about sixty feet high.* So the route still climbs. *From the summit we proceeded in an easterly direction through a very thick forest half a mile and reached an open prairie which is dry and covered with fern, dwarf sallal and some red top grass, with open timber around the sides.* The very grass seems the same. *From this prairie we pass through another belt of timber to another prairie lying in the same general direction as the first but somewhat lower and having the appearance of being wet and boggy. This was covered in its . . . lower portions with water grass and thick moss which yielded moisture on the pressure of the feet.* Step from the boardwalk and drops of moisture from James Swan's pen distill on our boots.

By now this second of the twin prairies possesses a name, and some winsome history. Maps show the eyelet in the forest as Ahlstrom's Prairie, where for fifty-six years Lars Ahlstrom led a solitary life as one more outermost particle of the American impulse to head for sunset. Through nearly all the decades of his bachelor household here, Ahlstrom's was the homestead farthest west in the continental United States.

Originally, which is to say within the first few dozen days after his arrival in 1902, Ahlstrom built himself a two-room cabin close beside the Ozette to Alava trail. That dwelling burned in 1916 and he lived from then on in the four-room structure which still stands, thriftily but sturdily erected with big tree stumps as support posts for its northwest and northeast corners, a few hundred yards from the trail.

Even now as Carol and I whap through the brush to this latter-day cabin, all signs are that Ahlstrom kept a trim, tidy homestead life. In his small barn on the route in, the window sills above a workbench are fashioned nicely into small box-shelves. At the cabin itself the beam ends facing west into the prevailing weather are carefully masked with squares of tarpaper. Inside, when Ahlstrom papered the cabin walls with newspapers, he wrapped around the pole roofbeams as well, a fussy touch that I particularly like. Summers in Montana when I worked as a ranch hand I spent time in bunkhouses papered this way, and neatness made a difference. Always there would be interesting events looming out at you—ROOSEVELT ORDERS BANK HOLIDAY or U.S. GUNBOAT PANAY SUNK BY JAPANESE—or some frilly matron confiding the value of liver pills, and the effect was lost if the newsprint had been slapped on upside down or sideways.

This rainbelt homestead of Ahlstrom's never quite worked out. Regularly he went off into the Olympic Mountains on logging jobs and other hire to earn enough money to survive the year. On the other hand, the homestead went on never quite working out for five and a half decades, until Ahlstrom, at eighty-six, cut his foot while chopping wood and had to move to Port Angeles for the last few years of his life.

Here in the drowsing cabin I think of Swan and Ahlstrom, who missed each other by forty years on this mossy prairie between Alava and Ozette, and judge that if time could be rewoven to bring them together they might be quite taken with one another. Swan promptly diaries down the facts of the life of *Mr Ahlstrom . . . arrived to America from Sweden at the age of 20 years . . . he and a neighbor have laboured to build a pony trail to the lake by laying down a quantity of small cedar puncheons . . . the rain here does not allow his fruit trees to thrive but his garden particularly potatoes grows finely. . . .* Ahlstrom, with his reputation for conviviality with travelers, pours coffee for Swan, watches to see whether he will take cream, Swedish style, or swig it black the way of the barbarous Norwegians. (Swan, resident of Neah Bay for a full two years before a milk cow arrived, takes cream whenever he can get it.) At slightest prompting, Ahlstrom entertains Swan with his story of coming face to face with a cougar here on the Ozette trail. *I yelled to scare him.* Instead it brought answer: the cougar snarled *and I could see plenty of room inside there for a Swede.* Ahlstrom spun and strode away—*It was no use to run*—without looking back. The next day Ahlstrom returned carrying a long-tom shotgun and discovered from the tracks that when he retreated, the cougar had paced along behind him for a hundred yards and then lost interest in Swedish fare.

The trail again, Swan's and Ahlstrom's and ours. *After crossing the second prairie we again enter the forest and after rising a gentle eminence descend into a ravine through which runs a small brook.* Exactly so. The little stream that dives under the boardwalk runs very loud, and sudsy from lapping across downed trees. Where the water can be seen out from under its head of foam, it ripples dark brown, the color of strong ale.

And now the lake, obscure and moody Ozette.

Here we found an old hut made in the rudest manner with a few old splits of cedar and showing evidence of having been used as a frequent camping ground by the Hosett hunters. An old canoe split in two was lying in front, and bones and horns of elk were strewed about. Now the premises which emerge into sight are a National Park display center and rangers' quarters.

At last at the lakeside, Swan recorded a curiously threatening experience.

It was nearly sundown when we arrived and I had barely time to make a hasty sketch of the lake before it was dark. We had walked out very rapidly and I was in a great heat on my arrival, and my clothes literally saturated with perspiration. I imprudently drank pretty freely of the lake water which had the effect of producing a severe cramp in both of my legs which took me some time to overcome, which I did however by walking about and rubbing the cramped part briskly. I said nothing to the Indians as I did not wish them to know anything ailed me, but at times I thought I should have to ask their assistance.

So he saved face, and evidently something more. What was it that struck at him with those moments of dismay in his legs? Uncertainty of how the Makahs might react to an ailment? That tribal habit of burying first and regretting later? The remoteness of Ozette itself, like a vast watery crater in the forest?

The next morning, the twenty-third of July 1864, Swan intended to go out with Peter and sketch his way along the Ozette shoreline, but awoke to heavy fog. *As I well knew that the fogs at this season sometimes last several days, I concluded that I had better return.* Their return hike to Alava was memorably soggy. *The fog and mist had saturated the bushes so that before I was a mile on my way back I was wet through and reached Hosett as well drenched as if I had been overboard.*

Well drenched, and better pleased. *I had accomplished two things   I had proved the existence of a lake, and had made a sketch of a portion and as I was the first white man who had ever seen this sheet of water I concluded I would take some other opportunity when I might have white companions with me and make a more thorough survey.*

Swan never did achieve that more thorough survey. But today, at least, he had the companions to Ozette.

DAY TWENTY-FIVE

I like about Swan that he has arithmetic in his eye.

When he and the Makahs dig around in the rubble of the short-lived Spanish fort at Neah Bay, the clay tiles they unearth *are 10 inches long 5¼ wide & 1¼ thick*. When Swan visits the lighthouse on Tatoosh Island, the Fresnel lens *measures 6 ft across* and *is composed of 13 rings of glass above   6 rings below*. When he is curious about how large the clearing behind the Indian lodges at Neah is, he finds out *by pacing it off . . . 235 paces long   60 paces wide   this will give at a rough estimate 2⁹⁄₁₀ acres*.

He scares me a little, though, about this winter's effort at precision, my try at knowing as much as possible of Swan. There is that easy deceit of acquaintanceship; in the months since *This House of Sky* was published I have heard again and again from schoolmates and Montana friends, "I figured I knew you pretty well, but . . ." (Echo: *never part of the time they were born into . . . walk their generations as strangers . . .*) If I myself am such an example of private code, how findable can Swan be in his fifteen thousand days of diary words? Findable enough, I still believe, for by now I have a strengthening sense of how it is that some of those coastal paths which for so many years carried him now hold me. But Swan does maintain boundaries, often numerical ones, with that deft pen. He may let me know exactly what size coat he wore, yet generally is going to make me guess about the inside of his head. Which perhaps is as much as one measurer can comfortably grant another.

DAYS TWENTY-SIX, TWENTY-SEVEN, TWENTY-EIGHT

The Neah Bay schoolroom once more, that wrestling site for Swan's tutoring and the Makahs' resistance to it.

My occupation is pretty regular every day, he reports on the sixth of February of 1865. *As soon as I get up, which is from half past 6 to 7, the Indians begin to come for medical treatment. Some who want prescriptions only I serve before breakfast but others who have sores to be dressed have to wait till I have done eating. Then it is dressing scrofulous sores, syringing out sore ears, bathing sore eyes and bandaging up wounds. Then round to visit patients. By this time it is eleven oclock & I then sit down to write, or if any children come in, try to teach them. And with the exception of a walk to Jones or Jordans, keep in the house all the time so as to be ready either as teacher or physician.*

Of these eithers, the Makahs plainly preferred Swan as physician, and logical choice it was. Mending an ill was welcome enough; changing the tongues of the tribe's children was not. For rickety and fumbling though it may have been, this new white men's governance of Cape Flattery, with the plow and schoolhouse as its cutting machines, meant rip after rip through the Makah way of life.

Swan himself once honed the metaphor. *We have indeed caused the plowshare of civilization to pass over the graves of their ancestors and open to the light the remains of ancient lodge fires.* Many of the Makahs must have known the consequences as well as Swan—probably better—and the wonder is that the tribe did not stiffen harder against the demand that they surrender their sons and daughters to alphabet and agriculture.

Part of the answer must be in the beguilement that Swan and his paper and pen represented. The Makahs respected any potent ability, and Swan as the reservation's deftest practitioner of paperwork flexed a right hand of magic. He it was who would provide a "paper" by which anyone who brought him an amount of firewood could be paid off in potatoes. Would draw up a document attesting that a canoeman had helped rescue ship-wrecked sailors and so deserved the favor of whatever white man was reading the words. (Or occasionally provide a some-what more wan endorsement: *Gave a "paper" to Shekaupt . . . that he is as good as the average but requires watching.*) Out of his books would reproduce those strange winged creatures and their stories. Swan had surveyed and mapped the Makah reservation, taken its census, noted down whenever a whale was killed and who the harpooner was, made arithmetic of the very weather by measuring rain and wind and temperature and giving them a history in his tremendous ledger. All his perpetual count-ing and scrawling added up to something the Makahs weren't quite clear on, no more than we would be if a tribe came out of the sea to us and spoke green sparks which hung in the air, except that it carried power.

The Indians have a belief that I can tell by referring to my book containing the census of the tribe what becomes of any Indian who may be missing, so last evening a great many came to ask me to look in my book and tell what had become of Long Jim and the others who had gone for seals and had not returned.

I told them my book told nothing but it was my opinion that Jim and his brother who are young and strong would return, but as for Old George and the boy who were in a small canoe I thought they would not get back so soon. . . .

His commonsense prediction proved right, and *the Indians now think that my book tells the truth and they have increased confidence in it.*

Some other matters about Swan must have been as puzzling to the Makahs as his ceaseless writing hand. He rejected coldly their attempts to bargain payments out of him for letting their children attend his school, yet he would pay rewards to have mere seashells brought to him from the beach. He scolded about the drinking of whiskey, indeed questioned the Makahs steadily about its purveyors so that he could report them to Webster, yet at Port Townsend it was said that Swan had a weakness for putting the potion into himself. Over the years Swan had arrived and departed among the Makahs casually, but now he insisted their children must live steadily with him in the schoolhouse. (*The boys will not come as day scholars, and there will have to be an entire change of things before the school will ever amount to anything.*)

All of which is to say, here at this point in his winter diary of unease, that Swan, who even by frontier standards stood out as something of a drifter, was irony's choice to bring white grooves of routine to the natives of Cape Flattery.

At last, the twenty-fifth of February of 1865, after a three-month absence Webster arrives with supplies for the reservation. Evidently Swan promptly made a fist at him about the gaping absence of authority at Neah Bay. Before Webster's next vanishing act a few weeks later, *he handed me a document which he had written placing me in full charge of the government property during his absence.*

Swan and diary ease out of their winter ire. *Some of the Indians have purchased umbrellas at Victoria and today there was quite a display on the beach. This is quite an innovation on their old style of warding off rain with bear skin blankets and conical hats.... Heard frogs singing this evening for the first time this spring.... At work trimming shrubbery, training rosebushes and transplanting currants, blackberries and gooseberries....*

Then, the evening of the fourteenth of April, a reverberation set off across the continent at Appomattox five days earlier: *we heard several reports of cannon which proved to be the swivel at Baadah but as it was raining none of us cared to go to ascertain the cause although we supposed Mr Maggs had received some news from upsound of some great victory over the rebels.*

And the next week the grimmer echo: *Mr Jones brings the sad intelligence of the Assassination of President Lincoln ... Dreadful news ... The result will be that the north will be more united than ever and will crush out the serpent that has been nourished....*

The reservation's potato field is planted. A day of fasting is observed in Lincoln's memory. Swan sets a hen on thirteen eggs in the schoolhouse basement.

The fifteenth of May, experiment by Swan's leading scholar. *Jimmy took the tips of the Bulls horns which were sawed off yesterday and set them out among the cabbage plants. He had seen me set out slips of currant & Gooseberries and thought if sticks would grow, the horns certainly would.*

Three canoes of Clyoquot Indians, faces painted red and black, arrive from Vancouver Island to visit. At Hosett, a Makah canoe splits on a reef, and a woman and a girl drown. Webster persuades Swan to stand for a seat in the territorial legislature, and Swan is trounced. Swan sets another hen on another thirteen eggs.

The eleventh of June, a Sunday of frustration and retribution: *Yesterday my cat killed all my chickens so this morning I shot the cat.*

Webster sends a number of Makahs to the halibut waters aboard the schooner *Brant*, hoping to encourage them to learn shipboard fishing. The British gunboat *Forward* anchors in the bay overnight. On the Fourth of July, Swan hoists the flag at five in the morning and bakes a gooseberry pie.

The sixth of July, a bit of provisioning. *Barker came from Clallam Bay this noon bringing some venison. I bought a hind leg....I strongly suspect it is our tame deer.*

Swan spends a week in Port Townsend, buys two sets of underwear and a pair of pants. A few days after returning to Neah Bay he suffers *a bilious attack*. He repairs to Victoria for a few days. School resumes. Annuities are distributed to the tribe's women: china bowls, bread, molasses, a chunk of beef and two blankets each.

The twentieth of August, the imaginative Jimmy once more. *Jimmy had his ears bored yesterday and since then has refused to eat anything but hard bread & molasses and dried halibut. The superstition of the Indians being that if other food is eaten the ears will swell to an enormous size.*

Then autumn, and unease among the Makahs. *Capt John tells me that the Indians predict a very cold winter. There will be according to his statement, very high tides, violent gales, great rains, much cold and snow. The Arhosets predict rain from an unusual number of frogs in a particular stream at their place. The Oquiets predict cold from the fact that great numbers of mice were seen leaving an island in Barclay Sound and swimming to the mainland.*

The natives and the mice and the frogs are promptly right. Nineteenth of November: *The wind this morning blew open my chamber door which opens out from the south side of the tower, and slammed it against the flagstaff breaking out the entire panel work.*

Next day: *Gales of wind . . . accompanied by a tremendous surf and the highest tide that I ever saw in the bay. The water was nearly up to the Indian houses. The Indians were out with their torches saving their canoes & other property.*

And the day after that: *Gale . . . lasted till sundown doing considerable damage to fences, and unroofing Indian houses. Frequent lightning with distant thunder during day and evening. . . . The Indians were badly frightened and brought their children to the schoolhouse for safety.*

The eighteenth of December. *Commenced snowing at 1 PM—6 inches* by six that evening.

The nineteenth. *Crust of ice on the snow. . . . The Indians have inquired of me frequently during the month when the sun*

*would begin to return north. They say the fish are all hid under
the stones and when the sun commences to come back, the
stones will turn over and they will be able to catch fish.*

This queer, jittery year of 1865 bites through its last days.
The diary entry for the twenty-ninth of December: *Katy was
taken sick on the PM of the 27th and I gave her medicine and
told her to keep in the house. But she went to the tomanawas &
took cold.* Katy was *a slave girl belonging to John's squaw* and
early in the year had begun to do household chores for Swan. He
found her intelligent and competent. During the summer and
autumn she cooked at the house of the Reservation carpenter,
then in early winter became cook for Swan at the schoolhouse.
To all appearances a stout and remarkably healthy woman, her
abrupt inclusion in Swan's running list of ill Makahs is disquiet-
ing. Then on the 31st, the final several hours of 1865:

*Katy died towards morning and was buried north of the
schoolhouse near the beach. . . . The attack was sudden and her
death unexpected. . . .*

DAY TWENTY-NINE

Seventy-nine pages later in the diary, this:

*I found that the dogs or skunks have been disturbing Katys
grave and that the body is partly exposed and flesh gnawed from
the bones. I spoke to John to have it covered up but as Indians are
very averse to such work, I shall probably have to do it myself.*

He then sawed up a plank, went out and protectively boxed in
the grave.

*I did this for the reason first that I wished to cover the body
from sight, then, as she was a slave I wished to show the Indians
that we considered slaves as good as the free persons, and lastly
I wished to give the natives an idea how we made graves among
civilized people.*

Possibly. Possibly something more than that nervous rattle of reasons. The next day after noticing the grave had been disturbed, Swan planted daisies on Katy's mound of earth.

DAY THIRTY

Year and year Swan's right hand shuttled on paper, pushing the quick daily threads into the pocket notebooks, the longer yarn across the broad ledger pages. In all his total of lines, forty steady years of them and tag-ends at either end of that, there exists not as much typewritten material as I produce in a week. But more handwriting than I would beget in four hundred lifetimes. Staring down into the diaries these weeks—a third of winter already flown; this man Swan is hour-eating company—I begin to learn this constant route of Swan's pen hand. Rather, his pen hands, for the weave of words on these pages proves to be not a constant tapestry: more like the output from some Hebridean isle of tweedmakers, steadily of a style but also of different and distinct wefts.

Pocket diaries: they generally are in pencil and the smallest several of them (1863 the size of a deck of cards) offer crimped little language indeed. One handwriting in these Swan simply tosses together of teensy stalactites and stalagmites. A word such as *Webster* jags along as if scratched onto the page with an icepick. This is Swan's casual-but-get-it-down hand, jab the day's doings into place and sit down to supper.

His second handscript comes slightly smaller—the comb from my pocket covers five lines at a time when I hold it across the page as a measure—but immensely more legible; the clerkly Swan, this one. These diary days procession along as if stitched by a sewing machine.

Lastly, Swan has a scrawling hand, evidently for use in a canoe or other deskless locales, and it asks a bit of cryptoanalysis. After a half minute or so of blank staring, something like *Prow & rum   wood 8* will seep through to me as *Snow & rain wind S.* Fortunately there is comparatively little of this written mumble.

The notebook hands have rich cousins: the two handwritings of the Neah Bay ledgers Swan began in 1862. (That tiniest of pocket diaries, 1863, he elaborated into ledger entries as well.) The more prominent of these is done in lines about as high as the thickness of a pencil, and slanted on the page as rain is with a brisk breeze behind it. These are pretty pages, each headed with the year and month—Swan showed real flourish here; the *M* of *March*, for instance, will begin off in space with a loop that seems to be going nowhere but then swoops in to make the central pillars of the letter and next curlicues off into a smaller farewell barrel roll—and the day's weather entries. Hard to believe that weather such as Cape Flattery's could be made decorative, but Swan has done it. Each day's temperature readings at seven in the morning, two in the afternoon, and nine at night are stacked within an elegant bracket which Swan draws beautifully, featherlike lines meeting in a precise pucker.

Rarely in these big pages is anything crossed out, and never blotched. Quirks do show themselves. Swan's alphabet tends to flip open at the top, an *a* or *o* only slightly more closed than his *u*; a *d* at the end of a word may have a quick concluding stroke away from its top, so that it looks as if a musical note has tinkled in from somewhere; commas, when they exist, are the briefest specks a pen can make. But overall this is a steady hand for which, again, the only word is clerkly.

His language is remarkably not out of date. He surprises me, for instance, by using *pretty* as loosely as any of us would: *worked pretty constantly all day*. The one off-word I trip over consistently is *eat* for *ate*, as when the schoolboys stay for supper with him: *I boiled a shin of beef with potatoes . . . and they eat heartily and washed it down with cold water*.

Swan's other handwriting in the ledgers, the fifth of the bunch, is simply more crouched than his standard ledger hand: about two-thirds in size. The reason could be in the deep springs of his psyche, Swan in these occasional scrimped pages showing some tightened mood. But my guess is lamplight. That when Swan wrote at night, he hovered to the page more carefully to be within the narrow yellow puddle of light.

All in all, Swan the so-constant diarist puts me in mind of a story he once records, of meeting a seaman named John Johnson who had sailed aboard an American ship with three other Scandinavians of the same name in the crew and who told Swan *I was called Johnson Number Four*. All of these days of pages are the shared craft of Swan One, Two, Three, Four, and Five.

DAY THIRTY-ONE

Point No Point is the tiny peg of map line from which Puget Sound measures itself southward. Southward and ultimately southwestward, for the Sound at its farthest thrust begins to fringe toward the Pacific as if swept in a steady breeze. Those streamers of water extend the measuring considerably; when the Sound has delineated its every last remote bay and channel, thirteen hundred and fifty miles of shoreline—the equal of the entire Pacific Coast from San Diego to Cape Flattery—edge the sprawling inlet's outline.

Evidently in derision, Point No Point was named by the Wilkes Expedition of 1841, when that American naval survey team sailed up to what seemed from a distance to be a promontory prowing into the Sound, one more bold shoulder of the northwest coastline, and isn't. The forested ridgeline lies a few hundred yards back from the shore, and the flat acres intervening between the dark bluff and the water, plus the nubbin of beach which provides a perch for the lighthouse, proved to be the maritime sum of the site. But eminent or not, Point No Point marks the main entrance to the great Sound, and nobody now remembers who Wilkes was.

Except for the four of us, Carol, me, Ann, and Phil, good friends newly moved to the height above our valley, today's visitors to the Point all cluster out on the water with salmon as

their purpose: twenty-five small boats in a bright shoal around
the lighthouse. Many are red rowboats from the resort nearby,
with dashing white script on their sides proclaiming *Point No
Point*. The fanciness reminds me of another prank of language,
that when his Mississippi townsmen used to scorn Faulkner as
an overelegant scribbler they would dub him Count No 'Count.
Here is a site in scansion I can see that sly squire enjoying, out
in one of the red rowboats with an antique bamboo rod and a
flask of sipping whiskey, affirming to fellow anglers that yes,
none other, he is Count No 'Count of Point No Point.

When the tide is down, as now, the beach can be walked for a
few miles southward from the Point into long views of the forested rim of Puget Sound. In fact an angled look across the
water to a particular patch of the quilled horizon on the Sound's
eastern shore exactly reverses my usual line of sight along the
gray plain of water: the view from the top of the valley which
holds our house, across into this Point No Point corner of the
Sound. Now, here on the western shoreline, bluffs align in se-
quence along the Sound's edge like sterns of a moored fleet.

We begin to do the leisurely beach miles and the friends' gab
that comes with them.

Ann performs a squinched-up impression which she assures
us is an abalone.

I retaliate with my imitation of a tenpenny nail being driven:
rigid stance, hands at side, shuddering winces as my knees
buckle downward.

Phil gently informs us that neither has much career ahead as
sealife or spike.

Carol is first to see an inbound ship. Freighters entering the
Sound pass close by the Point—indeed, emerging from Admiralty
Inlet to round the bluff they give the illusion that they are
going to carve away the lighthouse as they come—and this
beach offers one of the few sites where I can share in Swan's
fixation on passing ships. Windships sail day on day in his pages,
rocking into view with the hidden push of air against their
groves of canvas, whitely slicing the Strait's breadth of blue, the
very print of their names vivid enough to ferry the imagination

horizonward. *Willamantic* and *Alert* and *Flying Mist* and *Nara-missic*. The *Toando Keller*, the *Lizzie Roberts*, the *Jenny Ford*. *Orion, Iconium, Visurgis. Torrent. Saucy Lass. Wild Pigeon. Forest Queen. Maunaloa. Growler. Quickstep*. Up from San Francisco, *Nahumkeag. Aguilar de Los Andes*, eagle of the Andes and homebound to Santiago. *Lalla Rookh* and *Wavelet* and *Jeannie Berteux*.

Nothing in our world is so richly, gaily named any more, unless it would be racehorses, and the sails that come and go on these waters now fill for pleasure rather than commerce. Saturday spinnakers instead of daily broadsails. Swan would like it, though, that the region still is water-mad, in its way. To walk down to the shoreline of any Puget Sound community is to find mast-filled marinas, natural as coves of cattails. But schooners, barks, any of the working-canvas fleet that kited past him, sometimes several a day: no.

Our version of a *Quickstep* sheers past the Point No Point light like strap-iron passing porcelain, then steadies massively into the shipping lane of the Sound. We try, and fail, to pick the name off the freighter's bow with field glasses.

Ann tells of a handy powerful monocular her father carries with him on hikes. A spyglass, it would have been in Swan's time.

As if the first freighter was the outrider, others now show themselves from behind the bluff regularly each half-hour or so. The third black ship cuts past just at low tide, three P.M. As we have walked I have been watching a known place on the horizon for any glimpse of Mount Rainier, where I will be at this time tomorrow, but a squall in the center of the Sound's prairie of water is intervening. Soon the squall line moves north, off Whidbey Island, and try as we do to convince ourselves it can't boomerang toward us, it comes.

The Sound and sky go to deeper grays, the lighthouse begins sending out dashes of light, and we start back to the Point as the day's fourth ship, edges erased in the rain, passes indistinct as a phantom.

DAY THIRTY-TWO

As I carry groceries from the car to the cabin, the forest challenges me. *Rawf*, it barks, *rowf rowf roof. Rawf.* While showing me routines of the cabin, doorkeys and woodpile and pots and pans, Trudy and Howard had mentioned that a neighbor's small brown dog is fond of visiting. Solo and I would be instant friends, Trudy assured me. Dog friend is advancing on me now from the woods with his five-note salvo like a sentry triggering off warning bursts.

"Hullo, Solo, hey, Solo Solo Solo," I offer and coax him into being petted. At once he wags ecstasy, devotion, worship. But as I step down the path from the cabin Solo moves to my heels and yammers steadily all the way to the car.

Before gathering the next armful of cargo I again Solo Solo Solo him, stroke his back until the hair threatens to fray off, scratch his belly and the place between his ears, seem to have sent him irretrievably giddy. He then rolls to his feet and yaps me every step back to the cabin. One more round trip we make, Solo yawping determinedly whenever my hand isn't stroking him. I face the issue.

"Solo, goddamned if I'm going to spend four days petting you. Go home."

He wavers, somewhere between another aria of barking and a demand for further ransom of petting.

"Get-the-hell-outa-here."

Off Solo scampers through the ghostly alders, looking faintly regretful about having overplayed me. The silence that arrives along his retreating tracks fills the forest, reaches instantly down from the upthrust of fir trees and the hover of the mountain, vast Rainier, somewhere above their green weave. After the unquiet introduction, an avalanche of stillness.

I am here for stillness. For pause in this winter at Swan's heels and, I suppose, in my own strides across time. Coming to this underedge of snow country is a brief reflective climb back to

my first life in the West, the Montana life. I grew up in powerful winters of white, amid stories of even mightier ones: the
arctic seasons which have swept western Montana each three
decades since the first of them was registered, to the everlasting
shock of the rangemen, in 1886-87. 1919-20, which broke
our family homestead under its six-month burden of frozen
snow. 1948-49, when I watched my father struggle to save two
thousand sheep, and our future, on the blizzard-lashed ranch at
Battle Creek. Now, again, another thirty-year giant. For weeks
Montanans have been telling me by phone or mail of the deep
lock of cold in the Rockies, of snowdrifts across porch railings,
concern for beleaguered cattle soon to begin calving. Sentences
from a Missoula friend: "Anything bad about this winter in
Montana that you happen to hear, believe it. It is the worst ever,
and it started November 9. The ground has been under snow
since, and it hit -28 here on January 1, -50 in Butte."

I have had urges recently to return to Montana, go there for
the experience of the great thirty-year winter. It may after all be
the last to fall within my lifespan, and that ink of Swan's will not
drain away in spring runoff. But I would be returning on a
tourist's terms, on whim and mere spectatorship, which to me
are tarnished terms for such an occasion. Any honesty about
earthdwelling tells me I have not earned this Montana winter by
living with the land's other moods there, by keeping my roots
within its soil. Half my lifetime ago I decided the point, although
I did not then know how long-reaching the decision would be,
that the ranch-country region of my grandparents and parents is
no longer the site for me to work out life. I could not divide
myself, a portion to the words I wanted to make, another to the
raising of livestock and coping with furious seasons. Not winters
of white steel but the coastal ones of pewter-gray, soft-toned,
workable, with the uninsistent Northwest rain simply there in
the air like molecules made visible, are the necessary steady
spans for me to seek the words. Yet the white winters have not
entirely let me from their grip. A time or two a season, snowline
will help me see the margins of what I am doing and I migrate to
some place such as this, a silvered edge of the Northwest where I

can sit above my usual life for a few days. Hear what is being said in my skull. Watch mountain dusk draw down.

And scrutinize deer. The boldest of them wintering here is a doe which made her appearance soon after I arrived, and has ghosted back into the near-dark now. Black-tailed and gray-furred for winter she eases past this cabin a time or two each evening, Trudy and Howard told me, and can be recognized by the nick in her ear. A wide screened-in porch rambles about three sides of the cabin, a pleasant half-hidden promenade up among the first branches of the trees, and from it she can be seen for several minutes on her route.

As I watch down from the porch the motion of the doe's each step seems to recoil slightly into her as if some portion of poise is being pulled back each time in reserve. This tentative grace of deer which stops them just short of being creatures of some other element. Hoofed birds, perhaps, or slim dolphins of the underbrush. Who would have thought, on a continent of such machines of the wild as bison and elk and the grizzly, that it would be deer to best survive? For once, the meek have inherited.

Before bed I look up Swan on deer. The blacksmith at Neah Bay was undertaking to raise one from a fawn. The twenty-sixth of January 1865: *Mr Phillips tame deer has been missing for several days and I strongly suspect the Indians have killed it in retaliation for sundry dogs which Phillips and Mr Maggs have shot.*

But the next day: *The deer made her appearance this morning much to my satisfaction. . . . It is very tame and looks very pretty running about among the cattle.*

DAY THIRTY-THREE

New snow, two inches of dry fluff. The entire forest has been fattened by it, everywhere a broad white outline put onto all

branches of trees and brush. The effect comes odd against yesterday's green and gray of the forest, like a white blossoming
gone rampant overnight.

DAY THIRTY-FOUR

I intend as mild an afternoon as can be spent aboard snowshoes.
Whop around on the slope above the National Park buildings at
Paradise, watch the weather seethe around the summit of
Rainier nearly two miles above. When my thigh muscles make
first complaint about the pontoons at the bottom of my legs,
ease off the fluffy ridge, try to keep the car from becoming a
bobsled on the white-packed road down to Longmire Lodge and
coffee and pie: then the forest's miles back to the cabin, and
dusk and deer.

But halfway above Paradise I wallow onto rodent prints
stitching a path in and out of the stands of firs. Fate has jotted in
the snow. No choice but to become a tracker. Along tilts of
slope, over drifts, up, down, across. After several minutes I
glance back from the tiny pawprints to my wake in the snow. It
is what a whale might churn up in hot pursuit of a minnow.

Shameless, I plow on, occasionally deserting the tracks for the
pleasure of creating my own didoes in the white. I discover that
the south face of every fir I pass is gray-white with ice: frozen
melt at the very end of the branches, in fat cellular conglomer-
ates sectioned by the green fir bristles. Grenades of ice. A sudden thaw would put me under bombardment. Doves of peace—
no, gray jays ambling through the air to me, pausing just off my
shoulder as if kindly offering to search my pockets for any
loaves of bread which might be burdening me.

The jays sortie off to elsewhere and time drifts out of mind
after them, replaced by attention to the weather atop Rainier,
lowering, rising, brightening, darkening. As though the mountain
when it ceased being a volcano of fire became a cauldron for
weather. Like all else in this region of the Cascades, this casual

slope I am on, still not far above Paradise and its visitor center and lodge, points quickly up toward Rainier as if in astonishment at how the glacier-draped mound looms. I was surprised myself, far back along the highway when arriving to the cabin, how the lift of the mountain made itself felt even there, the road suddenly jerking into rising curves.

Inventorying the arc of mountains which surround Rainier, themselves lofty but less than half the giant peak's three-mile height, I come onto the thought that the geographical limits of my Northwest winter are Tatoosh and Tatoosh: Tatoosh Island offshore from the outermost perch at Cape Flattery, the Tatoosh Range of crags in view to the south here at the crest of the Cascades, jagging white up through the high-country fabric of forest. At Swan's first mention of a visit to the Tatoosh lighthouse I looked into a place-names guidebook, found that the derivation could be from the Chinook jargon word for "breast" or the Nootkan word for "thunderbird." Divvy the deriving, I decide: give these cleavaged profiles their due, let the thunderbird have the island.

Bulletins from below. Thighs are threatening open rebellion. Snowshoes still want more country. *Tatoosh-tatoosh tatoosh-tatoosh* the webs sing into the snow as I go onto a fresh drift.

DAY THIRTY-FIVE

Strange, to be again in a lodging of entirely wood. Under the rough brawn of ceiling beams and amid the walls' constellations of pine knots. Almost two decades of suburban wallboard intervene from when ranchhouse and bunkhouse nightly surrounded me with board walls.

What is it about a cabin within a forest or beside a shore that sings independence from the common world of dwellings? Something more than hinterland site or openly outlined strokes of beams and rafters; some inherent stubbornness against ever being thought an ordinary house shouts through as well. Cabina-

tion or antidomicility or some such rebellious shimmer of the
atoms of wall-wood; a true surmiser of cabins would have the
term. I simply know that cabin-y distinctness says itself and I
step across the threshold as if going into some chamber of a far
year. The broad central room of this cabin, for instance, trades
adamantly back and forth between the family who spend summers and weekends here and the abiding forest outside. A wall-
beam aligns the china plates which sit on it as if they were shiny
droplets on a branch; beneath runs a long bank of mullioned
window, the small panes fondling separate bits of the forest as if
they were scenes on porcelain. On another wall is the cabin item
that interests me most, a crosscut saw. Blazon of sharpened
steel, the crosscut is a remarkably elegant tool to have inspired
its epithets: "misery harp" the least profane description Northwest loggers had for it as, sawyer at either end, they ground the
blade back and forth through Douglas fir or red cedar. Having
caught from Swan the winter virus of measure-and-count I've
learned by yardstick that this slicer of forests is six and a half
feet long, by careful finger that it has sixty-eight beveled sharp-
nesses interspersed with sixteen wider-set prongs which make
space for the sawdust to spill away. A giant's steel grin of eighty-
four teeth and as innocent and ready in this cabin amid these
woods as a broadsword on a Highlands castle wall.

Sawed wood—firewood—decides my site when I am here inside the cabin. I settle at the kitchen table, close by the cook-
stove which must be fed each hour or so. (Howard has told me
he will harvest his own firewood when summer comes, from the
stand of alder woven within the mullioned window. A neighbor
who owns a team of workhorses will skid the downed trees in
for sawing. I wish the harnessed horses were there now, the
leather sounds of their working heft coming down the mountain-
side. Instead, if anything is out there, it will be either Solo on
reconnaissance to see whether I have mended my anti-dog ways,
or the slowly gliding deer.) Today out of the mound of mail
which has been building on my desk since Swan's diaries moved
into my days I finally have winnowed the letter from Mark, in
his faculty office in Illinois—we may be the last two American

friends who write regularly and at such length to one another—
and the quote which he found during his research on mid-nineteenth-century frontier missionaries. The Reverend John Summers, reporting from Benton County, Iowa, in July of 1852:

"A young man recently left for California, who for two years
has been very anxious to go, but during his minority had been
restrained by the influence and authority of his parents. They
offered, for the sake of diverting him from his purpose, to furnish him the means to travel and visit the Eastern cities. He
derided the idea. He would not turn his hand over to see all that
could be seen in the East, but he must go to the Utopia of the
New World; and he has gone."

Gone west and cared not so much as a flip of his hand to
know any of that lesser land behind him. In all but flesh, that
young Iowan was my grandfather, my great-uncles, my father
and his five brothers, me. After my Doig grandparents sailed
from Scotland and crossed America to a high forest-tucked valley of the Rocky Mountains, nobody of the family for two generations ever went to the Atlantic again. When I journeyed off to
college I was spoken of as being "back east in Illinois." My
father adventured to Chicago once on a cattle train and twice to
visit me. My mother, after her parents moved from Wisconsin to
the Rockies when she was half a year old, never returned beyond the middle of Montana.

This westernness in my family, then, has been extreme as we
could manage to make it. We lived our first seventy years as
Americans on slopes of the Rockies as naturally, single-mind-
edly, as kulaks on the Russian steppes. (Nights when I have
been at my desk reading Swan's pages I have noticed that my
square-bearded face reflected in the desk-end window could be a
photographic plate of any of those museful old Scotsmen who
transplanted our family name to the western mountains of
America. If we have the face we deserve at forty—or thirty-nine
and some months, as I am now—evidently I am earning my way
backward to my homesteading grandfather.) My own not very
many years eastward, which is to say in the middle of the Midwest, amounted to a kind of instructive geographic error. (In-

structive, literally: Montana as evaluated at Northwestern University in Evanston, 1957: "youse guys," confides my new college friend from the Bronx, "youse guys from Mwawntana twalk funny.") The journalism jobs in the flat-horizoned midland turned my ambition in on itself, impelled me to work the salaried tasks for more than they were worth and to sluice the accumulating overflow of ideas into pages of my own choice. Also, happiest result of my brief misguess of geography (chiding from a friend who had stepped back and forth among writing jobs: "It doesn't matter anymore where you live in this country." It matters.), I met Carol there, already edging west on her own, and when the two of us turned together, away from editorial careers and ahead to independence, we strode a fourth of the continent farther than any of my family had done. Puget Sound's salt water begins but a half mile from our valley-held house close by Seattle.

And so with Swan, I judge. When the Midwestern reverend wrote those opining words, Swan of Boston already had been on the Pacific shore for two years and was about to head onward to Shoalwater Bay and ultimately the Strait and Cape Flattery. Finding the place to invest his life meant, as it has to me, finding a West. (Roulette of geography, of course, that the American frontier stretched from the Atlantic toward the Pacific instead of the other way around. Erase *Santa Maria* and *Mayflower*, ink in Chinese junks anchoring at San Francisco Bay and Puget Sound four hundred years ago, reread our history with its basis in Confucianism, its exploit of transcontinental railroads laid across the eastern wilderness by quaint coolie labor from London and Paris, its West Coast mandarins—the real item—aloofly setting cultural style for the country.) What Swan and his forty-year wordstream will have told me by the end of this winter, this excursion back where I have never been, I can't yet know. But already I have the sense from his sentences and mine that there are and always have been many Wests, personal as well as geographical. (Even what I have been calling the Pacific Northwest is multiple. A basic division begins at the Columbia River; south of it, in Oregon, they have been the sounder citizens, we in Washington the sharper strivers. Transport fifty from each state as a colony on Mars and by nightfall the Oregonians will put up a school and a city hall, the Washingtonians will establish a bank and a union.) Swan on the Strait has been living in two distinct ones, Neah Bay and Port Townsend (and sampled two others earlier, San Francisco and Shoalwater Bay) and neither of them is the same as my own Wests, Montana of a quarter-century ago and Puget Sound of today. Yet Swan's Wests come recognizable to me, are places which still have clear overtones of my own places, stand alike with mine in being distinctly unlike other of the national geography. Perhaps that is what the many Wests are, common in their stubborn separatenesses: each West a kind of cabin, insistent that it is no other sort of dwelling whatsoever.

DAYS THIRTY-SIX, THIRTY-SEVEN, THIRTY-EIGHT

At Neah Bay, Swan writes on. Writes the daily diary entries, frequent newspaper articles, writes letter after letter in the series which, as I began to crank 120-year-old words into sight at the University of Washington library, filled a roll of microfilm thick as my fist. From the files of the Smithsonian Institution, "SWAN, JAMES G., Official Incoming Correspondence."

Eventually nearly half a thousand pieces of correspondence flowed from Swan to the savants within the Smithsonian's castle-like museum. It was—is—a spellbinding cataract of mail. Swan's machine-magnified handwriting reads like lines from a Gulliver who every so often pauses on one North Pacific promontory or another to empty out his pockets and his thoughts.

I have now ready to ship by first opportunity a case containing 16 birds skins, mostly large   2 Indian skulls   1 backbone of fur seal with skull   2 grass straps for carrying burthens   1 dog hair

*blanket   specimen sea weed   1 fur seal skin   2 fur seal skulls
4 specimen fossil crabs   2 miniature hats   2 down blankets
shells taken from ducks' stomachs....*

*The Indians here judge of the weather for the following day
by observing the stars whenever there happens to be a clear
night in this humid atmosphere. If the sky is clear and the stars
"twinkle brightly," they predict wind for the following day and
with uncanny certainty. If on the contrary the stars shine tran-
quilly they say there will be but little wind, and consequently,
prepare themselves at midnight to go off to their fishing grounds
some 15 to 20 miles outside Cape Flattery. They believe the
"wind in the air" makes the stars twinkle.*

*I have been reading with great interest the work on archaeol-
ogy by Mr Haven, which was received among other books from
the Smithsonian. . . . On page 148 Mr Haven remarks in his
conclusion while speaking of the Indians at the Columbia River
& Nootka, "There too prevails the singular and inconvenient
custom of inserting discs of wood in the lips and ears." Now the
fact is, that there is not an Indian from the Columbia to Nootka
who has, or has had, a disc of wood in either lips or ears....*

*. . . In 66 consecutive days there has fallen a little more than
2½ feet of water. I think that Astoria, which is usually accounted
the most rainy place on this coast, can hardly beat this quantity....*

*. . . I have got the names of the male decendants of Deeart the
chief from whom Neeah Bay or Deeah as these Indians pronounce it is taken. There are twelve generations and by a little
patience I can trace the various collateral branches and by that
means find out the relationship existing between the present descendants. But to ask these Indians as Mr Morgan lays down the
rule viz "what do I call my grandmothers great aunt" &c, the
answer invariably is "Klonas" or dont know.*

...2 Indian cradles   1 grass blanket   2 medicine rattles made of scallop shells   2 birds nests   1 little basket robins eggs   fossil crabs   baskets of shells   1 bark head dress   1 crab...

When we think of our once glorious Union, from its struggling commencement, to the culminating glory of its zenith, as Longfellow says, "We know what master laid the keel/What workmen framed thy ribs of steel ..." and then look upon the old ship of state as she now lies wrecked, broken, and apparently a total loss, it is almost enough to make a man doubt whether that Providence who has hitherto watched over us, has not for some national sin withdrawn from us for a season his protecting care. ... But I am digressing from a commonplace letter on bird skins into topics that have puzzled wiser heads than mine.

Most often these bulletins from Swan's persistent pen emerged onto the desk of an even more prodigious creator of mail: Spencer Fullerton Baird, assistant secretary and second-in-command of the Smithsonian. Swan had met both Baird and the secretary of the Smithsonian, Joseph Henry, during that interim of his in the national capital in the late 1850s. Henry and Baird added up to a most formidable museum team. While Henry, a practical scientist who had made pioneering discoveries in electromagnetism, enforced a tone of scientific enterprise for the Smithsonian, Baird was endeavoring to fill the place up like a silo.

He was one of those Victorian work machines, Baird, who could have run the affairs of the world by himself if he'd had more writing hands. In 1860 he noted in his journal that he had dashed off a total of 3,050 letters that year, without the aid of stenographers. And he soon got stenographers. Baird's passion was nothing less than to capture North American nature for the Smithsonian. When in 1850 he moved from his post as a professor of natural history to the Smithsonian, with him arrived two freight cars of his own bird specimens. Ever since, he had been welcoming, as the institution's annual reports testify, items ranging from dead garter snakes to meteorites. And perpetually, perpetually, churning out his messages of encouragement to an army of unofficial Smithsonian helpers who ranged from back-yards amateurs—"Never fear the nonacceptability of anything you may send," Baird once wrote to an enthusiast who had been mailing in insects from Eutaw, Alabama—to such scientific eminences as Louis Agassiz and George Perkins Marsh.

Swan's enlistment date was January 10, 1860. He put a box of seashells aboard a steamer at Port Townsend, *happy at all times,* he assured the Smithsonian's caliphs of science, *to add my humble collections to specimens in your museums.*

The Smithsonian and Baird of course were rare eminences to Swan's back-of-beyond existence while Swan was merely one, and a most distant one at that, of a battalion of science-struck gleaners. When the orb of microfilm begins to glow out its "LETTERS TO SWAN FROM SPENCER F. BAIRD," the difference between the epistles of the man in the frontier school-house and the man in the red-brick castle registers about as might be expected.

I should be pleased did your time permit it you could give me some reliable idea of the state of affairs at Washington, Swan will pen, exuberantly—wistfully?—filling all four sides of a folded broadsheet. *I can gather very little from the contradictory statements of the newspapers and know about as much of the doings of the Khan of Tartary as of our own government.* Back from Baird arrives a considerable fraction less of paper and bonhomie: *We had the very great pleasure today of receiving the box of shells from Nee-ah Bay sent by you....*

Master of perfunctory encouragement that Baird was, he nonetheless did enrich Swan's life at Cape Flattery. The speci-mens Baird asked for—birds and fish, particularly—made a welcome change of task from the Neah Bay routine Swan once summed as *attending to the sick, listening to Indian complaints of various kinds and looking after things generally.* (The Makahs occasionally held a dimmer view of Swan's break-the-monotony specimen collecting. *Last evening I shot a horned owl of the mottled grey species. . . . This forenoon I skinned it and prepared it for the Smithsonian Institution. The Indians think owls are dead Indians and I had quite a talk with some children who assured me that the owl was not a bird but an Indian.*) And as Swan freighted in his hodgepodge of promising items, Baird sent west to him an array of books of science, another bonus to a frontier life. (Swan was a reader. Through the years in the diaries I look over his shoulder to Stanley's account of tracking Livingstone, Mark Twain's *Innocents Abroad*, Thackeray's *Pendennis*, Melville's *Omoo* . . .) Most vital of all in these Neah Bay years, Baird's encouragement sat Swan down to an ambitious piece of scholarly enterprise: an ethnological study of the Makahs.

Swan likely did not even think of his intention as ethnology, or its mother science, anthropology. Only in the wake of Darwin's theory of evolution, not all that many years before, were such fields of study becoming recognized. Language, not the net of culture behind it, was the original lure for Swan, the Neah Bay diaries every so often showing self-instruction in Makah: *December Se-whow-ah-puthl January ā-ā-kwis-puthl February Klo-klo-chis-to-puthl* . . . Eventually Swan is complimented by a visiting tribesman *that he thought I was a real Indian as I could talk Makah so well. . . . I said to him that I could only talk the Makah dialect a little.* But Swan did have the necessary impulse, the flywheel of curiosity within him—or call it that penchant for eyewitnessing—to follow language into culture. *I know the importance of making these collections and writing the Indian memoirs now, while we are among them and can get reliable facts,* he once avows to Baird. *The time is not distant, when these tribes will pass away, and future generations who may feel an interest in the history of these people will wonder why we have been so negligent.*

The Indians of Cape Flattery took Swan more than two years to write, and his constant deskmate was interruption. *In order to have the work go on as rapidly as possible with the Government buildings I have been obliged to sink the teacher into the caterer for the mess,* Swan reported to Baird in the midst of the schoolhouse construction, *and a person arranging for the appetites of six hearty men who must have three full meals per day cannot find much opportunity for belles lettres.*

But on the thirteenth of April 1865, Swan could jubilate that *I have finished my paper on the Makah Indians at last and packed it with the sketches which accompany it in a snug parcel. . . .*

"Paper" barely described the work: a 55,000-word ream of manuscript about how the Makahs lived and spoke and believed. Swan's fetish for fact is on the finished result like a watermark. He describes the Makahs' canoes, how they fished and hunted seals and whales, what their ceremonies and legends were, how their masks looked, the tribal ailments, what games the children played, what the tribe ate and wore, how they told time, what they called the months of the year: think of a daily moment of life and Swan probably has set down for you how a Makah spent it. And what an interplanetary meeting of wordmen it is to imagine Spencer Baird being introduced, courtesy of Swan's pen, to Captain John: *About three years ago he had lost the use of one of his feet, probably from paralysis, but which he attributed to a "skookoom," or evil spirit, entering into it one day while he was bathing. He had been confined to his house for several months, and was reduced to a skeleton. I saw him during this sickness, and thought he could not recover. One pleasant day, however, according to his account, he managed to crawl to a brook near his house, and, while bathing, heard a rustling sound in the air, at which he became frightened, and covered his face with his blanket, whereupon a raven alighted within a few feet of him and uttered a hoarse croak. He then peeped through a corner of his blanket, and saw the raven with its head erect, its feathers bristled, and a great swelling in its throat. After two or three unsuccessful efforts, it finally threw up a piece of bone about three inches long, then uttering another croak it flew away. Remaining quiet a few minutes, till he was satisfied that the raven had gone, he picked up the bone, which he gravely informed me was of the Ha-hek-to-ak. He hid this bone near by, and returned to his lodge, and, after relating the occurrence, was informed by the Indian doctors that it was a medicine sent to him by his tamanawas, and this proved to be true, as he entirely recovered in three days. . . .* Swan now steps into the narrative with a bit of exegesis: *The tale of the raven alighting near him is not improbable, as ravens as well as crows are very plenty and very tame; nor is it impossible that the raven might have had a bone in its mouth, and finally dropped it; nor is it entirely uncertain that the circumstance so affected his superstitious imagination that it caused a reaction in his system, and promoted his recovery. The same effect might perhaps have been produced by a smart shock from a galvanic battery.*

The Makah manuscript done, Swan leaned back to await publication by the Smithsonian. It began to be a long lean. In the microfilm's blizzard of lines a year passes, two, three. Swan is writing heavier and heavier nudges to Baird. The second of November, 1868: *Can you give one any encouragement that it will appear within the next decade?* Yet another year: sixteenth of November 1869: *When that Makah memoir is published??!!! I should like some copies to send to several officers at Sitka who are much interested in Indian matters. . . .*

Either the deprivation of the Sitka officers or the explosion of punctuation did the job. At the start of 1870 *The Indians of Cape Flattery*, even yet the primary source on the historical Makahs, came into print.

DAY THIRTY-NINE

Time spent today in the words of other westerners, to try to see Swan within his lineage of frontier ink.

The journals of Lewis and Clark while their expedition sheltered in winter quarters at the tiny stockade called Fort Clatsop, just south of the mouth of the Columbia River. Like Swan,

Captain William Clark marks the daily weather scrupulously, but his has a terrible soggy sameness: in four months at Fort Clatsop it rained every day but twelve. A late February day in 1806 begins with typical lament:

we are mortified at not haveing it in our power to make more celestial observations since we have been at Fort Clatsop, but such has been the state of the weather that we have found it utterly impractiable.

Then the captain brightens and as Swan so often did, turns sketch artist.

I purchased of the Clatsops this morning about half a bushel of small fish—they were candlefish, an oily little species—*which they had cought about 40 miles up the Columbia in their scooping nets. as this is an uncommon fish to me and one which no one of the party has ever seen. on the next page I have drawn the likeness of them as large as life. . . .*

The candlefish swims delicately there among the words, eternally angled along the flow of Clark's handwriting as if feeding now and again on stray periods and apostrophes.

In Stegner's *The Gathering of Zion*, an excerpt from the trail diary of the Mormon girl Patience Loader. In the overland migration to the far half of America opened by Lewis and Clark she was pilgrimaging west to Zion with one of the handcart brigades of 1856, the travelers' tumbrils in heavy groaning tow all the thousand miles from the Missouri River to Utah. Having trudged six hundred of those miles Patience Loader and weary others began to ford the North Platte River in Wyoming: . . . *the water was deep and very cold and we was drifted out of the regular crossing and we came near being drounded the water came up to our arm pits poor Mother was standing on the bank screaming as we got near the bank I heard Mother say for God Sake some of you men help My poor girls. . . . Several of the breathren came down the bank of the river and pulled our carts up for us and we got up the best we could . . . when we was in the middle of the river I saw a poor brother carreying his child on his back he fell down in the water I never knew if he was drowned or not I fealt sorry that we could not help him but we had all we could do to save ourselves. . . .*

In my own scrawl, in one of the 4 × 6 hip-pocket notebooks which traveled western Montana with me the summer before last: *Day 2 . . . Gateway Gorg, Yosmit-lk rock c thrusts browing b o us. . . .* Curious to compare, I've dug out these notes of the backpack hike Carol and I made into the Bob Marshall Wilderness (and already notice two mighty alterations from Captain Clark's West and Patience Loader's West: now it is the wild places which are the enclaves hewn into America's geography, and now we count our "wilderness" experience by days instead of seasons). From my mix of speedwriting and single-letter Russian prepositions those scenes of the Rockies translate for me again: *mountainsides of colossal reefs and deeps like the ocean bottom tipped empty and left on its side . . . canyons everywhere . . . high narrow table of trail above the South Fork . . . Gateway Gorge, Yosemite-like rock with thrusts browing in on us. . . . Me: There's frost on the outside of the tent. Carol: It's on the inside. . . . 4th day of no people. . . . Made Badger Pass at 12—only slight incline to cross Continental Divide there   then climb for 1 hour over ridge to North Fork gorge. At top a sleet squall hit, we took shelter in trees; pellets of hail convinced us to put wool jackets on. Ate trail food, drank water and waited out squall . . . sound of rocks avalanching to the south . . . Another 10 mile day. . . . From the top of Family Peak through a notch to the east, farmland pattern of the plains could be seen. . . .* We came out of the mountains not having seen any other humans for five days; had not been dined on by grizzlies or entrapped by sleet; and felt a joy as huge as the peaks behind us.

Clark's winter of black rain brightened by a candlefish, Patience Loader's wade through horror; our own brief plunge into what-is-left-of-wilderness, to see how we would fare in it. Reminders to be kept in view while I saunter within Swan's orderly ledger that the edge of America can also be a brink.

DAY FORTY

A silver-bright day. Air clear and cold, ready to crinkle like silk, and for the second night in a row frost has daubed its way all across the ground and up into the first branches of the evergreens.

I have a queer edgy clarity in myself, consequence of so few hours' sleep: a grittiness like diamond dust. Luckily, sleeplessness comes to me in small seasons, two or three nights in a row then vanishes, else I cannot imagine what my daily mood would be like. These strange beings, ourselves. Needing the night but sometimes entirely at odds with it. My nights when sleep will not be coaxed I roll like a driftlog on one of Swan's beaches, and between last bedtime and early morning I wallowed a deep trough in the dark. In the bed beside mine, Carol's breathing form calmly ingested the blackness, channeled it on its smooth underskin routes. While my mind was a black blaze. Anything makes fuel; a walk taken around the neighborhood after supper, the day's writing, a letter from a friend. I steadily try a number of sleepmaking stunts. Breathe deeply, with forced regular rhythm. Let my tongue loll like a loosened strap. Try to sheet the mind with a white blankness. And have the success of a man attempting to win attention to his coin trick against the roaring backdrop of a three-ring circus.

The frustration is double. Sleep at best is a sharp cost of time, not-sleep is a cost to both. Yet not always; there is this morning's cold clarity, as if the white duff of frost had crept into me during the night too.

Swan on the Makah version of restlessness: *Last evening Peter wanted his Squaw to go home with him, she was then in Tahahowtls lodge. She refused, whereupon Peter pitched into her, pulled her hair and blacked her eye. Tahahowtl interfered and Peter went at him and they had a hair pulling match and finally separated to get their guns but friends interfered....*

Noon. The morning would not be calmed, kept shoving aside Swan's logbooks for its own. I let the hours roam back along the entire wordstream of this winter so far, turned them loose on the question of why the West takes hold of a James Swan, an Ivan Doig. Notions—they are not answers yet, if they ever grow up to be—tumbled like the scenes in yesterday's retrieved notebook of the Marshall Wilderness days: *... Perhaps the choice of place is in our body chemistry simply as other patterns of taste are, regulating me to dislike brussel sprouts, the color pink, and square miles of pavement. ... The west of America draws some of us not because it is the newest region of the country but because it is the oldest, in the sense that the landscape here—the fundament, nature's shape of things—more resembles the original continent than does the city-nation of the Eastern Seaboard or the agricultural factory of the Midwest. As for so much else, mountains account for it. They, and the oceans, are virtually the last pieces of earth we have not someway tamed, transformed. Although we are striving. Go in an airplane above the Cascade Range to see clearcut logging like countless patches of fur shaved off. Study the logging roads which incise the high edges of the Olympics. ... Or are we drawn west, or merely deposited? The way, say, spores drop into a forest: some spot is found in the immense environment, life is stubbornly established and clung to, whether the site turns out to be rich humus or up a tree?*

Enough. What counts for now, this winter, is to keep the question open, let the hours chase at it when they will.

DAY FORTY-ONE

The fifth of April 1866, in the elegant ledger diary: *Yesterday, Ahayah killed the first whale of the season....*

The next day: *I was much amused last evening with Johns moves. It seems he feels ashamed that he has not killed any whales and has concluded to go through the ceremonies to constitute him a skookum whaleman. Which ceremonies consist of going without sleeping or eating for 6 days and nights, to bathe in the salt water and run on the beach to get warm. John went into the water with his accoutrements on but soon got so cold that he was glad to come and warm himself by my fire. He had gone all day without eating and I think his courage was failing him for he admitted that he thought he could not stand it more than two days and if that would not suffice to make him a whaleman he could kill sharks. He intended to stop by my fire all night and occasionally go out and wash in the bay, but when I got up this morning he was gone and I learned that he was afraid to sit alone by my fire and had sneaked out about midnight with his courage completely cooled and has concluded that from shark killing he will be content with killing dogfish.*

DAY FORTY-TWO

God, how the blood strums in such weather. What it tingles out is: be truant.

Which I am. I woke with the sense that this would be another day brought pure by the cold and that I needed to be out in it at once. When daybreak came, a dry crackle of light onto the frost, I already had arrived here at Shilshole, a bay favorite to me for its head-on view west across the Sound to the wooded headlands and mountains. The Olympics, clouds caped on their backs, as yet are pale, wraithy, in the beginning day. Snow gods, asleep standing up, like horses. Going past is a big seagoing tug, in from the north and in a hurry. It seems to ride the floe of white water pushed up by its impatient bow. Freighter traffic is starting to procession past. Two ships inbound to the Seattle dockfront, two out. Three of the fleet are outlined in traditional lines of superstructure, masts and plow-pointed bow. But the fourth is squatty as a huge barge, some new fangle of containerized-cargo vessel. Swan would enter in his diaries' ship list an occasional *herm brig*; hermaphrodite brig, with a square-rigged foremast but a triangular schooner sail on its mainmast. The day now of the herm freighter?

One inbound vessel overtakes the other and as it begins to pass, the dark shapes merge, then slowly attenuate, pulled longer and longer like a telescope being extended, until they snap into two again.

After an hour or so of shivery wandering the Shilshole bayline, I go on to the dockside coffee shop at Salmon Bay, the fishing fleet schooled into winter berths all around.

"Breakfast, Bill?" the waitress asks the regular on the stool next to me.

"No, a doughnut."

"Any particular kind, or whatever I grab?"

"Whatever you grab, dealer's choice."

"Powdered sugar. There you go."

There you go: that western byphrase from waitresses and bartenders, sometimes from friends or just people in conversation. I hear it in Montana as I do here and like it immensely, the friendly release in the saying, the unfussy deliverance it carries. A very independent little trio of words, encouraging yet declaring okay-I've-done-my-part-it's-up-to-you-now. The best of benedictions.

Midmorning. Here at the desk, attenuation again. Swan has begun to pull from his five years at Neah Bay.

I am surprised with myself, he has recently mused into the ledger, *to find that I have so much patience as I have with these children. I get almost discouraged at times and then again I feel as though they were doing something. But they try my patience sorely and occasionally I feel like giving up my situation in despair of ever being able to do any good*. . . . In April of 1866 had occurred the tensest time Swan experienced at Cape Flattery, the arrival of troops to arrest Peter for the fatal stabbing he shoved as ante into the rivalry with the Elwhas. The Makahs resented the show of force, the soldiers resented being thunked down on the back porch of the continent, *and we are all heartily sick of their protracted stay.* Also, the month's weather was rampageous even for Cape Flattery: *11 7/10 inches Rain 3 pleasant days during month.* The diary pages twang more than a little. The Swan who liked to intone that he never carried the least caliber of self-defense among the Indians—*I have always found that a civil tongue is the best weapon I can use*—now inscribes something different: *Bought a Remington revolver of Mr Philips this PM....*

Nerves cool a bit in the next weeks but in midsummer Swan takes a twelve-day respite from Neah Bay, visiting in Victoria, Port Townsend, and Port Angeles; and a few days after his return there is the entry the year's diary pages have been marching toward. Wednesday, the twenty-second of August:

Notified Mr Webster of my intention of sending in my resignation as teacher when I send in my monthly report. The resignation to take effect on the 1st of October.

I want not to see Swan step from Neah Bay; not see this particular Boston bird drift back townward from the ultimate point of the West, Cape Flattery. Truth told, it may account for my own tautness of the past days. The glimpses I have had into the diaries ahead do not suggest the rhythmed richness of these regal ledger pages. Port Townsend, which will be Swan's next site, I think cannot be such a transfixing place as Cape Flattery, nor probably one to which Swan's talents are as steadily alert. There is grit in the ink to come, I judge. But 1866 is James Gilchrist Swan's cosmos, not mine. Whatever I might wish here in the ether of the future, he traces his own way with that ceaseless pen. And in the last few weeks of more than two hundred and fifty spent at Neah Bay that pen begins to record farewells.

First a ceremony of fabulous chumminess from exactly the quarter it could be expected. *This forenoon,* the twenty-third of September, *Capt John brought me in his box of "Whale medi-*

cine" which under promise of secrecy on my part he showed me
after going up into the tower and locking the door. . . . The
relics were in a box enclosed in a bag and had evidently been
under ground a long time as they were covered with mould
which stuck bag and box together so as to make it difficult to
open them. When at last the box was opened there a piece of
coal which had been rolled by the surf into an oval pebble as
large as a goose egg. . . . John very grandly assured me that it
was taken from a dead whale and was a great medicine. . . . The
other was nothing but the blow hole of a porpoise. . . .

. . . the great medicine came last, the bone of the Hah hake to
ak this was unrolled from some old trash and presented to me.
It was a shapeless piece of rotten quartz which had no resemblance to a bone of any kind. . . . John's father had been hum-
bugged by some smart Indian into this belief that the quartz was
a real bone, and John was firm in the same belief. I thought that
any animal who had such heavy bones must acquire considerable momentum in darting through the air, and it was not surprising it could split trees, or kill whales when ever it struck
them.

Then recessional, Neah Bay style. After closing up my business, the first of October, and packing my books and effects I
went to Baadah to pass the night with Mr Webster previous to
taking my final leave of Neeah Bay. I have been gratified and
surprised at the manifestation of feeling on the part of the Indians at my departure. They are not usually very demonstrative
but children and adults appeared very much affected, the former
shedding tears and the latter singing a chant expressive of their
sorrow.

I have tried to do my duty toward these Indians and these
friendly expressions on their part are more grateful to me than
the approval of others. . . .

The White Tribe

HOORTS
(The Bear)

DAY FORTY-THREE

Whidbey Island, this first dawn of February. Admiralty Inlet, with the Strait of Juan de Fuca angling like a flat blue glacier into one end and Puget Sound out the other. This promontory surge of the island's steep edge, lifting me to look west onto the entire great bending valley of water. And south to the trim farmland where on a summer midnight in 1857, Indians snicked off a head.

The beheaders were northern Indians: Tlingit warriors from an Alaskan island near Sitka, knifing downcoast eight hundred miles in their glorious high-prowed canoes. The victim they caught and decapitated was a settler named Ebey, a militia officer and member of the Washington territorial legislature. There was no specific quibble between the raiding party and Ebey; simply, one of their tribal leaders had been killed during a clash with an American gunboat the previous year and the Tlingits now exacted a chief for a chief.

Peculiar, for a timber and water empire which appears so everlastingly placid and was explored by whites and yielded by the natives with perhaps less bloody contention than any other early American frontier, that the practice of beheading crops up so in the Sound and Strait country. Recall the Makahs bringing home to Neah the pair of Elwha heads from Crescent Bay like first cabbages of the season. The earliest white expedition in from the Pacific, Vancouver's in 1792, was met with "A Long Pole & two others of smaller size . . . put upright in the Ground each having a Human Scull on the top." That trio of skulls rode

the air at Marrowstone Island, in direct line of sight across
Admiralty Inlet from where I am perched, and the exploring
Englishmen were blinklessly deferential about the display. Lieutenant Peter Puget, whose quote that is, proceeds to remark
that he does not wish to criticize a people "whose Manners
Customs Religion Laws & Government we are yet perfect Strangers to." Whether His Majesty's lieutenant would have been as
equable about the northern warriors' manners in carrying Ebey's
head away from here with them and eventually peeling the scalp
off it and swapping the skin-and-hair hank to a Hudson's Bay
trader for six blankets, a handkerchief, a bolt of cotton, three
pipes, and some tobacco—the trader then returning the grisly
prize to Ebey's family for burial—it would be interesting to
know.

Come look from this eminence of bluff now in the soft hour
before daybreak and you will declare on Bibles that the Tlingits'
act of 122 years ago was the last sharp moment on this landscape. The island's farm fields are leather and corduroy, rich
even panels between black-furred stands of forest. Tan grass
which broomed the backs of my hands as I climbed the path up
to here now whisks soundlessly against a four-wire fenceline.
The sky's only clouds are hung tidily on the southernmost Cascade Mountains at the precise rim of summit where the sun will
loft itself. Yes: Rural America of the last century, your eyes
say—or Westphalia, or Devonshire.

Directly below where I stand sits an aging barn with its long
peaked eave pointing southeast, like the bill of a cap turned
attentively toward sunrise. We will sunwatch together.

Across Admiralty the street lights of Port Townsend begin to
quench into the day. The timber-heavy shoreline angling westward out the Strait from the town seems not so black and barbed
as it was minutes ago. That shoreline is my reason—one of my
reasons; the other is sheerly that I love this blufftop arc above
the tiering horizons of water and shore and mountains—to be
here. Across there, invisible yet imprinted, curves the canoe
route which Swan traveled time on time during his Neah Bay
years.

A hundred water miles stretch between Port Townsend and Cape Flattery, and the journey along the fjordlike shore of the Olympic Peninsula usually took three days. *The Olympic range, recorded Swan from afloat, presents a wild forbidding aspect.* But then: *the line of foot-hills . . . disclosing deep ravines, with fertile valleys lying between them, and reaching quite to the base of the great mountains.* As for the long rough-hewn channel of the Strait itself, *Bays and points are bold, precipitous and rocky. The water at these points is deep, and, when the winds are high, dashes with tremendous force upon the cliffs, making a passage around them, at times, a difficult and dangerous matter.*

I can see exactly to where one such matter occurred, beyond the headland where Port Townsend nestles. Early in his years on the Strait, Swan was inbound from Neah Bay one afternoon when his Makah canoe crew pulled ashore to camp at Discovery Bay instead of paddling on the half-dozen miles to Port Townsend. Since the Indians' canoe pace seemed to be regulated part of the time by weather savvy and prudence and the other part by indolence, it required some knowing to tell the moods apart. (Swan had mused on a similar puzzle of canoe etiquette during his time among the Chinooks and Chehalis at Shoalwater Bay. *Speed will be kept up for a hundred rods,* he wrote in *Northwest Coast,* then the paddles put to rest *and all begin talking. Perhaps one has spied something, which he has to describe while the rest listen; or another thinks of some funny anecdote . . . or they are passing some remarkable tree or cliff, or stone, which has a legend attached to it. . . . When the tale is over . . . all again paddle away with a desperate energy for a few minutes. . . .*) This day Swan decided the crew was being entirely too casual with his time and insisted they continue. An old Makah woman in the canoe grumbled her disagreement, *for she said she knew we should have a gale of wind from the northwest.* As promptly as she predicted, the weather lambasted them. *We met the tiderips, and had a fearful time. . . . On we flew like an arrow, every sea throwing a swash into the canoe, keeping two persons constantly bailing. The old squaw began to sing a death song. . . .* The paddlers at last managed to teeter the canoe atop breakers which skimmed it to shore, and a shaken and wiser Swan hiked the rest of the way to Port Townsend.

Twin gulls break into my sight around the bend of the bluff. "Slim yachts of the element," Robinson Jeffers christened them, and taking him at his words these two are gentleman racers.

They stay paired, the inshore bird a few feather-lengths ahead, in a casual motionless glide past me, and on down the bluffline.

Then one flaps once, the other flaps once—evidently the rules of this contest of air—and they flow on out of my vision.

While I am monitoring birds the first full daylight has reached into the peaks of the Olympic Mountains, brightening the front pyramids of white and surely Olympus itself, eight thousand feet high but so discreet of summit it hides in the western backfile of the range. So a ceiling of sunshine is somewhere up there and in minutes I will be granted the floor of it down here.

I hurry north along the bluff, wanting to watch the light come onto the lagoon which bows out from the shoreline below. The lagoon is not quite like any other piece of coastwork I have ever seen: a narrow band of gravel beach which mysteriously has looped out from the base of the bluff—the curve of the gravel snare about two hundred yards across at its widest—and entrapped several acres of tidewater. Driftlogs by the hundreds float within it like pewter tableware spilled across marble.

At two minutes before eight the first beams set the lagoon aglow, the pewter suddenly becomes bronze.

The sun now rides clear of the mountains, but so far onto the southern horizon at this time of year that its luster slants almost directly along the Sound and Admiralty Inlet, as if needing the ricochet help from the water in order to travel the extreme polar distances to the lagoon and, at last, me.

The canoes that slipped through these water distances like needles; they stitch and stitch in my mind this morning. *Beautifully modeled,* Swan said of the crafts of the Makahs, *resembling in their bows our finest clipper ships . . . formed from a single log of cedar, carved out with skill and elegance. The best canoes are made by the Clyoquot and Nittinat tribes, on Vancouver*

Island, who sell them to the Makahs, but few being made by the latter tribe owing to the scarcity of cedar in their vicinity.... Propulsion was either the deft broadhead paddles carved by the Clyoquots or square sails of woven cedar bark, which caused the vessels to look all the more like small clipper ships, diminutives of that greatest grace of seafaring. The grace perhaps flowed up out of the cedar into the canoemen. Swan records that when the Makahs would convey him downcoast from Cape Flattery to the Hosett village at Cape Alava, for the sheer hellbending fun of it they would thread the canoe into the archways where waves have pounded through the big offshore seastacks. On one of these through-the-hole voyages Swan and the Reservation doctor *had an opportunity of witnessing the operation of three tremendous rollers which came sweeping after us and which I feared would knock us against the top of the arch. The doctor said he had his eye on a ledge which he should try to catch hold of in case of emergency, but fortunately we had no occasion to try our skill at swimming as the Indians worked the canoe through the passage beautifully.*

Makah canoemanship introduced Swan to Swell, dressed in that fresh suit of Boston clothes, bound out from Port Townsend to Neah Bay on a mid-September day of 1859 with a cargo of *flour, bacon, molasses and blankets.* Swan climbed in for the jaunt and ever after was impressed with Swell, wrote at once of him that line that *he is still quite a young man, but if he lives, he is destined to be a man of importance among his own and neighboring tribes.*

If he lives. Why those edged words amid the admiration, on a fine bright journey out this valley of water to Neah?

Whatever the reason for those three uneasy jots of Swan's pen, they were exact augury, Swell long since dead by the time seven Septembers later Swan canoed away from the Neah Bay teaching job, reversed that original route to arrive in from Cape Flattery to Port Townsend, across the water here.

A second illumination of this sunrise. I realize that I bring myself back and back to this bluff because here scenes still fit onto each other despite their distances of time. Becoming rarer in the West, constancy of this sort. What I am looking out over in this fresh dawn is little enough changed from the past that Swan in a Makah canoe, coming or going on the Port Townsend–Neah Bay route, can be readily imagined across there, the sailing gulls slide through his line of sight as they do mine. Resonance of this rare sort, the reliable echo from the eye inward, I think we had better learn to prize like breath.

DAY FORTY-FOUR

So to Swan's next frontier address: Port Townsend.

Port Townsend always has lived a style of boom and bust and that record of chanciness is a main reason I cherish the town. In a society of cities interested most in how svelte their skyscrapers are, Port Townsend still knows that life is a dice game in the dirt. I have been in and out of the place as often as I could these past dozen years and I can almost feel in the air as I step from the car whether the town is prospering or drooping. Small shops will bud in the high old downtown buildings. My next visit, they have vanished. A grand house will be freshly painted one day. When I glance again, peeling has set in. This time I was in town only moments when I heard that a few of the vastest old mansions have been trying life as guest houses. That seemed promising, but now the state is requiring that every room be fitted with a metal fire door, and the mansion proprietors proclaim themselves staggered toward bankruptcy by the prospect.

Reputation here has waned a bit, too, at least from what I can determine by reading around in Port Townsend's past. Swan once writes that in its early years the town was noted for whiskey so strong it was suspected to be *a vile compound of alcohol red pepper, tobacco and coal oil.* The quality of Port Townsend's early inhabitants occasionally was questioned in similar tones, as when a transplanted Virginian assessed his period of residence: "Suh, when I first came here, this town was inhabited by three classes of people—Indians, sailors, and sons of bitches. Now I find that the Indians have all died, and the sailors have sailed away." Those of us who grew up in small towns of such lineage ("Tell 'em"—the Montana rancher to me, sixteen-year-old ranchhand about to brave the community of Browning on a Saturday night—"tell 'em you come from Tough Creek, and you sleep on the roof of the last house") may become rare as mules in this citifying nation, but meanwhile a Port Townsend, adoze out on its end of the continent, reminds us of the vividness.

No ferry from the cities of Puget Sound connects to Port Townsend, and the road to its flange of headland on the Strait is a dozen-mile veer from the main highway of the Olympic Peninsula. In fogless weather I can very nearly see to the town, north past the jut of Point No Point, from the bluff above our valley. But driving here on this day of murk, the sky like watered milk and the road spraying up brown slush, Port Townsend seemed far-off and elusive as a lookout tower atop a distant crag.

From its initial moment of settlement, which happened in 1851, the remarkable siting has been Port Townsend's topic to boast, whenever not cussing it. As the first community astride the Strait of Juan de Fuca–Puget Sound water route, claiming a spacious headland with a sheltering bay along its southeastern side, Port Townsend looked to be a golden spot on the map. But the promontory site turned out not as the dreamed-of stroke of geography collecting all inbound ships but merely a nub of coast around which the lane of maritime commerce bent, like a rope pulleyed over a limb, and lowered cargoes onward to the docklands of Seattle, Tacoma, Everett and Olympia. Those cargoes still are going past.

The civic personality did not quite prove out as anticipated, either. Huge aspiring Victorian houses and unexampled views across water shoulder side by side with the scruff and shagginess of a forest clearing. The town is divided between the abrupt waterfront (brinklike in more ways than one: Swan once reports to his diary that *One Arm Smith the waterman fell through the privy of the Union hotel down onto the beach and injured him-*

self severely & perhaps fatally) and the expansive reach of bluff behind it, where the big old betrimmed houses rise like a baker's shelves of wedding cakes. Downtown is divided again, between the blocks of brick emporiums of the 1880s and a straggle of modern stores which look as if they have been squeezed from a tube labeled Instant Shopping Center.

I discover from the diaries that Swan achieved his move from Neah Bay to Port Townsend by way of Boston, a transcontinental detour not entirely surprising from him; if he had been paid by the mile in this Strait period of his life he would have made it to millionairehood. The holiday season of 1866 and the first months of 1867 Swan spent with his daughter and son, Ellen and Charles, and not incidentally was on hand to claim a windfall: an inheritance of $6,427.14 from an uncle. About half the sum he rapidly poured off for merchandise consigned to Port Townsend (*1 doz money belts,* the pocket diary begins enumerating day by day, *1 covered wagon . . . 1 set harness . . . cod lines . . . pistols etc.*). Much of the rest flowed away in gifts for Ellen and Charles and in an astounding number of $25 checks written to himself. By the first of June, 1867, he had his bank balance successfully decimated to $647.32, and took ship for the west again.

In mid-July Swan was back here at Port Townsend—he had shortcutted by way of Panama—and in mid-August drifted out the Strait to visit at Neah Bay. Near year's end he went off on a buying trip to San Francisco for one of the Port Townsend storekeepers. In 1868, at last I find pages where he begins to settle in to town life.

Swan has had another windfall, of sorts. The ship *Ellen Foster* smashed apart on the rocks near Neah Bay and he undertakes to salvage the wreck. Beachcombing in the truest sense of the word, this is, and Swan holds no illusions about it. The warehouse he rented on the Port Townsend waterfront to sort the *Foster's* bounty is consistently dubbed in his diary *the junk store.*

Simultaneous with the junkwork Swan begins to take on paperwork. As the customs port for the Puget Sound region and

county seat and the biggest dab of settlement between Victoria
and Seattle, Port Townsend had become a kind of official inkwell for the Strait frontier. Swan always swims best in ink. Rapidly he plucks up semi-job of some official sort after semi-job.

I have established myself here at Port Townsend, he soon
confides in one of his letters to Baird at the Smithsonian, *having
been appointed by the Governor as a notary public and Pilot
Commissioner, and by the Supreme Court as United States
Commissioner, and having appointed myself as a commission
merchant and ship broker. Thus you see honors are easy with
me. . . . I reverse the saying that a prophet is without honor for I
have the honors without the profit.*

DAYS FORTY-FIVE, FORTY-SIX,
FORTY-SEVEN

Swan has come down with railroad fever.

How strong and delusory a frontier ailment, this notion that
wherever you Xed in your town on the blankness of the west, a
locomotive soon would clang up to it with iron carloads of
money. I admit for Swan and Port Townsend that they had a
germ of reason for their railroad hopes: the attractive harbor
sited closer to the Pacific and its trade routes than any other of
the contending anchorages of Puget Sound. And a single germ
can bring on delirium. Swan's breaks forth in letters to Thomas
H. Canfield, an executive of the Northern Pacific Railroad:

*Had the most skillful engineer selected a site for a great and
magnificent city, he could not have located a more favored spot
than the peninsula of Port Townsend. . . . It may be of interest
to you as a meteorological fact, that while during the past winter, the snow on the Sierra Nevada has been so deep as to
obstruct the Central Rail Road, causing the mails and express to
be transported for a time on snow shoes, and while at San
Francisco, snow has fallen to the depth of two inches, yet in the
mountain passes north of the Columbia River, the greatest depth*

of snow does not exceed five feet, and on Puget Sound particu-
larly Port Townsend from whence I write, there has not been a
particle of snow this winter. . . . The whole of the rich valley of
the Chahalis, which empties into Grays Harbor, and the valley
of the Willopah the garden of the Territory, which connects with
Shoalwater Bay, would be tributary to a city at Port Townsend,
and could furnish supplies for a population larger than the
dreams of the most sanguine enthusiast. . . . A ship could sail
direct from New York with a cargo of Railroad iron, which
could be landed at any desired point on Hoods canal. . . .

Swan, I would turn you if I could from this railroad courtship.
I know its outcome, and you would be better off spending your
ink money and postage to bet on fistfights in your favorite waterfront saloon. The commercial future lay in wait here along the
eastern shoreline of Puget Sound, not across there with you at
pinnacle-sitting Port Townsend. Seattle and Tacoma, these
points where the westward flow of settlement quickest met deep
harbors—they became the region's plump rail-fed ports. (While
Swan still was busheling oysters at Shoalwater Bay in 1853, a
territorial newspaper already was crediting the barely born town
of Seattle with "goaheaditiveness.") Had Swan and his hamlet
of destiny been able to admit it, the very sweep of water which
served as Port Townsend's concourse, Admiralty Inlet and
Puget Sound, now made its moat.

The letters to Canfield flew on, however, and in the sixth of
the series Swan made bold to say that the Northern Pacific not
only needed Port Townsend, it required him as its local eyes and
ears:

I would respectfully submit to you whether it would not be for
the interest of the company to have some careful reliable person
to prepare a statement of all matters of interest relative to the
harbors of Puget Sound. . . . For $150. a month I will undertake
to furnish every information, and pay all the expense of obtain-
ing it, such as travelling expenses boat and canoe hire &c. . . .

Swan in this Port Townsend life is showing something I have

not seen much of since his time among the Shoalwater oyster entrepreneurs. He has a little bright streak of hokum in him, which begins at his wallet.

It is the thing I would change first about the West, or rather, about an ample number of westerners. Their conviction that in this new land, just because it is new, wealth somehow ought to fall up out of the ground into their open pockets. Such bonanza notions began with the Spaniards peering for golden cities amid buffalo grass, and surged on through the fur trade, the mining rushes, the laying of the railroads, the arrival of the loggers, the taking up of farmland and grazing country, the harvest of salmon rivers, and even now are munching through real estate and coal pits and whatever can be singled out beyond those. Besides a sudden population the West—the many Wests—have had to support this philosophy of get-rich-quicker-than-the-next-grabber-and-to-hell-with-the-consequences, and the burden of it on a half-continent of limited cultivation capacities has skewed matters out here considerably. The occasional melancholy that whispers like wind in westerners' ears I think is the baffled apprehension of this; the sense that even as we try to stand firm we are being carried to elsewhere, some lesser and denatured place, without it ever being made clear why we have to go. And the proper word for any such unchosen destination is exile.

Anyway, Swan strives on a central route of his era, a site he is not generally found at, in his current quest for bonanza. His problem is that nowhere among his skills is the knack for hitting it rich. This stone fact asserts itself in these Port Townsend years by not only keeping Swan unrich but chronically short of any income at all. He has tried to tap a field he knows much about, the native artwork of the Northwest, but without much success. In his periodic letters to Baird at the Smithsonian he attempts now and then, with more than ample justification, to pry whatever occasional collecting salary he can: *I know that I can do this work as well and probably better than any man on the Pacific Coast, but I cannot do myself or the subject justice, unless I am paid for my time, labor and expense.* Baird's thrifty fist stays closed. When Swan on his own contrives a trading trip to Sitka in Alaska, the venture seems not to produce much except some interesting new scenery.

Time and again the Port Townsend diaries have to make account of small borrowings, from Henry Webster, from a friendly storekeeper named Gerrish, most of all from the local jeweler, Bulkeley, who is steadily ready with a few dollars. The sum usually flits from Swan so promptly he scarcely leaves a fingerprint on it: *Borrowed of Bulkly $5.00 Paid wash bill $1.00. . . .* His credit plainly holds good; generally he notes repayment of his debts the same day he comes into any real cash and is himself then touchable for a loan. But chronic is chronic and so the Swan I watch in these railroad missives still is a fellow I would cheerfully accompany to Katmandu, but am not so sure I would buy a horse from, if he happened to be needy for funds at the moment.

Therefore his crowbar work on the coffers of the Northern Pacific. To my astonishment, which shows how much I know about financial sharpstering, Swan is hired, and at his price. I can only think that the New York railroaders wanted to overlook no chance, and if the shore of the Strait of Juan de Fuca somehow proved worthy of railroad iron, this *careful reliable person* who wrote such blarneying letters did know that outback shore.

Getting himself hired was different from maneuvering a railroad into town. Swan escorted the railroad moguls around when Canfield led a group of them out from New York, lobbied now and again in the territorial capitol at Olympia, tried to tout the prospect of transpacific trade with Siberia after talking with a barkentine captain who had come from the Amur River *in the very short passage of 28 days,* drew maps of the proposed rail route up from the Columbia River to Port Townsend, lined up local pledges of land if the town was tapped as the terminus. Then Canfield inexplicably telegraphed Swan to meet him at Ogden, Utah.

Swan, now no young man by any count of the years, jounced off into sage and desert on a 700-mile journey of horseback, steamboat and stagecoach. *Very hot and dirty,* the battered pocket diary of this trip mutters . . . *alkali plain . . . rattlesnakes . . . hottest ride I have yet had . . . desolate . . . miserable log house full of bedbugs . . .* At last at Ogden, a message meets Swan: Canfield has decided not to wait for him.

After that jilt Swan skidded downhill both fiscally and physically. Arriving back at Port Townsend from the three-and-a-half-week wild goose chase he jots constant notes of bad health—*Sick in house all day from the effects of my journey and a cold* and *sick for some time*—and probably despond as well. He also begins to record that the Northern Pacific has omitted to pay him several months' wages and he is having to nag for the sum.

It all spins out, Swan's several years of railroad fantasy, into a few words at the end of the summer of 1873. That spring, having thoughtfully bought much of the townsite first, the Northern Pacific had chosen Tacoma as its transcontinental terminus; now, on the eighteenth of September, the railroad underwent a financial collapse which took years to mend. Swan wrote unknowing prophecy in his diary at Port Townsend two days earlier: *Town very dull   nothing doing.*

I have some feel for Swan's railroad debacle, because the bulldozers on one of the slopes across this valley remind me steadily of futility of my own. My effort was to narrow progress, Swan's was to lure it in his direction, but in the end we are each as futile as the other.

The bulldozers are carving out housing sites. On any scale the slope they are swathing was no hillside of grandeur: scrub alder, madrona. But amid Seattle's spread of suburbs it made a healthy green lung, and its loss is one more nick toward changing the Puget Sound region into Los Angeles North.

At the hearing I spoke against the total of 107 houses designated for the site, suggesting if nothing else that half the number, on lots the same size as the reasonably generous ones on our side of the valley, made a more swallowable sum for the area. The zoning law, however, permitted that the size of the lots

could be averaged over the entire acreage, including slopes of
unbuildable steepness—a principle by which Los Angeles can be
averaged off into the Mojave Desert and it be proven that every
Angeleno owns a numerical rancho—and 107 houses it is going
to be.

Part of me has known the prospect is not bright that I can go
on and on through life as a suburban druid. Seattle, the city I
have most affection for, which until not so many years ago was a
green quilt of neighborhoods without much pretension beyond
that, has begun to overgrow, preen itself into metropolis. (I hear
the same of Denver, Portland, Boulder, Billings . . .) Probably,
too, I am at the point of life where, in this odd cottage industry
of making words, my velocity has slowed enough that I notice
society's more. Yet understanding the fact that change, altera-
tion of landscape and manscape alike, is a given of life does
nothing to make me think its consequences won't be particular
for me; everyone in the world has a nose but we all sneeze differ-
ently.

This attack of bulldozerphobia I know is a mood I should put
away, box it in the admission that I am sounding like a grumpy
homesteader who has just seen new chimney smoke on his horizon. (Make that 107 new chimney smokes.) Swan, you there
in mid-spiel of your wooing of a railhead for Port Townsend: you might tell me that I have western policy backwards,
that even yet "limits" is not a word to say, but you ought to hear
this much of my side of it, for it includes you more than you
know. While they were eating me like banqueters sharing a
cheese, the landholder's lawyer and the developer's experts and
the county's planners, the developer himself said least of all, and
I remember an instant when our glances met, baffled. I wore my
one suit, so as to look less like a beaver trapper among the
bureaucrats. The developer was in his rough shirt to show humble toil. Guises aside, we probably are not so very different; I
would guess I was piling hay bales at least as early in life as he
started pouring concrete. But the matter between us has become
one of mysterious creed—how many homeowners may dance on
the top of a surveyor's stake?—and the prevailing scripture is on

his side, not mine. Which is why his housing developments fell my forests, and tracks are laid to a town the railroad owns instead of one where a Swan dreams. Preach as we may in our own backyards, cottagers do not often sway a society's fiscal theology.

DAY FORTY-EIGHT

Rain trotting in the drainpipe when we woke up. Now, at ten in the morning, a gray pause has curtained between showers, a halfhearted wind musses among the trees. Today and yesterday are standard Puget Sound winter, rain and forty-five degrees, after the weeks of clear frost-rimed weather. A rich winter of two seasons, this. Time of frost, time of cloud.

Last comment unearthed from Swan on the railroad adventure. *Did not alter my opinion,* I come across him suddenly grumbling, apropos of nothing, during a visit to Tacoma years later. *That it is unfit place for terminus.*

DAY FORTY-NINE

A day that promises better weather one minute and reconsiders the next. The valley is sought out by wind every so often, but not yet rain, and the thermometer is nosing fifty. I would have known without checking that the mercury was up, for the cat is tucked atop a post of the fence at the far side of the neighbor's yard. More than ever he looks like a lion seen from far off, adoze at the edge of some thornbush thicket, waiting for a mouse-sized wildebeest to patter into his dreams.

What regulates this periodic cat, besides the day's warmth sliding in through his fur, or any other of the cats I have watched past my writing-room windows for the past dozen or so years, I have no conception. They are the most constant animals

I see and the most out of camouflage: they pace through our
wooded backyard in robes of color entirely unsuited to hunting.
Harlequins against the green. Yet unlike the neighborhood's
dogs which lollop around the street in dizzy concern for human
attention, cats are thoroughly in place within their routes. Only
other cats stir their imagination. Those aloof encounters by day
when any two, stalking like muffed-and-coated heiresses, will
ostentatiously keep the full length of my backyard between
them, then the shrieking rites by night when they try to murder
one another as inventively as possible. Otherwise it takes the
profoundest kind of intrusion to nick into a catly routine. The
gray-and-white wanderer who one day tiptoed into the garden
dirt, scratched a hole, daintily settled atop the tiny pit in
hunched but poised position—Queen Victoria on a thunderbox
—to do the necessary, did it, scratched the lid of dirt into place,
gandered uneasily around, spotted me watching from the window, and fled as if aflame. (No such episode from the tan cat; it
would not be lionly.) Probably the mind of cats is territory we
are better off not knowing. The winter Carol and I lived in
London, I stretched back from my typewriter one morning and
looked directly up at a cat on the ceiling. Our flat was the below-
stairs portion of a Georgian townhouse, a long warren of rooms
with plumbing pipes and electrical wires vined along the walls
like root systems and a splash of daylight at the rear, a kind of
glassed-over porch with frosted panes as its roof. The cat was
roof-sitting. Ceiling-sitting, from my point of view. Into the middle of the roof-panes of glass a light fixture had been webbed, on
the English electrical principle that unless the electrician has been
specifically told by the householder not to expend 238,000 miles
of wiring he will proceed to rig a bulb to the underside of the
moon, and the light as it glowed threw upward a small circle of
heat. By some instinct the cat had gravitated up from the alley
to curl itself to the warmth. (Is it Eiseley?—"In the days of the
frost seek a minor sun.") The rest of the day I would glance
overhead every so often and find the cat absorbedly licking its
paws, its midnight-and-snow face dabbing in and out of focus
through the frosted glass. That time of an alley tabby in wavery

orbit over me convinced me forever that whatever their thousand daily pretences, cats all are secret Cheshires.

To Swan of Port Townsend now, another here-again-gone-again countenance of my wintering. His effort to woo the railroad was mostly told in spare pages of the ledger diary he had used at Neah Bay, evidently a special effort to keep straight the skein of blandishments being tried on the Northern Pacific executives. Otherwise, the Port Townsend years are an era of pocket diaries: lines jotted instead of composed. Low water in the forty-year river of words. Scrawled small as they are, these entries will be day upon day of decipherment. But beyond doubt, worth it. I lift pages to the start of 1869 and find:

Stormy day. Commenced to occupy office on the lower floor of old Post Office building Pt Townsend, as the office for Commissioner of Pilots. US Commissioner. Notary Public &¢ rent $5 pr month.

I check the final night of 1874 and learn:

One Arm Smith & I worked this PM sodding Bulkeley's grave & planting shrubbery around it.

Even for Swan these seem broad enough brackets of endeavor.

DAYS FIFTY, FIFTY-ONE, FIFTY-TWO

Pleasant day, nothing of interest occurred except a fight . . . between Ginger Reese and Sam Alexander in Reeses saloon. . . .

Dave Sires   Lieut Paige and several officers of the Cutter gave me a serenade about 12 oclock PM. . . .

Col Larrabee & Col Pardee passed the evening with me discussing Swedenborgianism. . . .

Swan's frontier Americans as they clumped themselves together into the barely-in-out-of-the-weather settlement they called Port Townsend. To the local Clallams and visiting Makahs they must have seemed exotic as albino bears, this white tribe.

Their customs and rites of leadership are sporadic but frenzied. (Most memorable, at least by Swan's report, would have been the election of 1860: *The Republicans burned a tar barrel in honor of the supposed victory of Abe Lincoln.*)

They have a fixation on honorific titles: officers from the army post near town always addressed as "Colonel" and "Major," those from ships on station in the harbor as "Captain" and "Lieutenant"; at the courthouse, it is "Judge" and "Sheriff." (Swan himself in these years served for a time in charge of a municipal court and became thereafter on the streets of Port Townsend "Judge Swan." Such distinction was not without drawbacks: *Tom Butler and I had a talk in Jerseys saloon this evening in which he made threats that he would hold me responsible for my decision in case of Butler vs Butler.*) This they extend with guffawing generosity to the Indians, renaming the local Clallam chief Chetzemoka as "the Duke of York" and one of his wives "Queen Victoria."

This white tribe's sacred notions focus not on the earth and its forest and its roof of sky, but on obscure ancient quibbles among humans. (White humans, at that. Swan early makes note of an Oregon tribe who shook their heads firmly when told the story of Christ's crucifixion. The Indians had enough trouble getting along with each other without borrowing conflict, they declared to the missionary; this Jesus matter was a quarrel the whites would have to settle among themselves.) They hold as well a strange sense of territoriality, strong as that of wolves, basing it on invisible boundaries: not the borders of common sense where you know yourself liable to ambush from another tribe, but seams on the earth somehow seen through a spyglass mounted on a tripod.

Their weaponry is potent and mysterious, and growing more so all the time. (*Lieut Hanbury US Topographical Engineer called on me today he is engaged on steamer* Celilo *taking account of force of current at various points on the Sound for the purpose of ascertaining if it is practicable to make use of torpedoes as a means of harbor defence.*)

Their boats are even more prodigious. Long schooners—the

admiring Makahs have told Swan their word for them is *bar-bethl'd: house on the water*—which moor at the sawmill settlements and take aboard what had been sky-touching groves of trees. Steamboats which with their thrashing sidewheels can travel without the wind.

Their food ranges from disgusting—hard salted beef which the sailors call "mahogany horse"—to marvelous: molasses, rice, coffee.

Their views on whiskey are inconstant: some Port Townsend whites irate about the Indians sharing in it at all, others making a commerce of the liquid fire. *(Thomas Stratton brought a bottle of whiskey to me which he took from a Clallam Indian this noon under the wharf of the hotel. The Indian said he got it at Sires saloon and it was lowered through the floor to him.)*

So too their notions on sex: the white men are ostentatious about preferring women of their own skin, yet Port Townsend has a growing population of half-breed children. (This matter and the previous one meet once in Swan's pages, when he reports that an elderly couple of the Dungeness area have complained of their neighbors *that Squaws and Whiskey were legal tender among them.*)

These whites are showy as well about their dead, keeping the corpses about for a day or more for the sake of ceremony instead of putting them instantly to rest in the earth.

A good many whiteskins, particularly those along Port Townsend's waterfront, are several baths per annum less clean than the Indians. (Especially less so than the Makahs, of whom Swan at Neah recorded that whenever a grimy task such as flensing a whale carcass was completed, they at once scoured themselves in sand and surf and *came out clean and bright as so many new copper tea kettles.*)

Above all, this: they are a moody people, hard to predict, their community sometimes boisterous, sometimes dead silent. The afternoon, make it, that Swan and the other townspeople learned that the iron wagons of the railroad would not be coming: watch them from the eyes of Chetzemoka the Duke of York, how the bearded men cluster and mutter and slump away to their houses, how the street stands emptier than empty after them, how even the whiskey voices in the saloons cannot be heard.

You might imagine, the myth already finding words inside your lips, that this odd white tribe had abruptly got aboard one of its wheeled boats and gone away.

DAY FIFTY-THREE

And then Port Townsend would jerk awake again and scarcely blink between excitements. In one span of a dozen weeks Swan inscribes these doings:

...Edwin Jones died during the night of heart complaint. He had been playing in the band at a dance in Masonic Hall and was on his way with the rest to Allens to get supper. He stopped in at Urquharts Saloon where he had a room, laid down and died immediately.

. . . About Midnight Wednesday night Bill Leonards cow came into my entry and I drove her out. Then Ike Hall brought a drunk man into his office and I got up to see who it was and took cold by so doing....

...A Clallam Indian was cut in the head by another Indian and the squaws came and complained. The Sheriff took the guilty Indian and locked him up.

. . . John Martin stabbed Poker Jack this morning about 2 oclock in Hunts Saloon....

. . . Joseph Nuano the half breed Kanaka—Hawaiian—who murdered Dwyer on San Juan—was hanged today at the Point near the Brewery....

... The 6 canoes of Haida Indians who have been camped on Point Hudson for several days left this morning—They first went to Point Wilson where they burnt up the body of a Hydah man who died in Port Discovery 3 days ago—then they gathered up the bones and carried them off all leaving for Victoria and thence to their homes on Queen Charlottes Islands—

DAY FIFTY-FOUR

Lot of Hydah Indians with me this day in office, the tenth of May of 1873. *I copied the tattoo marks on the back and breast of Kitkune....*

He did indeed, and the creatures from Kitkune's epidermis writhe up at me now, from the pages of *Smithsonian Contributions to Knowledge No. 267.* The breast tattoo is a head-on image of a dogfish, twin tails looping beneath its gills to both sides: it is a broadline cartoon of some tropical mouthbreather which might gape at you from an aquarium tank. The creatures of the back—a pair of them, sitting up and facing to opposite directions like book ends—are crossbreeds of killer whales and wolves. They have snouted heads with teeth like sawpoints, claws long and pointed as fork tines, broad curved scimitar-like tails, and an extra eye just beneath the neck.

The skin art of the visiting Haidas plainly captivated Swan. He sketched a dozen of the patterns—the most decorative visitor seems to have been a canoeman named Kit-ka-gens, who displayed a thunderbird across his back, squids on each thigh, and frogs on each ankle—and lamented that they were *but a portion of the whole which were tattooed on the persons of this party. . . .* Soon another of his letters was away to Baird at the Smithsonian proposing the article for *Contributions.* (Proposing a bit nervously, given all these whalewolves and ankling frogs: *the Haidas,* Swan assured Baird, *are no more grotesque in their attempts to imitate nature than are our designs of griffins, dragons, unicorns and other fabulous animals.*)

His fascination with the Haidas is more than understandable. They surge in the history of this coast as a Pacific Northwest version of Vikings. Writers are habitual about the analogy of raids down from northern waters, canoes like small dragonships, fur-shirted warriors bursting up from the thwarts to do battle. Swan never blazons that comparison, and I think he was right. The Haidas of his time amply deserve attention entirely as Haidas. Undo the past and disperse a few hundred thousand Haidas along this coast from their home islands of northern British Columbia, the Queen Charlottes, south as far as the mouth of the Columbia River between Washington and Oregon, prime them with firepower equal to ours, and white civilization still might be waiting to set its first foot ashore here. The Haidas from all I can judge would have warred implacably as long as we could have stood it, then negotiated us to a frazzle.

The actual arithmetic is that as late as 1835 perhaps as many as six thousand Haidas dwelled in the Queen Charlotte Islands and by 1885 there were eight hundred. Alcohol and other allurements of white frontier society had made their usual toll of a traditional way of life, but more terrible harvest yet, civilization's diseases killed these warrior people like kittens. A smallpox epidemic in 1862 spread north out of Victoria and devastated what was left of the natives of the British Columbia coastline. No one knew the total of corpses—a ship's captain counted a casual hundred scattered along the shores like flotsam on his voyage from the Stikene River to Victoria—but the estimate has been that of a coastal Indian population of perhaps sixty thousand, one-third perished. Among the Haidas that smallpox outbreak obliterated several particularly strong villages along the remote lengthy western margin of the Queen Charlottes archipelago. That west shore population, reported a visiting geographer in 1866, "has become wholly extinct"; every Haida had left in terror or stayed and died.

If the Haidas were a diminished tribe, in unaccustomed baffled retreat to the safest of their shores, they remained a profound academy of artists. Besides the tattoo pages in Swan's *Contributions* article he drew a few of the stone carvings the visiting Haidas had brought with them, miniatures of the carved cedar columns which soared in their villages, and I can barely pull my gaze from the one that proffers four fantastic figures lined one atop the other. Just what the merry hell is going on here, it is not clear at first. Count on Swan to explain the foursome into two sets of two creatures: . . . *the lower one is* Hoorts *the bear holding in his paws the* Stoo *or crayfish. The upper figure is the* Tsching *or* Tsing, *the beaver, holding the* Tl-kamkostan *or frog.* . . . *The Indian, however rude or grotesque his carvings or paintings may be, is always true to nature. He knows that the bears eat crabs, crayfish and other littoral marine crustacea, and that the frog is the fresh-water companion of the beaver.* . . . *If the carver had reversed the grouping, he would have been laughed at by his friends.* . . . The linework is as fluid as the logic; no inch of the carving is without some thrust of action, something amazing about to begin. The beaver could be some creature of Mayan art gone mad; the frog he holds looks like some semi-human doing a handstand while wearing a gas mask; the bear could be a South Seas version of a jolly grizzly; the crayfish being plucked up backwards into his jaws is clearly from some far star. Restless skilled minds move behind this deftly stacked menagerie; minds which took magic from the forest, had the power to draw the coastal fir wilderness and its beings into the brain like fog into a cave and joyously make them art.

Swan caught an idea from the Haidas during that day of tattoo tracing in his Port Townsend office, and it became the underpattern of his *Contributions* article: the Haidas were a most intriguing tribe—*of larger stature, better proportion, and lighter complexion* than the natives of the Strait—whose home villages in the Queen Charlotte Islands—*a healthy picturesque territory*—ought to be visited—*if the Government would empower some person here, and appropriate sufficient funds to be expended*—by someone probably named Swan.

That notion persisted, I find, as if one of the Haida tattooists had engraved it on the inside of Swan's forehead. Entrancement with the Haidas' vivacious art surely has gripped Swan here, but I wonder whether something more is not urging him as well: a longing to step away, if only temporarily, to a new horizon. To the next West he can find (*a healthy picturesque territory*). Catching his third wind, so to speak, after having moved his life to California and then to the Washington coastline, Swan looks to me ready—yearnful—to venture again, and he would be typical enough of his era (and mine, now that I count up my own veers) to do so.

Whatever ran in his mind here in 1873, over the next years Swan's letters to Baird say steadily this: *I am more desirous of making explorations in the Queen Charlotte Island Group than of doing anything else.*

And Baird's to him say as steadily only: *I hope that one of these days . . .*

Later: something remembered as I stare at Swan's sketch of Beaver fondling Frog, Bear sampling Crayfish. When we returned from our time in Britain six years ago Carol brought with her a recording of *African Sanctus*, the fusion of African songs and dances with Western choir music, and began to use it in her semantics course to show the queer capturing power of rhythm, the vast sophistication of "primitive" folk art. The Haida work is something like that awesome *Sanctus*: anthems of existence, modulation upon modulation of the creaturedom which we too belong to. Carved music.

DAY FIFTY-FIVE

Storm. Fencefloater. Goosedrowner. None of which is fractionally enough word for such weather. Nightlong, rain swatted walls and windows, the wind pounded and ripped among the valley trees. Carol and I yanked awake at the gale's first try at peeling the roof from the house, never fully slept from then on. I was certain that the birch trees outside the bedroom would be bending, eluding, as they always do in southwest blows. I was equally certain I would be greeting one or more of them in through the rafters any moment.

After breakfast—the birches still stood, although branches thicketed the lawn as if someone had spent the night up in the limbs with a pruning saw—I slumped away to try for sleep, Carol drove up the hill to meet her classes. The wind roared on. In minutes I admitted myself more or less awake for good, managed to decide that I would head for Shilshole to see this weather at full run on the Sound.

In the car: full run hardly says it either. Wind-flung clouds dive almost into the streets. Just beneath their reach traffic lights dance like lanterns swung by frantic trainmen. People waiting for buses try to squeeze themselves narrow enough to fit the lee spaces behind telephone poles. Everywhere a sprinkle of ever-green branches has sifted down, as if the city has been seeded with them by a giant foresting hand.

In restaurants I pass, people are talking to each other with their hands. "Famous weather," a man brogued to me on a Killarney street one wan but rainless spring morning, "famous weather." This gale, the unruliest in the dozen years I've lived beside Puget Sound, is going to have a name of its own sort. It takes much to draw a gesture from a Puget Sound resident, but steaming mugs of coffee are being waved around in there to punctuate the expostulations that somebody's daughter and son-in-law got up this morning to find a Douglas fir limb exploded down through the carport roof, that they themselves will not even attempt driving to the job at Boeing this morning, that there's been nothing like this christly wind since the Columbus Day blow of, what was it, '62?

At Shilshole: I lean my way out onto the fishing pier. A bird lifts hazardously in front of me near the boat ramp. Incredibly, it is a kingfisher, blown in from some forested river bank or another and looking very weary of wind. I glance west, north, south, and find the Sound absolutely empty of ships and boats, the first time I have ever seen it so. The next surprise is that the weather is not the steady rage down here that it is in our valley.

A harsh uneven chop ruffles the water, but no higher than a tugboat's bow, and not much breakage of wave along the shoreline. I realize what is happening: instead of crashing the waves ashore here, the southerly wind is skidding the water the length of the Sound. When all the miles of chop finally fetch up against the banks of Whidbey Island the banging spray must be colossal.

Out of the wind which whangs among the harbor's sailboat masts seeps a high agitated whistling, like the cry of mournful birds. Souls of displaced kingfishers, most likely. In the clouds to the west the Olympic peaks pop through into whetted outline every so often, and unexpectedly, sunshine through some loophole in the vapors is beaming onto a stretch of the shoreline across the Sound. But quickly full storm again. The new rain front hits, rolls along the wavetops, resists me every waterlogged inch of the way back to the car; I could lay forward into the storm as if it were a wall of wool.

Homebound: against my habit the storm has me listening to the car radio. The announcer has just said the Hood Canal floating bridge has vanished. A mile of it, strutwork, giant pontoons, roadway, the bunch, blown beneath the waters. I count the number of times I have driven across the span to the Olympic Peninsula this winter, to Neah Bay, Alava, Port Townsend, Dungeness; once just back and forth over it to see where Swan made some of his incessant canoe jaunts with the Indians. With its linkage of barge-sized pontoons sitting across the broad surface of Hood Canal the gray floating bridge has always reminded me of a blockade chain across some river being contested in the Civil War. No more. This storm was the iron wind to snap it.

DAY FIFTY-SIX

Innocent weather today. Clouds wander sheeplike along the horizon as if unacquainted with rain, never any lust to meet the wind and go dancing raucously on the grave of a bridge.

* * *

In one or another of his earliest sojourns at Neah Bay, Swan had watched a Makah pageant of marriage proposal. According to what he wrote later for the Smithsonian, into the bow of a beached canoe stepped a man with a whaling harpoon. Another Makah sailor climbed in amidship and held a sealskin buoy as if ready to cast it onto the waves. A third man, the steersman, alertly knelt in the stern with paddle poised.

Onto the shoulders of eight men were hoisted the canoe and its crew of three and through the air in its above-sand voyage toward the lodge of the family of the girl being wooed, the whaling pantomime slowly sailed.

In front led a fourth Makah actor, a man beneath a blanket and creeping on all fours, *occasionally raising his body to imitate a whale when blowing. At intervals the Indian in the canoe would throw the harpoon as if to strike, taking studious care, however, not to hit him.*

Behind the man-whale and the airborne sailors strode a chorus of the suitor's friends, singing, drumming, shaking rattles. *The burthen of their song was, that they had come to purchase a wife for one of their number, and recounted his merits and the number of blankets he would pay.*

At last, as the procession reached the lodge of the intended, the mock whale scuttled to one side; there was an instant of poised expectation among the entire tableau; and the harpoonist with full might whammed his harpoon into the cedar plank door.

This operation, deadpanned Swan, *may be said to be symbolical of Cupid's dart on a large scale.*

Evidently some splinter of that great dart flew and buried itself years deep within the watching guest. Just before Christmas of 1874, into Swan's diary pages arrives the name of Amelia Roberts. Fifteen times in the next two months it sparkles there, and oftener and oftener "Amelia" is fondly burnished down to the attractor's nickname, "Dolly."

This is new. Over the years Swan's words on women have been scant. In 1863 when the Neah Bay employees invited ashore to Fourth of July dinner the captain of a trading vessel it was rare exuberance, perhaps lubricated by a holiday bottle, for Swan to note that the captain was companioned *by a very handsome specimen of savage beauty in the person of a Stikene squaw whom he had brought down in his schooner.* . . . There are the warm diary entries about the Makah housekeeper, Katy. A single wisp on a spring evening at Port Townsend in 1869, when Swan had gone calling on friends: *Mrs. Phillips and her sister from Whidbey Island were present. I was much interested in Mrs. Phillips from her strong resemblance to my late wife.* But little else. Until now these drumbeat inscriptions of Dolly, Dolly, Dolly.

Gifts to her begin to dollop from Swan like honey from a pitcher: sewing box, market basket, inkstand, writing desk, earrings, a painting, collections of seashells. *Dolly full of fun,* the diary exults. *Dolly weighs 127 pounds and measures 5 ft 4½ inches,* it commends.

One other reckoning does not reach its pages. That winter of 1874–75, James G. Swan reached his fifty-seventh birthday. Dolly Roberts was sixteen.

That canyon between their ages perhaps did not gape as widely as it would in later eras, but it made chasm enough. There were Swan's other fissures as well: his thin finances, his drinking. Visiting Indians sometimes slept—good gracious, sometimes *lived!*—in his office. Swan himself periodically dwindled across the horizon to Sitka or Utah or somewhere. Plenty, in short, for Dolly's mother, and maybe even Dolly, to mull about Swan the swain. And Port Townsend being the compound of New England small town and muscular western port it was, whatever could be brought up against Swan stayed in the air a doubly long while, as tittle-tattle among the mercantile families on the bluff (Dolly was the niece of prominent merchant F. W. Pettygrove, one of the town's founders), heavy winks and nudges among the waterfront saloon constituencies.

Unpromising odds. Yet as the ongoing diary lines about Dolly indicate, Swan had a bridgehead in the situation. He had been smitten with young Miss Roberts in, of all locales he ever can be found at, the Port Townsend Episcopal Church choir.

Against Port Townsend's night in, night out whiskey baritone, that choir must have been a very wavery Sunday trill. Sometimes the hymning voices were six or seven, sometimes as few as four. But consistently in late 1874 and early 1875—the diary begins to show dogged stints of churchgoing by Swan as long ago as 1869—they included Mrs. Roberts and her daughters Dolly and Mary, and Swan. (Mr. Roberts is a mysterious absence, both from the choir and the household. Deceased? Absconded? A sea captain?) Swan quite promptly begins to drop by the Roberts home for rehearsal of the church music. Then he begins gifts of food—scallops, salmon—and naturally is invited to share supper. Henry Webster, also at loose ends in Port Townsend just then and still Swan's stalwart, might be asked to join in as well. One fine February Sunday there even is a morning's genteel stroll, Swan and Webster and Dolly and Mary, in the course of which the young women probably heard more than they wanted to know about the singularities of life at Neah Bay.

What came of Swan's season of romantic hovering was just what could be expected: letdown. The choiring goes on but the gifts and visits slow a bit, and then become more widely—more respectably?—spaced.

Swan never speaks it in the diaries but the increasing intervals say it for him. Sometime here the moment occurs, invisible but sharp, when the fact registers on Swan, as it probably already had on Dolly with some help from her mother, that the choirgirl and the white-bearded frontiersman are not a likely match. I find ahead in the diaries that for a number of years to come Swan will continue a fond proximity to Dolly and the Roberts family. Not this daily nearness of an infatuated suitor, however. More like the weekliness of a favorite bachelor uncle.

So then. Who would have thought the clerkish whiskeyfied aging dabbler had such steam in him? But of course he did, exactly because he had never shown so, and to me his infatuation is as entirely enchanting as it was foolish. Wish such a season to any of us, man or woman, so long self-locked into aloneness. Let the blaze come out for once from within the bones. I say emotional paroles are due the alone of this world even if, like Swan's, the outing turns out to be quick and bitter-sweet. Better that than simply bitter.

Meanwhile, early in that spring of 1875 a territorial news-paper carries this item:

MARRIED: In Portland, Oregon, April 3d, Henry A. Web-ster and Mary E. Roberts, both of Port Townsend.

DAY FIFTY-SEVEN

I am negotiating for the purchase of the largest canoe ever built on this coast, Swan to the Smithsonian's Baird, another spring day of 1875. *It is at Alert Bay, Vancouver Island. It measures 75 to 80 feet long....*

The great canoe's reputation proved to be somewhat vaster than its actual dimensions—sixty-five feet in length—but it still was a titanic craft, said to be able to carry a hundred persons. What was more, Swan himself could jaunt north in pursuit of the canoe and whatever other tribal items caught his fancy along the coast of British Columbia and southeastern Alaska. Baird had caught a glint of opportunity: the U.S. Indian Bureau wanted to sponsor a major exhibit at the Philadelphia Centennial Exposi-tion in 1876, and after the Exposition the exhibit items could pass to the Smithsonian. The way they would reach the Indian Bureau exhibit was from Special Commissioner James G. Swan, salaried at $200 a month and offered the U.S. revenue cutter *Wolcott* to convey him around the North Pacific.

Left for Victoria on Steamer . . . with Lieut Kilgore, to pur-chase charts and other articles for Wolcott & for me to get some silver to take north to make purchases, the seventh of June, 1875. That same night the *Wolcott* docked long enough to take the pair of them aboard, and *about 12 Midnight* the cruise began.

You would expect that this luckstroke from Baird, steamship and silver and all, might be the change of western scene Swan seems to have been angling toward. Certainly it provided distance and fresh enterprise: for the next forty-four days Swan records ports of call all along the broken coast of the North Pacific and buys busily, hundreds of items ranging from the giant canoe for $225 to wooden berry spoons for 25¢ each. (Only the wonderfully carved columns of the coastal villages eluded him. At last, at Howkan village on Prince of Wales Island, he is given a forthright explanation. *"These posts are monuments for the dead and we will not sell them any more than white people will sell the grave stones or monuments in cemeteries but you can have one made for you."* Swan at once put his order in.) But his account of the *Wolcott* cruise does not read revivified to me. The scrupulously-daily-as-ever journal is somehow perfunctory about the new tribes he was among, the Bella Bella and Tsimshian and Tlingit, vivid artistic peoples all; the pages show duty but not bounce of spirit. It may have been that Dolly Roberts still was on Swan's mind. She definitely poises there on the seventeenth of June, her birthday. A pair of *Wolcott* officers—with straight faces or not, I cannot tell—join Swan in toasting *the handsomest, liveliest, and most lady like* belle of Port Townsend. There was this, too: Swan undoubtedly spent time in gab among the *Wolcott*'s eight officers and crew of twenty-nine which otherwise would have gone into diarying. Swan's pen for once simply may have been visited to distraction.

DAYS FIFTY-EIGHT, FIFTY-NINE, SIXTY

After these steady days of my sorting within their pages, the Port Townsend diaries at last begin to annal themselves.

1869: the year's page-edges shine with gilt respectability. After a decade of daybooks imported from Boston or New York, this is Swan's first western diary, printed by the H. H. Bancroft firm of San Francisco. Plump as a pocket Bible and with a neat flap to bring the covers closed, it is fancier than anything Swan has been writing into since the Neah Bay ledgers, and his entries start off more neatly, purposefully, than the previous year's. He is churchgoing. Has begun to woo the Northern Pacific Railroad and bought some land on the edge of Port Townsend in case the courtship is consummated. Makes his mercantile jaunt to Sitka.

The first half of 1870 stays as steadily sunny—Swan at last sees his Makah monograph brought into print by the Smithsonian, and on June 30 hoists a flag to celebrate the marriage of his son—until the mystifying pilgrimage to Utah on behalf of the Northern Pacific. The diary, another Bancroft and near-twin of 1869, shows its own consequences of that journey: hard-used, spine nearly worn through, the covers flaking and fraying.

1871: this diary a "Pacific" imprint; smaller and an enlivening dark-green after the parson-black Bancroft covers. Swan begins the year with scrupulous routine once more, the tidbits of good news—a lock of hair from his new grandson, sale of the last of the *Ellen Foster* scrap iron, admission to practice as a lawyer—steady until September. Then he is taken ill again. (*First day for nearly 10 days that I have felt like a return to health. I have not been well for some time past, but hope that from this time I may recover both mentally and physically for I am in much need of both.*) Perhaps worse, the Northern Pacific has not come through with the salary he has been trying to obtain for months. Gaps riddle the rest of the pages. Swan ends the year literally at sea, en route home to Port Townsend after a steamship journey to Olympia: *At 12 midnight while about midway between Steilacoom and Tacoma . . . the pilot blew three long and loud blasts with the steamer whistle for New Years.*

A brighter year, 1872. The Northern Pacific at last pays up, Swan buys still more land, settles his bills and borrows no more. He does much walking of the Port Townsend headland; is impressed with a touring temperance lecturer and evidently takes another of his periodic vows of dryness. This year the Pacific people have inserted a credo on the calendar page at the front of the diary: "Make your words agree with your thoughts."

For 1873 the Pacific diary featured across the top of each day's page a decorative band of colored lines, red-blue-red, reminiscent to me of the battle ribbon rows on the chests of World War Two servicemen. Combat says it for the year, which arrived on the heels of a New Year's Eve gale and swept on to bring the Northern Pacific's collapse. Swan records long bouts with neuralgia; Peter's wife, Dukwitsa, arrives from Neah Bay, suffers hemorrhage, and has to be put up in Swan's room for nine days. Except for the visit of the tattooed Haidas from the north, the best that can be said of the twelve months is that a brewery has opened at Port Townsend—*tasted the first brewing made ... found it a very fine quality and it reminded me of the home made beer I used to have at home when I was a boy*—and that Swan was given the civic honor of sending the first message on the new telegraph line to Seattle: *Flags flying here and every one rejoices.*

1874, a Bancroft diary again but the biggest and gaudiest of this group: about the size and fatness of a thick paperback book, and bound in purple with angled streaks, like the pinstripe suit of a colorblind gangster. Swan is gaudy himself. Another inheritance is to be claimed in Massachusetts and for the first time he travels east by train. (Only seven days now, the journey from Pacific to Atlantic.) As before, Swan lavishes money and gifts on his daughter Ellen as if he were practicing to be rich; also dips down to Washington, D.C., to call on Spencer Baird at the Smithsonian; and up to sightsee New York with son Charles. Swan is back in Port Townsend by late September, spends the autumn getting interested in Dolly Roberts, closes the year on that queer note of the New Year's Eve sodding of the grave of the Port Townsend jeweler, Bulkeley.

1875: the year of Swan's collecting trip to Alaska aboard the *Wolcott* but also the year the matter of Dolly Roberts comes to nothing. In this diary's calendar pages the publisher, who chose anonymity, decorated each month with some scene of gods or gamins. Swan must have looked with rue upon Miss August, a robust unbloused lady around whom a troupe of cupids perform acrobatics on trapeze lines of flowers.

Sick, robust, drunk, dry, infatuated, thwarted, railroad-hopeful, railroad-undone, off now to Alaska and now to Utah and now to Boston, perpetually yearning north toward the Haidas, still ambassadoring occasionally among the Makahs and Clallams from his own white tribe, esteemed author at last for his Makah memoir and dabbler as ever amid piddling paperwork. I take back the slander that Swan's Port Townsend years are more dozeful than his time at Neah. Not as much of it a life I would trade for, though. The periodic illness, the steady lure of too much whiskey, the seesaw finances, all or any would be as perpetual earthquakes compared to my even days. (Nor does Dolly Roberts, sweetly though she trills, sound like the best prospect I can imagine.) But I do envy Swan the historical moment, just there before America marked that centennial which he went collecting for. (Although historical moments may be less different from our own than we like to think: the quote recovered from a notebook I put it in during the Bicentennial hoopla of three years ago: humorist Mose Skinner in 1875, on the eve of the American centennial, proposing a ceremony to match the popular mood: "Any person who insinuates in the remotest degree that America isn't the biggest and best country in the world, and far ahead of every other country in everything, will be filled with gunpowder and touched off.") Both of my grandfathers, in Scotland and Illinois, were born amid the years spanned by these half-dozen diaries, and with them the family's western impulse. It seems a time when the American landscape had not yet been swathed so hard (although the frontier populace was busy enough at it); a time yet of a green tentativeness about the country, and particularly the West, as if we were still deciding what to make of it, or what it might make of us.

This odd community of time I mentioned at the start of this book of days. Since then I have spent a pair of simultaneous spans with James Gilchrist Swan, the first two months of this coastal winter and the quarter-century after he detached himself from Boston for the Pacific shore. By now I know of him, what?

That he has failed at two major tasks, teaching to the Makah children and butlering for the transcontinental railroad. The oyster venture at Shoalwater, he seems never to have got engrossed enough in for his abandonment to qualify as failure. His collecting of specimens for the Smithsonian is "attended with success," as Baird periodically hurrahs him, but as a way of earning is a slow dollar indeed. Swan fends rather than amasses. With his Port Townsend collection of not-quite-livelihoods he reminds me of a householder with a leaky roof, distractedly positioning a washbasin under this drizzle, a battered pot under that one, until the plinks somehow are all, or at least mostly, caught.

That he is a spree drinker, dry for weeks, months—at Neah for years—at a stretch. No constant souse can have written his thousands of diary entries, hundreds and hundreds of letters, frequent newspaper articles, the Smithsonian treatises, and *The Northwest Coast.*

That he is mildly forgetful, having a tendency to leave behind a book or a spare pair of pants in a hotel room. The big Neah Bay ledger diary once goes into a fluster: *This evening I lost or mislaid my spectacles in a singular manner for which I cannot account. I had given two of the boys some medicine and entered it in my book which was the last time I had them on. A few minutes afterward I could find them nowhere. The boys and myself hunted for over an hour without success.* Next day: *I took down my prescription book and to my great pleasure found my spectacles which I had placed in the book and had unthinkingly shut....*

That he is not a chronically jokey man, but laughs at the frontier's humor probably more than a sound Bostonian ought to. The Olympic Peninsula settler who has a prized rooster named Brigham Young is cheerfully in Swan's pages, as is the sailor—*a Dago or a Russian Finn*—who notices the carcasses of skinned fur seals on the shipdeck and asks, *Captain will I throw them cartridges overboard?* Swan can ping a nice note of irony, as when he stepped from the Neah Bay schoolhouse to watch a Makah tamanoas ceremony *and was much edified to notice that two of my scholars   Jimmy, who had just recovered from a severe attack of cold, and George, were performing on the beach entirely naked....*

That, in the frequent way of solitary persons, he loves song. His regular choiring began long before Dolly Roberts was there to share a hymnbook, and at times he vocalizes in the living room of one friend or another, an occasion he is apt to record as *a grand frolic.* I imagine his voice as a bit nasal and, the twenty-five frontier years notwithstanding, notably Yankee in accent.

That he can get very full of himself, particularly when his own evidence on a matter is contradicted. During a dispute with a Smithsonian scientist who maintained that fur seals all birthed their young at the Pribilof Islands off the Alaskan coast, Swan tetchily writes to Baird: *I do not believe all the fur seals of the North Pacific Ocean assemble on the Pribiloff Islands any more than I believe all the flies of this coast alight on one or two carcases of dead animals. . . .* (Current science suggests Swan somewhat misjudged the seals' independence; the Pribilofs are considered to be the single birthing grounds.) But other times he can drift into a dress-blue funk: *the great care and anxiety I feel . . .* Evidently not for long, and perhaps most often when he has to count another birthday (*I trust that the remainder of my life may be passed more profitably than it has so far . . .*), but he does know gloom.

That all the regularity in him is channeled down his right arm into his pen. He may pass from job to job to job with the liquid hops of a squirrel, but his diary account of his days and his record of effort to learn from the Indians are the steadiest kind of achievement. Constantly I am impressed with Swan's care to be exact; the steady spatter of arithmetic through the diary pages as he measures and totals things, for instance, and the fact that as early as his stint at Shoalwater he made it policy that whatever lore was given him by a tribal member, he would check by

later asking others about it, one by one. A scrupulous corre-
spondent, Swan is perpetually eager for mail and often answers
instantly, putting the reply on the same mailboat. No question:
the stickum that holds his life together is in his inkwell.

That he has a quality I do not know what to call except
gallantry. An ingredient of it must be New England manners. In
the diary he misters even as old a friend as Webster, and is an
instinctive caller on friends, welcomer of strangers, visitor of the
ill (white or Indian), sharer of magazines and books and undoubtedly bottles. But it goes beyond that, into the attitude he
seems to hold that the human race is a kind of fascinating com-
monwealth. Swan does not have this perfected; the Indians
periodically exasperate him into an inked mutter of *savages*.
Consistently, however, he respects their skills and lore and is
able to see and judge them, and for that matter his own white
tribalists of Port Townsend and the Strait country, as individuals
rather than a corps. Which must be the most valuable possible
discernment for a diarist.

What escort he has been. The ancient woman Suis whom
Swan in his Shoalwater years had questioned about the natives'
names; she spoke to him of the carrying influence of ancestors,
first people. For those of us on this long coast now, successor
tribe to Suis's in our pale thousands and thousands, Swan is of
our own first people. (Making those of us of this moment, in
T. H. White's term, the after-people: the ones for whom "music
and truth and the permanence of good workmanship . . . the
human contribution to the universe" are inheritance to try to
add to.) Swan is doubly valuable to me because the people of
my own blood are gone now, buried in Montana, the storytell-
ers, reciters of sayings, carriers of the Scots lowland voice that is
scarcely traceable on my tongue, and Swan filling his days and
mine with his steady diary lines is an entrancing winterer—a tale-
bringer, emissary from the time of the first people—such as I
have not been around in the years since. He seems a kind of
human bonus, a dividend to me for making this chronological
passage. And there still is a month of him to collect.

DAY SIXTY-ONE

Capt John came to my house this afternoon, the sixteenth of November of 1878, and told me the following queer yarn. He says that at the time Ah a yah's son died at Hosett, Peter, whose sister is mother of the boy, and Ah a yah were putting the body in a box for burial. They had that portion of the lodge screened with mats and fastened the door so that no one but themselves should be present. A woman however who was in the lodge unobserved made a hole in the mat screen and looked through. She first heard the dull sound of something chopping, and saw Peter and Ah a yah cut off both the boys arms below the elbows and then put the body in the box and bury it.

Some time the past summer the Indians found near a small brook which runs near Ah a Yah's house two human fore arms & hands or rather the bones, one end of which rested in a tin plate and the hands rested on a stick held by two forked sticks, so they could be roasted before a fire, the remnants of which were plainly seen. The marrow which had melted into the plate had mostly been removed but some remained which was hard and white.

These were lethal doings, Captain John solemnly explained to Swan. With the substance in the plate Peter had cast a spell—bad medicine—which took the life of a boy of the tribe.

I listened very attentively to the recital of this fabulous tale just to find out to what lengths Johns superstitions will lead him but the idea of Peter roasting the arms of his own nephew to extract grease to work bad medicine to kill his enemies, is too monstrous and absurd for me to believe without better proof than Capt John.

Captain John's busy tongue: the mysteries of Peter: Swan's recording pen. Unmistakably, life at Neah Bay.

Swan returned to Cape Flattery in mid-August of 1878, once

more kited on the wind of Henry Webster's political fortunes. Newly appointed as collector of customs for Puget Sound, Webster named Swan his inspector at Neah Bay, a job at last exactly Swan's size and fit. The first several months of each year a small fleet of schooners in the fur seal trade now worked out of Neah Bay. Swan was to make sure their sealskins were the harvest of Makah canoe crews launched from the vessels, rather than any catch from the natives of alien British Columbia across the Strait. Another trader at Neah dealt in the oil of the small sharks called dogfish, a useful lubricant for sawmill machinery. Swan similarly was to see that the dogfish oil remained all-American, or had the proper import fee paid. As to the Makahs themselves, original merchants of Cape Flattery, they were to be regularly cautioned against trading dutiable goods with the British Columbia tribes. Those few tax sentry tasks made the sum of Swan's new job. Otherwise, he was free to read, write, and, finally, collect one single salary he could live on.

His new prosperity wasn't fancy; as assistant customs collector, he received about a hundred dollars a month. But it could not help but be steadier than his life had been in Port Townsend the past few years. The diaries of 1876–77 show a number of gaps, the dangerous silences when Swan is either ill or in whiskey; one month-long void follows the note that he has been enjoying *Scotch whiskey punch* with some chums. Then he begins to regain himself when Neah Bay becomes a prospect again, in late 1877. His welcome back to Neah the next year was generous. A former Puget Sound steamboat captain named Charles Willoughby now held the job as agent of the Makah Reservation, and Willoughby promptly dealt Swan into the doings of the agency by calling on him to interpret to the Makahs. Swan in turn thought well of the Willoughby style of administration, as when an election process was set up to choose tribal leaders: *One feature in the election was that several women voted by permission of the Agent*—this a dozen years before any state permitted women the vote, and forty before the nation did—*thus establishing a precedent in this tribe of womans suffrage   which is right, as the women of the tribe always have a voice in the councils. This is the first election ever held by the Indians here, and will be followed by similar elections in Waatch Tsooess & Hosett.*

Another amendment to Makah life Swan's pen liked not at all. *While at the Lighthouse yesterday, Capt Sampson informed me that whales have been quite plenty around the vicinity of the Cape this Spring but the Indians have not been after them as they devote themselves exclusively to sealing. I think the business as now conducted is a positive detriment to these Indians. They neglect all other avocations during the sealing season, from January to June, and the money they receive for the skins they secure is either gambled away or is spent for flour, bread, sugar &c, is distributed in potlatches to their friends.*

Not only in their lapse from whale hunting did the Makahs seem less dramatic and turbulent than in the past. After twenty years of persistent Reservation administration, they had become not quite citizens of either their ancestral world or the new white world, but of some shifting ground between; as though the Cape Flattery "earthshakes" Swan used to record in his schoolhouse tower were sending tremors up through the tribal society as well.

On the one hand, the customary ceremonies of the tribe lived roaringly on:

The Indians had a great time last evening. They visited the various lodges and performed some savage scenes one of which was eating raw dog. A lot of boys imitated raccoons and climbed on Davids house and entered through the roof throwing everything down from the shelves and making a deal of mischief. Other boys imitated hornets and had needles fastened to sticks with which they pricked every one they met. Today they had the thunder bird performance and a potlatch. These Makahs are as wild and savage in their Dukwalli performances as when I first knew them twenty years ago.

But another day, Swan is startled when the schoolgirls, playing in a corner of his office, pretend they are holding a tea party and begin by primly reciting grace.

There is a moment in the diary when the tilt—to the Makahs, perhaps a lurch—toward the future can almost be seen to be happening. Swan is called to interpret as Makah mothers bring in youngsters who are to begin school. The schoolroom baffles the little newcomers. *They were as wild as young foxes and some were quite alarmed and struggled and bellowed. The school girls were standing outside to receive them and they looked so nice and neat, that it reminded me of what I have read about tame animals being taught to tame and subject wild ones.*

And one mark further of change in the tribe. Neah Bay in these years has a chief of police, and he is Peter.

In other areas besides Peter's psyche Neah Bay showed itself as a greatly tamer place now than in the early 1860s.

Regularly each week, a steamship chugged in; no more three-day canoe trips to Port Townsend. Another vessel was on station in the bay with pilots to go aboard ships entering the Strait. There was even an official but underfunded lifeboat station. (When Swan and the Makahs watched a few annual practice rounds being fired from the station's mortar, *Old Doctor told me he thought the mortar would be a fine thing to kill whales with.*) Willoughby's Reservation staff of whites was much expanded from Webster's original shaggy little crew of bachelors. Wives and children, even a woman schoolteacher, were on hand now. This new Neah Bay is capable of social whirl which reads almost giddy in the pages where Swan used to record the pastime of warring on skunks:

Mrs Brash and Mr Gallick came up today and dined. After dinner Mrs Willoughby, Miss Park, Wesley Smith and I sang, or tried to sing the Pinafore but with poor success as I had a bad cold and a head ache and the others were not feeling well and to crown all our discomfort the organ was badly out of tune, but we blundered through it some how and our audience said we did well, but I did not think so. . . .

Mr Fischer, Charley Willoughby and Mr Plympton came in this evening and I read from Scribners magazine the "Uncle

*Remus" stories which amused them very much particularly Mr
Fisher who pronounced them "Doggoned good yarns."*

If Neah Bay was changing, so was Swan, at least the diarying
part of him, and tremendously for the better. After years of
crabbed pocket diaries, these thirty-six months at Neah, August
of 1878 to August of 1881, are exquisitely, almost artistically,
penned. Swan returned to the grand 1866 ledger which he had
been using only to copy letters of almighty importance, such as
his blandishments to the Northern Pacific, and resumed the day
by day superior script he had practiced in the last years of his
previous Neah Bay life. When he reached the bottom of the
ledger's final page on the thirtieth of June 1879, he procured an
identical leather-covered volume and invented even more elaborate diarymanship, now annotating events in the margins and
summarizing each month with a stupendous double-page
weather chart which recorded Cape Flattery's every nudge of
temperature and drift of breeze.

In more than penmanship, these are high years for Swan. He
is puttering usefully, staying sober and enjoying health. His days
seem not only better kempt, but glossed.

*Last night was very calm and at 11 PM there was but little
surf on the beach and the air being perfectly still the least sound
could be noticed.... As the swell of the ocean gently fell on the
sands and receded it sounded like harmonious music. I laid
awake an hour listening to it. The air seemed at times filled with
...the steady notes of some great organ.*

*Indians out again tonight after ducks. Their torches make the
bay look as if a number of vessels were lying at anchor.*

*Called on Capt John. ... He then gave me the words of a
wedding song, which originated with the Nimpkish Indians in
Alert Bay.... When a Nutka man buys a Nimpkish woman and
she is brought home, they sing,*

"Ya ha haie, ya ha haie
Halo hwai kook sa esh
Yaks na artleesh, mamats sna aht
Cha ahk wyee, cha ahk wyee,
Ya ai ho   ho ho ho ho   hoo hoo"

and may be rendered thus. I have a strong house on an island full of presents, and I will toss you there as if you were a bird.

The final word is a jingle like row de dow dow in an English song.

John could not give me the full explanation of the words but said there would be some Nutka Indians here before long and I could find out from them the exact meaning, but I inferred that it was as difficult for him to explain what the words meant as it would be for me to interpret Mother Goose's melodies to him....

Capt Dalgardno, Pilot Stevens and Mr Fisher made me a visit this evening and we had a pleasant time telling stories in which Fisher as usual carried off the palm. He told about firing a 4th of July salute in a mining camp in California with a quicksilver can, which at the last discharge kicked through a pine stump then flew into a miners cabin knocked the top off a loaf of bread and finally jumped into a bunk among the blankets.

Fisher, the Reservation farmer, proves a particular boon to Swan, the kind of rumbustious frontier character he has savored ever since the days of the oyster boyos at Shoalwater Bay. *Fisher shot two very fat wild geese a short time since and eat them both at one meal and drank up about a pint of Goose oil. It rather loosened him up for a couple of days. . . . Fisher sent an order to the "Toledo Blade" for a book on horse diseases and received by mail yesterday a copy of Pictorial Bible Biography with a postal card that they had sold out all the horse books. . . .*

But Fisher is a now and then performer, showing up when Swan's assiduous pen takes time off to chuckle. The most frequent figure in the diary of this second Neah Bay stint is Swan's most affectionately written ever.

Little Janji and Joe Willoughby amused themselves this forenoon in my woodshed splitting sticks for kindling. while so engaged they hear a noise and ran in and slammed the door too. Joe said "Something out there will bite us. —What is it, a squirrel or a rat? I asked   No said Janji "big bee bumbel bee." I went out and saw nothing and told the boys there was no bee there. "Yes said Janji, hear him sing." Just then the fog whistle blew at Tatoosh Island and the distance made the sound hum like a bee. I explained to the little fellows what it was but they didnt believe me and Joe ran home. Ginger said, "Josie fraid, I not fraid I big boy I not fraid Bumbel bee." He then went out and caught a bee in a fox glove blossom which he killed by stepping on it and then showed it to me in triumph. . . . I told him he is the chief of the bumble bees, and he is very proud. He still thinks the fog signal is an immense bee in my woodshed which he intends to kill with a hatchet. . . .

He reminds me of my own boyish days . . . is constantly in motion never at rest from the time he gets up till he goes to bed and is as healthy a little boy as there is. . . . Jimmy's relatives were at Capt Johns house, they were telling little Ginger how kind I am to him, when to the surprise of every one the little child said "I love Mr Swan and when I am a big man I will marry a Boston kloochman and have a big house and Mr Swan shall come and live with me and I will take care of him when he is old. . . ."

Janji is very polite and will open the gate for me to pass through. The only instance of an Indian's politeness that I ever knew. If he lives, he will be a superior man and may be of great service to his tribe.

Jangi Claplanhoo, "Ginger," was the son of Jimmy, Swan's first student nearly twenty years before. Swan, refugee from Boston family responsibilities for nearly half of his life, now becomes a kind of honorary frontier grandfather. The diary is open about it: Ginger, he writes, *is a dear little fellow and I love him very much. . . .* Or, more open still, that fretful little earlier phrase about the boy: *if he lives*. Swan had written that of another Makah once, when he met Swell.

One other significant newness in the pages of this second Neah Bay life of Swan's. The Indians of the past—*elip tillicums, the first people,* the woman Suis had called them at Shoalwater all those years before—are having their effect on Swan's night hours. The incident of Swan's-dream-of-the-dead-and-subsequent-gift-of-clams occurs, and another as well. The twenty-seventh of February 1879:

I had a dream last fall that . . . Boston Tom came to me and requested me to move his wife's remains so that the salt water should not wash them away but I did not know till today where she was buried. A few more storms will wash the grave away. Dashio promised to have the remains removed as soon as the weather gets settled....

Swan seems not to know what to make of these nighttime visitations. Nor do I. Evidently Captain John is going to have to be our final source.

DAY SIXTY-TWO

In Cardiff I remember hearing of the Welsh custom of nicknaming by item of livelihood. It was said that in one village, the mechanic was known as Evans the Garage, and his father, local purveyor for a medicinal liquid of some sort, as Evans the Oil. By that standard, in 1880 this winter companion of mine truly becomes Swan the Pen.

He is sixty-two years old, hale, sufficiently salaried at last, away from Port Townsend and its tempting aroma of whiskey, among the Makah community he knows perhaps better than his own white tribe. He celebrates all this in ink, ink, ink.

This forenoon, the third of January, *called to see Capt John. Mary Ann made me a New Years present of a cap of Sea otter skin which she had just finished. It is a very nice one and very warm. Little Janji was very well and very lively, and told me the cap was a present from him.*

Peter, David, Albert & Lechessar, of the newly elected chiefs came up, the fourteenth of February, *to get their "papers" or certificates of election which Capt Willoughby gave them in my office. They were then told to choose one of their number as head chief for one year and they chose David.*

Today, the nineteenth of March, *I commenced painting a Thunder Bird and whale on the top of the chest I bought from Fannys father. I made up the design from the drawings of whales and Eagles done for me by Haida Indians....*

This remarkable year, even mishap amends itself. *This forenoon,* the twenty-first of March, *while splitting a stick for kindling it flew in my face injuring my right eye, and cutting my eye brow and nose. I expect a weeks black eye in consequence.... I thought it would be imprudent for me to go up to the house to dinner this evening as it was raining and I feared I might take cold in my eye So Mrs Willoughby sent my dinner down in grand style. First the Captain came then Mrs. Willoughby and with her 16 school girls each one bearing something. One had soup, another meat, another bread, the 4th one had pie, 5th had pepper, 6th salt, 7th vinegar and so on ... and the smallest one Emma, had my napkin.*

With the arrival of spring, Swan does his *summary of the seal fishery for the quarter ending March 31—1,474* seals harvested by the Makah canoe crews and the schooners *Lottie, Champion, Eudora, Teazer* and *Letitia.* Then back to notes of pleasure:

Frogs in full blast tonight for the first time, the twenty-second of April.

One of the Rhododendron plants which came from Port Townsend and was set out by me Dec 31 1878 has blossomed, and today—the thirtieth of May—*is in full bloom. This is the first time a Rhododendron ever bloomed in this portion of Clallam County. They are found at Port Discovery but I think not farther west than Sequim Bay. I have 30 plants and think nearly every one will blossom next year.*

Neah Bay is not yet so domesticated it can pass a year without commotion. In late June, the body of a visiting Quillayute Indian is found in the forest, murdered and robbed. When the investigation proceeds more slowly than the Quillayutes think it should, Swan has a talk with Peter. *Said he "you remember when I killed a man at Crescent Bay for helping to kill my brother Swell   I thought I was right but Mr. Webster put me in the fort at Steilacoom and kept me there a year   I have learned better since then and now I am the head of the police and Washington pays me to look after the bad people."* In a week, Peter is stepping aboard a schooner to take the Makah accused of the murder to Port Townsend for trial.

Swan does his second quarterly report, the final one, on the seal harvest, calculates that the total is up to 6,268 skins.

This has been another delightful day, the sixteenth of July, *the temperature just about right, with a refreshing breeze and everything looking charming. My flower garden looks very pretty   Fox gloves, white and purple, and blue Canterburybells ... My roses are beginning to bloom and Lillies ready to expand. ... If our season is later than up sound it is very welcome, for while everything here is green and fresh, at Port Townsend and on Whidbey Island the ground is parched and flowers are done.*

Swan has reason to find charm in his Neah Bay days. By regular steamship, he can jaunt to Port Townsend once a month, tend to a few office chores there, see friends and be back at Neah within a day or so. Visits across the Strait to Victoria are an equally simple matter now. So dinky are his official duties that he can spend as much time as wanted on personal correspondence, and letters constantly ripple off, to Baird, to Ellen and other relatives, to any number of ink-addicted acquaintances out of his past two decades in the Pacific Northwest.

Brief aggravation on the nineteenth of August: *The calves have annoyed me so much by running in my back door whenever it is open that today I put up a temporary fence of poles but I doubt if it keeps them out.* But then the year purls along again. Swan draws a salmon as the pattern for the new weather vane put atop the schoolhouse. Sends off to a tailor in Boston for *a suit of Navy Blue Beaver Cloth.* Cheerfully reimburses Webster, that dogged practitioner of patronage, $24 *as my assessment to National Republican Committee.* . . . Has a chortle when the chief of the Makahs reports his impression of Rutherford B. Hayes, the chief of the whites making a visit to Puget Sound: *David returned from Seattle & Port Townsend. Says he saw the President, but had about as lief see me.* . . . *I think David expected to have seen him in uniform.* Discovers that he himself has unsuspected white-tribal standing: *Mrs Webster told me that when President Hayes and wife called on her, they expressed their regret that I had not come up from Neah Bay as they had heard of me at Olympia. She said that President Mrs Hayes, Gen Sherman & Daughter, Gov & Mrs Ferry, Secretary Owings & others of the Presidential Party called at my office but I was not there and they then learned that I was not in town.*

Even early winter seems just dandy to Swan. *Driving NE Snow Storm 3 inches fell to 7 AM,* the fifth of December . . . *I think it auspicious to have winter set in at this time of year. The more cold weather we have now, the better the prospect there is for an early spring.*

By the end of 1880, Swan has filled 366 sumptuous ledger pages with daily entries, done twelve elaborate tables of day-by-day weather, kept account of the seal harvest, written 413 letters (and received 185), and had the president of the United States knock on his door. Writ large in more ways than one, this year of Swan the Pen.

DAY SIXTY-THREE

A quiet rain, which hangs bright beads on the birches. At the end of every branch, and strung at random between, elves' balloons of silver against the evergreen valley slope.

Swan's weather at Neah this date, the twenty-first of February, in the winter of 1881: *very heavy rain during night 3.25 inches fell stormy dull day. This is the perihelion of Venus Jupiter & Mercury and the last quarter of the moon The weather is quite warm and buds are well started.*

Another 1881 entry: the twenty-fourth of May:
The Teazer *brought the "Intelligencer" and "Argus" in which is the announcement that Mr H A Webster Collector of Customs has been removed from office and this will of course remove me. . . .*

The twenty-seventh of July:
Arrived at Port Townsend from Neah Bay at 2 oclock PM. Called at Custom House and reported myself to the new Collector A W Bash. . . . Received an invitation to tender my resignation as Inspector of Customs which I took into consideration. Dined at Mr Websters and gave Mrs W a boquet of flowers which I brought from my garden at Neah.

The first of August:
Left Port Townsend at 11 AM for Neah Bay to get my things. . . . Before leaving I handed Collector Bash a letter in which I declined tendering my resignation and he in turn gave me a notification that my services were no longer required. . . .

The second of August:

Very pleasant morning and smooth all night. Arrived at Clallam Bay at 6 AM and after leaving mail proceeded on to Neah where we arrived at 9 AM. Capt Munroe blew the whistle before we reached Baadah, and on rounding the point Mr C M Plympton   teacher   came off in a canoe and took me ashore.

I immediately commenced packing my things and was assisted by Jimmy and others.

I gave Jimmy all my floor mats, an empty barrel, a lot of coal oil cans and a variety of stuff.

I gave all my little garden tools to Ginger and distributed a lot of other things to Martha, Ellen, and some other children and to Martha I gave many of the flowers in the garden particularly my white lillies and Tiger lillies.

I feel more regret at leaving my flowers and plants than anything else, as they have been to me a source of pleasure the past three years.

At last all was packed, and boxes and packages taken to the beach and put into Kichusams canoe, and soon the Dispatch *came up and anchored and my things were taken off. It took two canoe loads. I went on board in the last canoe after bidding good bye to the family and friends I have lived with the past three years. The school children will miss a kind friend.*

I do not regret leaving Neah Bay as I think I can do better elsewhere....

DAY SIXTY-FOUR

As it is better late than never—Baird of the Smithsonian, the last day of January 1883, blandly about to incant a miracle—*I may perhaps be able to arrange for an exploration under your direction during the present summer....*

Not simply an exploration: *the* exploration, Swan to the home islands of the Haidas, the Queen Charlottes.

Swan had tugged at Baird's sleeve about the topic for ten

entire years. Now there was some quick back-and-forthing on money—Swan: *Will you kindly allow me to remind you that I have received no salary for my work . . . I support myself wholly by office work which in a place like this is but a mere stipend, and I cannot leave to go on any expedition to make collections but I find on my return that I have lost business. . . .* Baird: *I am not unmindful of the very great service you have rendered . . . our funds are either so limited or tied up that it is extremely difficult to use them as I would like*—until they worked out that Swan would receive $300 a month for at least three months in the Queen Charlottes, plus an allowance for expenses and purchases of Haida artifacts. Baird made it plain he wanted his money's worth: *You will understand that we want the fullest collections of all kinds, especially of objects connected with the fisheries and with hunting, to include models or originals of boats and canoes, weapons, hunting and fishing dresses, &c. As stated, I want you to make the most exhaustive memoranda as to the manufacture and application of the various articles gathered by you.*

Swan, at age sixty-five, is about to have the one more West he has wanted.

DAY SIXTY-FIVE

The water route to Port Townsend, hastily re-created after a lapse since steamship days now that the Hood Canal bridge lies tumbled beneath three hundred feet of riptide. That void atop the waves has made Port Townsend more queerly isolated and central than ever: without the bridge, the drive to Port Townsend and the Olympic Peninsula beyond is so long, south all the way around Hood Canal, that the state ferry system has installed this nautical shortcut.

The big green and white ferry *Kaleetan* spins northwest out of the Edmonds ferry slip as if having decided to make a break for Alaska, and the newness of direction sends itself up from the deck plates through my body, a vibrant return to the time when passenger craft skimmed up and down the Sound and Strait in purposeful daylong voyages instead of flat across the channels in quick commuters' hops. The fresh sense of surging out onto the water world is not illusion; the *Kaleetan*, running almost at its maximum eighteen knots, will take an hour and a half to reach Port Townsend.

The day is dark enough that the first of the lighthouses to slide past the ferry, Point No Point, still has its light winking. Behind it, the shoreline of the Peninsula juts blackly along the gray canyon of water and sky, Whidbey Island its mate-shore to the east. I have brought along Swan in scholarly tatters, notes and photocopies and snippings, but the wide water and its dikes of forest keep my eyes. Time enough for Swan's future at the two coffers of it waiting for me in Port Townsend.

Some dozens of minutes and Foulweather Bluff, named by Captain Vancouver as the North Pacific rain ran into his ears. Strangely, Puget Sound and now Admiralty Inlet seem broader, out here as the ferry goes along the center of their joined water like a zipper up a jumpsuit, than when I look across from either shore; the wave-ruffled distance in both directions somehow adds up extra.

More midchannel minutes, until the *Kaleetan* sprints north past Fort Flagler, opposite Port Townsend, as if still determined on Alaska, then at last yields slightly west with a graceful dip and begins to wheel direct onto the hillside town.

Seen here from the water, Port Townsend stands forth as a surprising new place. It regains itself as the handsome port site of its beginnings, the great water-facing houses appear correct and captainly on their bluff, the main street is set broadside along the shore as it ought to be in a proper working wharftown. Instead of the dodgy glimpses along its downtown through too many cars and powerlines, this Port Townsend looks you level in the eye and asks where you've sailed in from.

Docking this ferry is also from maritime days of the last century. *Kaleetan* is far too massive for the tiny ferry slip, like an ocean liner coming in to moor to a balcony, and the crew must show seamanship. One ferryman fishes out with a boat-hook, snags a larger hawser off pilings at the port bow. With that our vessel is snubbed while a tugboat hustles in and butts the stern around until, slotted just so, the ferry can make a final careful surge to the little dock ramp. The elephant has landed.

Many of us who step off as foot passengers could be our great-grandparents traipsing ashore at Ellis Island, Montreal, Boston: beards, duffel coats, parcels, suitcases. A number of us, as I am, in watch cap and waterproof jacket, which I suppose would mark us as crew of an immigrant windship. Three ministers are prim among us, over from Seattle for the day on some missionary duty or another. Women carry children ashore, mothers greet daughters, husbands wives, huge trucks ease off the ferry, others snort aboard, turmoil of drayage and pilgrims such as the town hasn't seen in eons.

But a block or so from the ferry landing, within a dozing quiet from some other vector of the last century, the carved cane reposes in its glass museum case. I squat and begin to inventory. The handle is ivory carved into a perfect fist the size of a child's right hand. Through the grasp of the fingers, like a held rattle, and out the circling grip of thumb pressed onto forefinger, twines a snake. The ivory reptile then writhes through air down onto the wrist. There above where the tiny pulse would hammer, the snakehead rests. Except that it is not at rest, but in midswallow of a frog, eternally doomed in its try to escape around the rim of wrist.

I check my notes. Swan first saw this creation in the village of Masset in the Queen Charlotte Islands on the tenth of July 1883. The carver, one of the Haida magicians either *in wood, stone, or in gold or silver,* still was at work on the cane.

A second snake, this one of wood, drives up the cane from the bottom in three precise writhes covering most of the length, until the head poises very near to the carved struggle of snakehead and frog. After snake eat frog, the outlook seems to be snake eat snake. This deft crawler along the cane length has a broad scal-loped design along the middle of its back, with cross-hatched scales along either side of the broader cuts. It also has tiny blue-green abalone eyes, a gentle everlasting glitter.

Snakes white and brown, contorting a stick of wood into struggle, legend, art. I very nearly reel back from this example of Haida blade magic.

Over lunch in a restaurant which confusedly has tried to rig its interior as a shipdeck, I think of Swan coming upon the snake-cane six hundred miles to the north of here. Keen as he was about art of this coast, he must have felt like a prospector whose boot has kicked up a potato-sized nugget in front of him. The carved scene ripples the other way in me, from art out into life. I see back to the instant when a jay attacked into the garden outside my window, its flash of blue and black and the high excited *HEEP HEEP HEEP* cry and then the toss of the garter snake which had been sunning on the warm dirt. In combination of grappling and chopping, the jay finished off the snake in an instant, then undertook to pull it apart, like a man trying to stretch an inner tube he is standing on. After a few minutes of tugging, the jay dropped the loop of corpse in disdain, bounded across the garden in three arrogant hops and flew off. When I went out to look at the snake, I found it as long as the span of my hand, nine inches: gray-green with three strings of yellow down its length. In places the jay had frayed through the body, small ruptures like those a knife makes in rubberoid wiring. Even as I bent in study of the snake, not two minutes after the jay's ambush had begun, an ant clambered on like a pirate coming aboard a derelict schooner, dashed in and out of the snake's open mouth and up to a quick circle of the flat skull, then raced off in exploration of the first body-rip. How sudden it all, the same eternal suddenness of the ivory frog sinking down the ivory snake's gullet.

End of the Port Townsend day, the *Kaleetan* churning a fast white current away from the town. In the early dusk—hard to tell this day's darkness from its daylight—I can see from the afterdeck back to today's second reference point of Swan's em-

barkment toward the Queen Charlottes that early summer of
1883. The bespired red-brick courthouse, and in it the records
of the municipal court which Swan himself presided over in
some earlier years, and within those records this verdict from
the twenty-sixth of May 1883:

*It is Ordered, Adjudged and Decreed that . . . James G. Swan
is an Habitual Drunkard as described in Section 1674 of Code
of Washington Territory. And it is hereby further ordered . . . to
every Dealer in Intoxicating Liquor and to all other persons
residing in the County of Jefferson . . . not to give or sell under
any pretence any Intoxicating Liquor to said James G. Swan. . . .*

DAY SIXTY-SIX

Unfold a map of the North Pacific, and you notice, some six
hundred miles north of the British Columbia capital of Victoria
and not far under the overhang of Alaska, a large stalactite-like
shard which has fallen free of the continental cliff of shoreline.
The illusory plummet has carried the chunk fifty miles to sea,
striking its western edge into some of the trickiest weather of the
entire Pacific and shattering the landmass into a hundred and
twenty-five fragments from the size of rocky hummocks to big
adrift peninsulas. Swan's telling of these geographic proportions:
*The extreme length of the group from North Point, North Island
to Cape St James the southern extremity is 156 miles. The Islands
of the main group are North, Graham, Moresby and Prevost.
Graham and Moresby, are the largest and constitute nearly eighty
five per cent of the whole area. . . .*

White seagoers had arrived in the late 1780s—the islands
received their name from the British captain who sailed in on
the trading vessel *Queen Charlotte*—but except for the Hudson's
Bay post at Masset and a dogfish oil refinery at Skidegate, white
enterprise and settlement across the next hundred years remained strangers to the Haida homeland. (This changed sharply
at the end of the nineteenth century, and on into this: the Queen

Charlottes now count a population of about 6,000, the majority
of it non-Haida.) Here in 1883, then, the archipelago still was,
as Swan so heavily had hinted a decade before in his Smithsonian article on Haida tattoo patterns, not familiar territory to
whites, and his own prime intention lay with the least known
geography of all: the west coast of the Queen Charlottes, that
region swept peopleless by the smallpox epidemic among the
Haidas two decades earlier.

The idea wafted to Swan out of the report of the most recent
previous white expeditionary to the Charlottes. Geologist
George M. Dawson in the mid-1870s had been able to sail and
clamber at will among the Charlottes, except: "The time and
means at my disposal did not enable me to make a survey or
geological examination of the west coast of the islands, which
would require to be carried on during the early summer . . . the
least boisterous portion of the year. It is a very dangerous lee
shore for sailing craft. . . ." Swan pointed out to Baird at the
Smithsonian the west shore's defeat of Dawson, *nor has any one
visited this Coast or examined it who has made any reliable
report*. Since he, Swan, would be in the Charlottes anyway . . .

Running a little late in life as usual, Swan at six and a half
decades intends an expedition which I, twenty-five years younger
and with the advantages of modern equipment, can never hope
to duplicate. The point is moot this winter, since this season is
not the necessary "least boisterous portion" of the weather year,
but precisely its most. The still-unpopulated western coastline of
the Queen Charlottes remains one of the remotest loose ends of
North America, and winter flogs it with surf, gust, downpour.
Telephoning to the Queen Charlotte communities to ask about
hire of a fishing boat or airplane or helicopter to glimpse some
of that shore, I am roundly advised to put even that notion out
of my head, wait for a summer. Which, remembering the one
near-drowning this North Pacific coast warned me with a few
years ago, I decide I had better accept as gospel. Even in summer, as Swan is aiming for, I cannot have the means he did. The
advice had been held out by Dawson to whomever adventured in

next: the Queen Charlottes' west shore "would, I believe, be most easily dealt with in one of the canoes of the country manned by a good Indian crew." To Swan, rider of canoes throughout the frontier half of his life, those words chimed exactly right. To me, footsoldier of a considerably tamer West, they can only be rue, and useful comparison of some of Swan's capabilities and my own.

As to why Swan decided to dare the Charlottes' western shore, when the Haida population and the material he sought to collect for the Smithsonian were peppered along the eastern coastline, the answer does not show itself in his diaries or the letters to Baird. My hunch is that whatever he told himself in his justifying Boston way, he wanted to do it for the edge of challenge, as the Makahs canoeing downcoast along Cape Flattery could not resist darting themselves through the tiderip tunnels in the searocks. Swan held no small estimation of himself as a coastman; *a true coastie*, in the Dungeness lighthouse keeper's sudden fine phrase to Carol and me; and here lay one of the last unknown rims of western shore. An extra West, one more over-the-horizon territory for the curiosity that worked in him like a second heart. For certain, this is greatly the broadest leap I have been close enough to see Swan take—his 1849 decision to cast himself west to California being lost to time—and I settle in with anticipation to watch how he will manage it.

From under that Port Townsend civic cloud of decreed drunkenness, which at least was newly lined with the Smithsonian's silver, Swan sets off for the Queen Charlotte Islands in mid-June of 1883. He voyages in rare style, out of Victoria aboard the *Otter*, a Hudson's Bay Company supply steamer. In effect, he is traveling to the Queen Charlottes as the invited guest of British Columbia's Superintendent of Indian Affairs, Dr. Israel Wood Powell. Of their time, Powell and Swan are perhaps the two white men of the Pacific Northwest most ardent and informed about the coastal native cultures, and long have known each other through Swan's visits across the Strait to Vic-

toria. Powell's cachet, particularly in vouching for Swan to the
Hudson's Bay Company whose ships and trading posts were the
supply line into the North Pacific, was ideal, and with it came
the suggestion that Swan be accompanied by one of Powell's
field agents, James Deans. The one hitch in this supremely hos-
pitable arrangement is that Deans missed the boat.

Swan shrugs—*watched for Mr. Deans till the Steamer was
under way but he did not appear,* the diary reports, and lets it go
at that—and settles back to savor the cruise of the *Otter.* Not
much of event has happened to him in the almost two years
since leaving Neah Bay. Wait, there is this: Henry Webster's
death, which Swan inscribed and then drew triple lines around,
crosshatching them darkly at the corners and center until the
result looked eerily like the sketch of a coffin. But otherwise,
except for a dab of added enterprise when a Haida bracelet
maker named Ellswarsh worked for a while out of the back
room of his office, Swan's Port Townsend routine consisted
of the minor paperwork chores of old, and the bald patches in
the diary which led up to the citation for chronic drunkenness.
An overdue change, this shipboard life which Swan is more than
veteran at; since his jaunty voyage to Britain four decades earlier, I count more than a year of his life spent on vessels breast-
ing off to somewhere or other. The *Otter's* seven-day slalom of
supply calls along the North Pacific coast, to Metlakatla and
Fort Simpson in British Columbia and Fort Wrangell in Alaska,
promise a particularly cozy round of visits for Swan, who by
now seems to know every living soul, Indian and white, from
Shoalwater Bay to Sitka.

Swan, it ought to be reported, is writing now in triplicate. Or
rather, in three versions which add up to triplicate and then
some. During each day he pencils into a pocket diary, and in it
flash his touches of mood, occasional grumbles (the Metlakatla
stopover: . . . *the hour was too early for these settlers who had
but just got up. I notice this listlessness, and desire to lie in bed
mornings to prevail in Victoria and every where I have been in
British Columbia and Alaska. Sit up late at night and get up late
in the morning;* worse at Fort Wrangell: *Arrived . . . at 8 AM*

and found the whole town asleep) or frets or chuckles. At first chance he transcribes, in that brown ink, into a small squarish hardbound composition book. This version is narrative at fuller flow, expansion of the pocketed days. Next exists the fifty-page report he later drew up for the Smithsonian, typed—shakily— and with historical background of the Queen Charlottes periodically swatched in. I have had no small amount of decipherment to do on James Gilchrist Swan the past two months, but never before triangulation.

What is happening is this: in a sense, just as Swan is being whetted against a new edge of the continent now, so are the diaries. As I have begun to go through the simultaneous three, it occurs to me that with their blend of detail and elucidation and reprise they are truly taking their place with those supreme westering pages, Lewis and Clark's and young Patience Loader's. To tell his Queen Charlottes journey in any higher style, Swan would have to hymn it. And after the ledgerly reports of contentment from his 1878–81 stint at Neah Bay and the unreported discontents of his Port Townsend life of 1882 and early 1883, these diaries' frank completeness is unexpected and welcome, like having a trout begin to warble to you up through its pond. These next days I am going to stand back a bit and give the busy pages vocal space.

At the end of the afternoon of June twenty-fifth, a shore which appeared *low and quite level, but as it was very rainy we did not get a good sight.*

The dim landfall is Graham, largest island of the Charlottes.

Arrived at Massett at 5 PM. . . . Delivered my letters of Introduction . . . took account of my freight as it was landed— wisely: *2 sacks flour short in my count & notified Purser Sinclair —and then went to a very comfortable cottage in the enclosure of the HB Co. . . .*

Off the *Otter's* gangplank with Swan steps the one expeditionary companion he has hired, described in a letter to Baird as *a*

very intelligent young Haida man, a worker in jewelry, a painter
and a tatooer who has been with me about 3 months. . . .
Johnny Kit Elswa is the keg-chested fellow beside Swan in the
second Victoria studio portrait, and his jacket-and-trousers at-
tire does not hide that he is a new example, perhaps in his mid-
twenties, of the outdoor artists in which the Haidas had been
so rich. Johnny (Swan calls him so in the diary, and I will follow
that) has become the latest in Swan's line of Indian confidants
—Swell, Captain John, the Port Townsend Clallam chieftain
Duke of York, Jimmy Claplanhoo—and promises to be especially valuable to Swan as hired helper on this expedition. *The*
most faithful intelligent and reliable Indian I have seen, as Swan
touts him to Baird, Johnny is from the village of Cumshewa on
an eastern midpoint of the Queen Charlottes shoreline *and can*
show me things of Indian manufacture that the foreign collectors
never have seen.

He at once proves to have less exotic talents as well: *This*
forenoon the roof of the house I am occupying, took fire from
old stove pipe falling down. Johnny & another Indian put it out
with buckets and Mr McKenzie furnished new pipe which
Johnny fixed all right.

Swan is advised at Masset that the canoeman he needs is the
chief who, before smallpox emptied the area, ruled on the absolute northwesternmost fragment of the Charlottes, then called
simply North Island, now on the maps as Langara Island. With
that chief and his canoe crew North Island could serve as the
piton for the journey along the western shore: relatively calm
waters from Masset to North, assured shelter there on the chief's
home isle, then the headland to headland descent by canoe
seventy-five miles down the coast to Skidegate Channel, the
passageway between Graham and Moresby Islands, and through
to the settlement at Skidegate at the southeastern corner of Graham Island.

The one omission in the smooth plan echoes the absence of

Deans back at the Victoria dock. At the moment, the chief is away somewhere on another canoe errand.

On wait at Masset, Swan begins to entertain himself typically, with his pen. Goes out and counts the Haida community: *Sixty-five houses old and new nearly all of them with a carved column or pillar in front, covered with heraldic devices ... of the family residing within, and representing some legend. ... * Does whatever collecting is possible: *Johnson brought me a fine model of an ancient war canoe with mat sails, paddles and every thing complete. The Haidahs were formerly a warlike people and a terror to all the Coast tribes ... but they have become peaceful lately and no war parties are now sent out, and the ancient canoes have all decayed and gone. ... Johnny was of great assistance in trading and purchased everything much lower than I could. The Indians remonstrated with him and asked him why he liked the white man better than his own people? Because, was the reply, "the white man pays me, you pay me and I work for you." This logic did not suit them but they let Johnny alone and I succeeded in obtaining some very interesting specimens.* Visits companionably with Masset's handful of white residents, *Alexander McKenzie trader, Charles W. D. Clifford of the Indian Service who was there on a visit and Reverend Charles Harrison the Episcopal Missionary and his wife all of whom were most courteous. ...*

Swan also passes his tests, Haida and white, as a guest. One item I noticed especially in Swan's consignment of supplies taken aboard the *Otter* in Victoria was a copper tank for specimens of fish he is to obtain from the waters surrounding the Queen Charlottes. A Baird idea, of course. Besides his duties at the Smithsonian, where he had become secretary after the death of Joseph Henry several years before, Baird in his spare time had assumed charge of the U.S. Fish Commission. He had tapped Swan into the Fish Commission payroll for occasional collecting of fish in the Cape Flattery region, and now Baird wanted samples from the North Pacific. Swan, nobody's amateur when it comes to packing for a journey, filled the fish tank with oranges bought in Victoria, opens the lid and bestows the fruit on the gratified Hudson's Baymen and local Haidas.

Next, the first of July, *An Indian sold me 2 halibut heads for 2 pieces of tobacco and I made a real old fashioned down east chowder which we had for breakfast. Mr McKenzie and Mr Clifford pronounced it delicious. . . . Then I showed Johnny how to make a plum pudding which was done by 5 PM & served with baked salmon. . . . This being "Dominion day," which is celebrated by the Canadians & provincials they considered that my cooking was done in compliment to the day, which however I knew nothing about till this evening.*

Clifford, the Canadian Indian agent, walks Swan to the burial ground near the entrance to Masset Inlet that afternoon. Beyond the gravestones—the Christianized Haidas now were importing them from Victoria—they see the platforms which elevate the remains of a trio of tribal *skagas*, medicine men. The skeletons show through the rotting plank coffins, rather as if the skagas are getting restless about eternity. Together with their sacred bones, Swan knows, will be the carved instruments of magic, *medicine sticks and implements of office. . . . But we did not care to examine too closely at this time for fear of giving offence, so we turned our attention to examining the surrounding scenery.*

Ceremonies of Canadian-American amity aside, Swan paces the Masset shoreline day upon day, because still there is no sign of his canoemen. The site at least has its beguilements. Wild strawberries, fat little pellets of flavor, virtually carpet areas of the island. *Elsewhere, for miles as far as the eye could reach were acres of wild roses in full bloom.* McKenzie told Swan he had been visited the previous summer by a Russian traveler who marveled: "This is Bulgaria, the land of roses!"

Swan's own comparison is less exotic but as emphatic:

The whole region about Masset reminds me of the appearance of the land of Neah Bay . . . covered with the same kind of

forest and shrubbery. It is an Indians paradise, plenty of fish and
berries in summer, wild geese and ducks in myriads in the fall
and all winter, and with but little physical exertion their every
want is supplied.

The pause; the propositional line which is as close as Swan
ever comes to disclosing calculation:

If there was a regular communication between this place and
Victoria by steam so that one could come and go at least twice a
month, I would as soon reside here as at any place I know.

Two weeks and a day after Swan's arrival at Masset, para-
graphs of promise. The ninth of July: *The old chief for whom I*
had been waiting returned home today. His name is Edinso or,
as the whites pronounce it, Edin shaw.

Edinso. There is a story of him terrible as any mythic lightning flung down from Olympus. When smallpox erupted in Victoria in 1862 a group of Haidas led by Edinso was there.
Whether to clear the Haidas from the disease's ravages or simply
to get the obstreperous Edinso out of town—the Victoria *Daily*
British Colonist once called him "a perfect fiend" when he had a
few drinks in him—it is not clear, but the governor of British
Columbia ordered in a gunboat to tow the Indians home. Not
far north along the coastline of Vancouver Island, Edinso pulled
out an axe and hacked free his canoes. He put to shore with his
followers, they made camp, defiantly returned to Victoria, and
smallpox swept them. When Edinso eventually led home to the
Queen Charlottes those who had survived, the epidemic went
with them.

Which of course is only to say that horror came to the Haidas
on one wind rather than the next. Yet that wind was Edinso's, as
if fate couldn't leave him alone.

Edinso likely was in his early seventies when Swan met him
and started to talk canoe charter, and for decades had been a
name in the North Pacific for the sumptuous potlatches he had
staged; for whirling a Tsimshian chief into the path of a gunshot

intended for him during a tribal fracas; for traveling about the Queen Charlottes in his glory days in a canoe "twelve fathoms in length, elaborately carved and painted at both ends, manned by a large number of slaves and dependents." By now, however, he also was a fading figure, an aging sea-soldier who was merely one of a dozen chiefs basing themselves at Masset since their villages had died or dwindled and trying to accommodate to the tribe's narrowed future. In the mid-1870s a missionary had arrived at Masset and impressed some of the Haida leaders with Christianity's magic of inoculations and other medical care. Within a few years a number of the chiefs and even some of the shamans who had most desperately resisted the missionaries came into the new fold. Edinso, with whatever level of enthusiasm, was one of these Haida leaders to decide that the gospel-bearers were a milder plague than the horrific invisible diseases. He made his peace as well with the officialdom in Victoria, even erecting a carved column topped with the figure of the governor of British Columbia in frock coat and silk hat.

But political accommodations with the white world were one matter, canoe charter was another. Swan will just have to wait longer, Edinso serenely tells him, until he completes a trading trip to Fort Simpson on the British Columbia mainland. Meanwhile, wouldn't Swan care to look over *a lot of ancient things he had for sale?*

The tenth of July, in probably not the best of moods, Swan shops through Edinso's items. *As he asked too much I did not purchase,* the diary says shortly. What did seize Swan's interest was the project of the chief's nephew, Charley Edinso, a carver at work on a pair of caneheads made from the ivory teeth of a walrus. *Two beautiful canes nearly finished,* Swan records, *each representing a serpent twined around the stick which was a crab apple sapling . . . on top of one was a clenched fist*: yes. The writhing Port Townsend museum piece in gestation.

The depiction, Charley Edinso enlightens Swan, is the hand of Apollo's priest Laocoön, vainly grappling the serpent as it crushes him to death for trying to warn his fellow citizens against the Trojan horse. Although I would not put it past the best of Haida artists to tune in from the very air whatever lore they wanted for the day, the Haida carver did not possess an advanced knowledge of Greek mythology; simply a picture from a London illustrated newspaper which had found its way across the planet to Masset.

As for the other canehead, Swan squints close to find that this one is the head of an elephant. Newsprint provided these astounding details—thrust of tusks, bend of trunk—too: *a picture of Barnum's Jumbo, representing the hoisting on board a steamer when bound to New York.*

Veteran shopper of Indian art that he is, Swan is dazzled. *Beautifully carved*, the diary says again, then the cautious prod to Charley Edinso about price. *He asks $10 each.* Swan may even manage to keep a straight face as he says he'll think on it.

Edinso pushes off across Dixon Entrance and Hecate Strait toward Fort Simpson, Swan strolls down to watch a Haida canoe maker at work. As a canoe connoisseur, Swan is closely interested in the process of molding a hollowed log into a craft of honed grace. The builder *first softened the wood by filling . . . with water which he made to boil by putting red hot stones in it. The canoe was then partially spread and allowed to remain for a day. . . . The next morning after heating the water again with hot stones he built a slow fire of rotten wood and bark on the ground along the sides of the canoe to render the wood perfectly soft, or as he said, "to cook it," and then stretched the sides apart as far as was safe and kept them in position by means of stretchers or thwarts. I measured this canoe before he commenced to widen it and found that amidship, the opening was two feet eight inches wide, after he had finished the canoe I again measured it at the same place and found it was four feet nine inches. . . .*

Days peel this way from Swan's Queen Charlotte summer

with practically no effort at all. On the twenty-first of July, a canoe at last glides up Masset Inlet. Not Edinso; out steps the tardy James Deans, by way of a supply steamer which brought him as far as Skidegate. Swan shows no measurable enthusiasm about the arrival.

Instead, now that he has been beached at Masset for a solid three weeks, Swan's thoughts turn inward. Stomachward.

Not that his menu thus far hasn't been fertile as usual. *Johnny cooked a nice breakfast,* runs one diary report, *a stew of Potatoes and onions, Griddle cakes or "Slap Jacks" as Johnny calls them, and nice coffee.* Another: *Made some clam fritters for breakfast which were very fine.* And again: *Today I made a pudding of the roots of the brown lily . . . first boiled the root, then mashed and mixed with eggs, milk, sugar and spice and baked. . . . I think it is the first pudding ever made of this kind of root.* But if his own palate is faring splendidly, the victuals of the Hudson's Bay colony horrify him. *Prior to my advent, the H.B. Company people were content to live on Indian dried salmon cured without salt, canned meats, beans, peas and salted fish. . . .* In other words, like a colony of Martians bivouacked in an orange grove and eating galactic K rations. *So I thought to give them a treat.*

The diary pages now whoosh with Swan's marine gathering and garnishing . . . *some clams which I put in a tub of water for two days to get rid of the sand . . . large crabs nicely boiled in salt water. Some fresh trout and fresh salmon. . . .* A soda-biscuit stuffing prepared for the trout, enhanced with *dried herbs . . . fat bacon chopped fine . . . three cloves of garlic bruised,* pepper and salt and water, *the whole rubbed into a uniform mass with a potato masher.*

Swan chefs on to crabs, clams, salmon. *When all was ready, I called the gentlemen to the repast which may be enumerated as follows, clam chowder, baked trout, roasted salmon and deviled crab, with a dessert of wild strawberries and strawberry short cake, coffee and tea; a banquet of natural products which elicited encomiums of praise from the guests.*

Even the glazed encomiums are not his final word. Where

food is concerned, there seems never to be one with Swan. Two days later he is busy preparing an octopus salad and serving it up to his Hudson Bay converts with chutney sauce and another of his culinary perorations: *when one knows how to render such food palatable it will be found that many a relishing and nutricious meal can be had from articles which previously excited disgust.*

DAY SIXTY-SEVEN

Swan's sunny idyll of strawberries and roses begins to be over. The final Thursday in July at Masset:

Mr. McKenzie succeeded in harvesting his crop of hay this afternoon.... The Indian children ... Minnie and Charlotte were full of fun and frolic this PM I told Mr. Deans it was a sure sign of rain, as children and little pigs and kittens always were unusually frolicsome at approaching changes of the weather....

Friday: Rain ... commenced at 9:30 PM. It being a dull day I remained in the house drawing sketch of Johnsons fish trap.

Saturday: Weather showery. Swarms of gnats were very troublesome all night. This morning I killed quantities on the window with the fumes of burning matches....

Sunday: No prospect of Edinso getting here so long as this gale lasts ... must be windbound somewhere between here and Fort Simpson.... I think if he does not get back by Tuesday that I will get Weeah to take me to North Island. Swan tries to take his mind off Edinso with the youngsters of Masset. *After church some children came to look at some pictures of the Zuni Indians in the Century Magazine of December 1882, when they looked at the dancing scene and masquerade performances in the February number they chatted like magpies....*

* * *

On Tuesday, the last day of July, the details pause as Swan notes a favorable wind and hopes *as I am very anxious to be starting off* that it will waft in old Edinso.

It does not, and the next day Swan sits back and listens to McKenzie and Johnny Kit Elswa discuss a Haida method of fixing guilt. *When a person is taken sick and foul play is suspected two men, not doctors but relatives, drink salt water for four successive days. In this water a frog dried and pulverized is stirred and mixed. This causes purging and vomiting. This cleansing of the system enables them to see clearly both mentally and physically. . . . A wood mouse having been caught is put in a little cage, and set up on a box or table. Its first impulse is to retire to a corner and setting on its hind legs it remains immovable for a short time. While it is quiet the men question it to learn who made their relative sick. They name the persons suspected. . . . The person whose name causes the mouse to nod its head is considered the guilty one, and unless he or she pays a number of blankets or give a present of equal value they will have the same sickness and die.*

By now, Swan has been encamped at Masset long enough for hair to grow down to meet his collar, so Johnny Kit Elswa trims him *as well as any barber and better than most. . . .* The young Haida shines steadily in the triple diarying. I like particularly his imaginative moment early in the Masset sojourn: *Johnny . . . procured a bottle of Lime juice and a bottle of Raspberry syrup at the store and made a drink which he said was to celebrate the fourth of July. . . . A good interpreter, a good cook and good valet,* Swan praises him to the diaries, *and a splendid hand about a camp and managing a canoe, young active and strong, and faithful in looking after my interests.* It might be added, no slouch at other interests, either. Before their time in the Queen Charlottes is ended, Swan will act as scribe for his helper: *Wrote to Rev Charles Harrison   Massett   that Johnny wants to marry Charlotte. . . .*

* * *

Friday, August fourth, no Edinso. *Wrote letters and packed specimens today.*

On Saturday, Swan buys the pair of Charley Edinso's extraordinary canes. *They are beautifully carved and when varnished will look finely.*

DAY SIXTY-EIGHT

"In Northwest coast art, perhaps more than in any other art, there's an impulse to push things as far as possible."

"Haida artists worked mostly within a rigid, formal system, but occasionally burst out and did crazy, wild things which outcrazied the other people of the Coast."

"They weren't bound by the silly feeling that it's impossible for two figures to occupy the same space at the same time."

As accompaniment to Swan's notes on Haida art I have been reading *Indian Art of the Northwest Coast: A Dialogue on Craftsmanship and Aesthetics,* by Bill Holm and Bill Reid. In my kingdom, the pair of them will be the highest priests. Holm of the University of Washington's Burke Museum and Reid himself a Haida artist, they sat to discuss item by item one of the great exhibitions of Northwest Indian art—the Haidas, Kwakiutls, Tlingits, Tsimshians, Bella Bellas, and Bella Coolas created so much there has come to be a kind of academic subindustry based on numerous museum holdings—and the talk of Holm and Reid as they pass back and forth incredibly carved pipes and dagger hilts and ceremonial masks is as exuberant and nuanced as their topic. The quotes are from Reid, who has done a carving surely as great as any of those of his ancestors: a depiction of Raven, as the Haida legend vows, discovering mankind in a clamshell; the clever bird poised atop, wings cupped out in shelter—or is it advantage?—while tiny mankind squirms to escape the birth-shell, pop forth from the sea-gut of the planet. Reid's insights make me wish for more rumination from Swan while ensconced at Masset, with those dozens of carved poles looming as skyline around him. What Swan does say of that most soaring of Haida art is this:

These carved columns are pictographs, and the grouping of animals illustrate Indian mythological legends. . . . They are all made of the cedar (Arbor Vitae), which abounds on the Islands and attains a great size. In order to relieve the great weight of these massive timbers they are hollowed out on one side and the carving is done on the other or front side, so that what appears as a solid pillar is in reality but a mere shell of about a foot in thickness, thickly covered with carvings from base to summit. . . . These columns are generally mentioned as "totem poles" without regard to their size some of which are six feet in diameter at the base and ninety feet high, and to call such great monuments poles is as inapplicable as to apply the term to Pompeys pillar or Cleopatras needle or Bunker Hill monument.

DAY SIXTY-NINE

Monday, the eighth of August 1883, 8:30 that morning, a plash of canoe paddles at last. Swan, Johnny Kit Elswa and Deans push off from Masset, in company *with Edinso and his squaw, three men and two boys. I am to pay Edinso $1.00 per day. His wife and the three men 75¢ each and the two boys 50¢ each and canoe 50¢ per day . . . which makes a total of $5.50 per day,* plus rations.

The expedition's start had not been promisingly smooth. Edinso *did not give instructions about stowing the things and when I got in I found myself perched up on some boxes with Mr. Deans. Old Edinso asked in a curt manner why I sat so high up. I told him . . . if he wanted me to stow his canoe I could do so. I then ordered several packages placed properly and made myself comfortable and we proceeded on....*

After that bit of bramble, the canoe rides before *a fair but light wind* west past Wiah Point, its passengers let out fishing lines *with spoon bait and trawled them astern and soon caught three large salmon. Edinso's squaw had about two gallons of strawberries and a lot of red huckleberries and she gave us as many as we could eat.*

The floating picnic crosses Virago Sound by midafternoon and a stop then called *to cook a meal for the canoe crew. Mr. Deans and I lunched on strawberries, sardines, bread and cold coffee.*

They go on to make their first-night camp at a village called Yatze; *little to recommend it even to Indians,* Swan thinks. The Haida villagers of Yatze are gone somewhere, a few wan potato patches and one lonely carved monument the only signs of life. Human life, that is. *Mosquitoes and gnats were plentiful and . . . quite lively.*

As if not wanting another clear look at the place, the canoers paddle out of Yatze the next morning before dawn. Edinso complains of having sprained his back while launching the canoe and, Swan notes perhaps a bit apprehensively, is *quite cross,* but the expedition progresses west several miles to the Jalun River before breakfasting.

The queer beach there impresses Swan as *a singular exhibit of volcanic action in which the lava had burst up through the upper strata of rocks as though the region had boiled up like a pot. The lava . . . of a brick red color and a pale sulphur yellow in places, filled with boulders and pebbles of stone blackened outside with the heat and looking like a gigantic plum pudding. This is the first instance I have seen of such an evident volcanic action on the direct sea beach.*

In early afternoon Pillar Rock is passed, and Swan hurriedly pencils a sketch which shows it as a ninety-foot-high spike of stone driven into the offshore shoals.

A few hours later the canoe eases ashore at Edinso's own

village, Kioosta, deserted except for *many carved columns the handsomest of which are in front of Edinso's house.*

Swan is in his tent after supper this second night out from Masset, possibly congratulating himself on the expedition's unruffled progress, when Edinso drops by to inform him of new terms of canoe hire: he and the crew desire hot biscuits and coffee to be served them every night.

I knew the old fellow put on considerable style with strangers and I determined to settle our status at once. I told him I did not wish him to dictate to me what I should do, and he knew that since we left Masset we had no time for any cooking but the most simple kind, and it was no use to talk to me about hot biscuits till we got to camp where we would have leisure.

Edinso huffs from the tent and Swan falls asleep to the mutters of the crewmen debating the biscuit issue.

In the morning the dietary squabble wakes with them. *Had a good blow up with old Edinso,* Swan's pocket diary begins forthrightly. This time the chief tries Swan on the angle that the canoe crew wants to eat with him *and they want flour and potatoes and pancakes, and want Johnny to be their cook.*

They might as well have wanted Swan to pare their toenails during supper every night, too. If there is one matter in the cosmos that Swan has a clear doctrine about, it is the sanctity of his meals. He fires back to Edinso and the other Haidas the ultimatum—bluff, more likely—that *if I heard any more complaints I would return to Masset and get another crew. . . . When they found I was determined they gave up and all became good natured.*

Good-natured or not, Edinso defers on biscuits and hotcakes and begins showing Swan and Deans the long-awaited shores of his North Island, today's Langara.

He takes them first to a site called Tadense, a deserted village rapidly expiring back into the forest. *Even the more recent houses built fifty years ago are fast decaying: the humidity of the climate causes a growth of moss which, freezing in winter and seldom or never dry in summer, rots the soft cedar and rapidly reduces it to a pulpy mould.* Then from the oozing-away village, along the waterline to a burial cave. *A dry cavern some 60 feet in length,* as Swan jots it, *the entrance to which is 25 feet above high water mark and approached by a rough path over conglomerate boulders.* Edinso, who is proving to have a rhetorical formula for every occasion, assures them that no white eyes ever have seen the hallowed spot before this instant.

They clamber in among *some 28 or 30 burial boxes of various sizes. . . . In one of the boxes of skeletons which had been opened by age, a puffin or sea parrot had made its nest. . . . Some of the burial boxes were ornamented with the crests of the occupants carved and painted in colors, others were merely rough boxes. Some of the bodies were rolled in Hudson Bay blankets, and some of the heads were mummified like AZTEC mummies. . . . That of a Chief or doctor, was well preserved the hair tied in a knot on the top of the skull, and the dried ears still holding the abalone shell ornaments. . . .*

Yet one more stop in this funereal day: Cloak Bay, sheltered by a small island which thrust up a conglomerate cusp of cliff astoundingly like a round medieval tower, *everything but the want of windows made this appearance complete.* Sharp rocks fanged around the island. One pinnacle displayed a hole bored through by the ocean's action. Edinso at once advertises the cavity as the work of an immense fish gnawing a doorway to its house. That reminds him that he hasn't adequately explained the castellated island, and he relates to Swan and Deans that here lived an Indian slaver named Teegwin, *and for his misdeeds he was turned into this big stone, and his sister coming to see him was also turned to stone.*

After this recital we hoisted sail and returned to camp.

Two days after that, on the tenth of August, Swan makes a find which is among the oddest in his thirty years of nosing along the Pacific shoreline. Edinso and crew had steered Deans and him to the deserted village of Yakh, there to see the burial place of a medicine man named Koontz. Inside his plank box,

Koontz in a shirt of caribou skin reclines in full dignified length, *not doubled up as is the practice. Bodies of doctors alone being allowed to remain in the position in which they die.* Deans potters around the corpse a bit, but Swan is less interested in Koontz's posture than a pair of items among the skaga's burial trove. Two large curved teeth which he thinks resemble those of a beaver, but which seem too long, too . . . odd. The baffling incisors, he subsequently learned *were tusks of the African wild hog . . . probably procured from the wreck of a Japanese or Siamese junk which was lost on Queen Charlotte Islands in 1833.*

Swan has on his mind even another mystery of Africa-in-the-North-Pacific. Back at Kioosta he noticed among the carved column figures a creature with a rolled-up snout. Except for the lack of tusks it looked for all the world like the head of an elephant. Beginning to wonder about the pachydermic enthusiasms of the Haidas, Swan at last questions Edinso and is enlightened when the chief points toward a flutter on a nearby bush. The carved creature was a colossal butterfly, the snout its proboscis.

Swan of course asks for the legend, Edinso of course has it ready: *that when the Hooyeh or raven was a man, he lived in a country beyond California, that he got angry with his uncle and lit down on his head and split it open. Then fearing his relatives he changed to a bird and flew to Queen Charlotte Islands where he was told good land could be found. The butterfly, a creature as big as a house accompanied him and would fly up in the air and when he saw any good land he would unfold his proboscis and point with it.*

Just the way, Edinso drives the point home to his white questioner with a tap of mockery, *Johnny was going with me showing me places.*

DAY SEVENTY

Recited in turn by each of Swan's three sets of diary pages during their early weeks in the Queen Charlottes, a legend, a belief, and a lore:

Towats was a great Haida hunter, and once while hunting he found the house of the king of the bears. The king bear was not there but his wife was, and Towats made love to her. Arriving home to a much disordered house the king bear charged his wife with unfaithfulness. She denied all. But the king bear noticed that at a certain hour each day she went out to fetch wood and water and was gone long. One day he tied a thread to her dress. By following the thread through the forest he came upon his wife in the arms of Towats. The king of bears slew the hunter Towats by tearing out his heart.

Called on Kive-ges-lines this PM to see her twins which were born on the 10th. They were pretty babies but the Indians are sure to kill one. Next day: One of the twins died during the night as I predicted. The Indian who told me said . . . "It died from want of breath" which I think very probable. These Haidas like the Makahs have a superstition that twins bring ill luck. . . .

Old Stingess . . . came to my house and . . . I asked her to tell me about tattooing and when the Haidahs first commenced tattooing. She said it was always practiced . . . as long ago as the most ancient legends make any mention. Formerly the Indians procured the wool of the mountain sheep which was spun into fine threads which were stained with some black pigment either pulverized charcoal and water, or with lignite ground in water on a stone, as at present, then with needles made of copper procured from the Sitka Indians, these fine threads were drawn under the skin producing indelible marks. When white men

came they learned the art of tattooing with steel needles from
sailors on board the vessels, and have adopted that plan since . . .
here the old woman became tired and went home.

How elliptical, literally, the past becomes. Stingess culls from
what may have been an evening-long narrative an answer for
Swan. Who chooses as much of it as he thinks worth cramming
into his diary pages. At my hundred years' remove, I select lines
from his and frame them in trios of editing dots. From her
Haida tradition to Swan's white tribe to my even paler version.
The logical end of the process signaled by my ellipses, I suppose, might be for the lore of Haida tattooing to compress down
to something like a single magical speck of print, perhaps the
period after the news that Stingess has got tired of all the chit-
chat and hobbled home. But I've heard it offered that a period is
simply the shorthand for the dots of an ellipsis. That a story
never does end, only can pause. So that would not complete it
either, the elliptical transit from Stingess to Swan to me to
whomever abbreviates the past next.

The Cracked Canoe

TCHIMOSE
A mythological animal residing in the ocean.

DAY SEVENTY-ONE

I flip the month on the photo calendar above my desk, and the room fills with lumberjacks. The calendar came as a gift, a dozen scenes from the glass plates of a photographer who roved the Olympic Peninsula lumber camps in the first years of this century, and I've paid no particular attention to the scenery atop the days: January a stand of age-silvered trees, February a few dodgy sawyers off in the middle distance from the camera. But March's four loggers, spanned across the cut they are making in a cedar tree as big in diameter as this room, hover in as if estimating the board footage my desktop would yield.

The chunky logger at the left stands on a springboard, his axe held extended, straight out and waist-high, in his left hand and the blade resting almost tenderly against the gash in the cedar. He is like a man fishing off a bridge beam, but absent-mindedly having picked up the camp axe instead of the trout rod.

The next man is seated in the cut, legs casually dangling and crossed at the ankles, a small shark's grin of spikes made by the bottoms of his caulked boots. His arms are folded easily across his middle; he has trimly rolled his pant legs and sleeves; is handsome and dark-browed with a ladykilling lock of hair down the right side of his forehead.

The woodman beside him is similarly seated, arms also crossed, but is flap-eared, broad-hipped, mustached. Surely he is the Swede of the crew, whatever his origins.

The final logger, on the right edge of the photo, is a long-faced giant. As he stands atop a log with his right foot propped on the cut, broad left hand hooked into a suspender strap where it meets his pants, there is unnatural length to his huge stretched body. The others must call him Highpockets. Or Percival, if that is what he prefers. His shirt is work-soiled, his eyes pouchy but hard. Unlike his at-ease mate across the tree, he clenches his axe a third of the way up the handle, as if having tomahawked it into the tree just over the left jug ear of the Swede.

Down the middle of the picture, between the seated sawyers, stands their glinting crosscut saw. If the giant is six and a half feet tall as he looks to be, the saw is ten; the elongated great-granddaddy of the crosscut in Trudy and Howard's cabin. Under its bright ladder of teeth are strewn the chips from the cut. The foursome has not much more than started on the great cedar, and already the woodpile is considerable.

Twenty days until spring in the company of these timber topplers, and by-God forceful company they promise to be. I want all at once to see the Peninsula woods that drew whackers like these, if only to reassure myself that they're not out there now leveling daylight into whatever green is left. Late tomorrow, Carol will be finished teaching her week's classes. We will head for the Hoh rain forest.

Swan at Kioosta, his forty-eighth day in the Queen Charlotte islands and his fourth on the venture along the western shore: *Very disagreeable morning, thick with misty rain.*

He decides to sit tight and do such diary matters as ruminating on the blessed *total absence of fleas and other annoying insects so common and universal in Indian camps and villages.... Edinso says that formerly fleas were very numerous, and at Masset they were so plentiful as the sand on the beach and they remained as long as the Indians dressed in otter skins and bark robes, but when the white men came with other kind of clothing and bought all the old fur dresses, the fleas began to disappear. At last the Indians all went to Victoria, and on their return they found that the fleas had entirely left.... Edinso said perhaps the world turned over and all the fleas hopped off.*

DAY SEVENTY-TWO

Sunshine, bright as ripe grain. Just before lunch as I looked out wishing for birds, a cloud of bushtits and chickadees imploded into the backyard firs. I stepped into the yard to listen to their *dee dee dee* chorus, watched them become fast flecks among the branches.

No sooner had I come inside than the lion-colored cat, pausing for a slow slitted look in the direction of the sun, lazed up the hillside into the long grass.

Three times in four minutes he tried to nest himself. Then sat casually and eyed a number of items he evidently had never noticed before, such as his own tail, a bug in the grass, every nearby tree. Sneezed, and was astonished about it. I have decided there is no worry about him marauding the birds. More prospect the birds will mistake him for a fluffy boulder, perch atop him and drown him in droppings.

Now to Swan. Sunday, the twelfth of August, he arises at five intending an early start downcoast from the North Island waters, the cornering turn which will take the expedition at last along the Queen Charlottes' west shore. Arises and feels a southeast wind on his face and peers seaward to *a brilliant and perfect rainbow, a double one, which indicated rain.* Within half an hour the downpour has begun.

I am disappointed as there is nothing to prevent our going but the rain, and I am anxious to be moving.

That double rainbow, signal to Northwest rain, indeed must have been an "anxious" omen to Swan. Dampness is a price humankind hates to pay. ("Eleven days rain, and the most disagreeable time I have experienced," wrote an edgy Captain William Clark on November 17, 1805, and that was at the very *start* of the Lewis and Clark expedition's sodden months in

winter camp near the mouth of the Columbia.) Perhaps it is
because rain tugs all that is human in us too far back to our
undry origins. If it has taken this long to encase us, set us
upright and mobile on frames of bone, and all that evolving can
be pattered back to sheer existence by drops of water, we are
not safe. No, I think the private red streams in us do not at all
like that call of commonality, and the unease of it now must be
in Swan.

Monday, thirteenth of August, *a most disagreeable day, misty
rain and alternate showers. I remained in my tent most of the
time, writing and drawing, but the rain prevented out of door
sketching.* Edinso's sprained back also remains a bother. *Yesterday he put some hot sand in a sack and . . . sweated the part;*
now evidently has taken cold. *This makes it disagreeable to us
as well as painful to him.* The ailing chief passes the day by
having *several messes of boiled halibut served up till Mr. Deans
and I were surfeited.*

Meanwhile, Swan adds, one of the paddlers is busy at the fire
forging *a lot of square staples to mend our canoe which had got
split along the bottom.*

The cracked canoe creates a new fret, and Swan's most serious yet. Cedar canoes such as those of the Haidas were so finely
honed, so extreme an alchemy of tree-into-vessel-of-grace (recall the Masset canoe maker Swan watched stretching an amidship portion to double its natural width) that their beautiful
tension of design became a kind of fragility. For all their length
and capacity they were thin, thin craft, leanest of wood. Think
of this: you are in a twin-engined aircraft and one propellor
begins to stutter, semaphores an erratic pattern in from the wing
to your solid stare. There, maybe, is something like the jagged
message Swan must read now from the canoe bottom.

To me, Swan exactly here is tested as a true explorer, for this
is the first deep nip of predicament. Predicament somehow
shadows an expeditionary in strange forms that cannot be imagined until the pounce happens. The Antarctic explorer Mawson,

the bottoms of his feet dropping off like insoles, forcing him to bare his body for periods so the polar sun might bathe germs from it. Meriwether Lewis, on his way home down the Missouri after the two-year expedition to the Pacific, wounded in a buttock when one of his hunters mistook him for an elk. Swan's confrontation with predicament is not yet so dire, but as odd: the canoe which he has chosen as the single capable implement to carry him along the west shore now becomes threat to the journey. And dependent for safety on Edinso's canoe, which like its owner has endured considerably past spryness, are Swan, Johnny Kit Elswa, Deans, the chief himself, the chief's wife, the five crew members: ten persons, plus full supplies, plus Swan's hefty tanks of fish specimens.

It can be imagined that Swan watches carefully, hawk-intent, as the copper staples are tacked into place along the fissure through which the Pacific could come in, and the entire expedition dribble out. Then that he puffs a long moment on his white meerschaum before saying aloud that in the morning they will push on.

The rain has gone by morning, and on the ebb tide they set out again, Swan uneasy about the canoe bottom *but as I know Edinso is careful I don't think he will take any chances although I expect we will get some of our things wet, and we may have to lighten the canoe by throwing some part of our cargo overboard.*

That put away in the diary, *we moved and paddled along, noting everything of interest in this, to me, most interesting region.*

Rounding Cape Knox, a long promontory which on the map looks ominously like a canoe flipped on its back, Swan and crew meet a headwind which forces them to land on a rocky point and scramble for a camping site. They find a place sheltered from the rain by spruce trees and high grass. With tents up and a fire going, Swan decides to lift the party's spirits. *This is a pretty rough time, with wind and rain, so to mark the event I had a ham cut and some slices fried for supper.*

The ham and a good campsite warm Swan's sense of whimsy.

This same place had been occupied as a camp last summer by Count Luboff, a Russian who was looking at lands for parties in Victoria. He had put up a notice on a board, that the place was taken as a coal claim. Some of the Indians not knowing what the board meant, split it up for fire wood, which was the best use that the board could be dedicated to, as there is no coal or any indications of coal at this place except the charred remains of Count Luboffs fire.

I have said Swan's trio of diaries tell very nearly as much as possible about this expedition, but there is an omission noticeable by now. The phantom of these pages is Deans. Johnny Kit Elswa and Edinso receive their ample share from Swan's pen, but the British Columbia Indian agent is mentioned only when he goes prospecting or accompanies Swan into a burial cave. The notations are unfailingly polite: too polite, as though the diarist does not want any commotion if wrong eyes find the pages.

Swan, I am beginning to think, may wish that Deans still was on the dock back at Victoria.

The rain keeps on—*Our situation is more romantic than pleasant*—and the expedition hunkers in for another day.

Swan passes it by sketching *the stone doctor . . . a sandstone reef washed by the surf into a form that certainly does not require much imagination to make one think as the Indians do that it is a giant doctor of ancient times petrified and fossilized. . . .*

Perhaps inspired by the offshore medicine man, Swan now concocts a salve of spruce gum and deer tallow for Edinso's ailing back. If not cured, the chief at least is assuaged. He bestows a pair of shark teeth ear ornaments on Swan in return.

The weathered-in site atop Cape Knox begins to pall on Swan. *This delay, and Edinso's sickness makes me feel pretty blue . . . as I must pay for every day these people are with me. . . .*

At 2 P.M. a schooner on the offing bound south with all sails set . . . A pleasant sight as there is nothing between us at this camp, and Japan, nothing but a dreary stretch of wild and monotonous ocean . . . the swiftly moving vessel gave a feeling of life. . . . I am quite tired of this place and long to leave it.

The last of dusk on the Olympic Peninsula. Beyond Lake Quinault, northward along the Pacific edge of the Peninsula, we are passing through miles of tunnel of high firs. The line of sky is so narrow between the margins of our deep road-canyon that it looks like a blue path somehow hung along the treetops. I am sagging from the day of deciphering Swan's travel, readying for our own; Carol with her better attention to the dark drives this last blackening stretch of distance.

Mapping in my mind as the road slits the forest, I realize that the coast here, off through the timber to the west of us, is the single piece of Washington's ocean shoreline never visited by Swan. He came as far north as the mouth of the Quinault River in 1854, on that jesting report from the Shoalwater Indians that a British steamship was carrying on a smuggling trade with the Quinaults, and he once canoed down from Neah Bay to the Quillayute tribe at La Push. Between, the stretch of shore where the Hoh River flows into the Pacific, Swan somehow did not attain. But the two of us in this fat pellet of metal have, on some tideline wander or another. I think over the fact of having set foot anywhere along this continental rim where the wandersome Swan didn't, and of sleeping tonight beside a fine Peninsula river he somehow never saw, and the surprise of it whirls to me out of the rushing dark.

DAY SEVENTY-THREE

The Hoh park ranger, stocky and red-mustached, recites for us new numerals of the February windstorm that unbuilt the Hood

Canal bridge. Here in his domain those hours, ninety trees were blown down across the first nine miles of the trail Carol and I are about to hike. Twenty-two more barricaded the road we have just come in on from the coastal highway. When the wind hit its wildest, the ranger heard seven trees topple within a total of five seconds.

I try to imagine the blizzard of wood, tons of cudgel falling at every eyeblink, and ask the ranger what he did during it, hole up somewhere and try pull the hole in after him?

"Wasn't anything to do, just drink a little wine and listen to them fall."

If the Alava trail is a miniature Roman road and Dungeness Spit a storybook isthmus between saltwater and glacier ice, these Olympic Peninsula rainforests, the Hoh the most northerly of four, are Atlantises of nature. Communities of myriads of life which thrive while enwrapped in more than twelve feet of rain per year. Their valleys are fat troughs to the Pacific. In from the ocean the rainclouds float, are elevated by the terrain beginning its climb to the Olympic summits, and let down their water. The moisture produces a whopping northwoods jungle, a kind of Everglades grown to the height of fifteen-story buildings. Here in the Hoh, for instance, Sitka spruce are the dominant giant trees, and they measure big around as winery vats and more than two hundred feet up.

The power and loft of the Sitkas, however, are merely the might above the rampant details of the rain forest, like crags over delicate valleys. Nature here tries a little of everything green. Variety and variety of moss and lichen, sprays of fern. The fascination of the rain forest is that all flows into and out of all else; here I can sense how the Haidas, whom Swan went among in their own clouds of forest, could produce art in which creatures swim in and out of each other, the designs tumble, notch together, uncouple, compress, surge. This forest's version is that an embankment with a garden of fir seedlings and ferns sprouting from it will turn out to be not soil, but a downed giant tree, its rot giving the nurture to new generation. Moss-like growth romps its way up tree trunks, and from amid the fuzzy mat spurts licorice fern, daintily leafing into the air sixty feet above the ground. Alders and broad-leaf elm are adorned with club moss, their limbs in wild gesticulation draped with the flowing stuff. So laced and lush is this ecosystem that we walk our several miles through it today without making a footfall, only scuffs.

Carol tells me that these Olympic rain forests and the rough coast to their west provide her the greatest calm of any place she has been. That she can walk in this rain forest and *only* be walking in this rain forest, moving in simple existence. Surprising, that, because neither of us thinks we are at all mystic. Perhaps, efficient dwellers we try to be, we simply admire the deft fit of life systems in the rain forest. The flow of growth out of growth, out of death ...

I do not quite ease off into beingness as she can. Memories and ideas leap to mind. I remember that Callenbach's young foresters of *Ecotopia* would stop in the forest to hug a fir and murmur into its bark, *brother tree*. ... This Hoh forest is not a gathering of brothers to humankind, but of elders. The dampness in the air, patches of fog snagged in the tree tops above, tells me another story out of memory, of having read of a visitor who rode through the California redwood forest in the first years of this century. He noted to his guide that the sun was dissipating the chilly fog from around them. No, said the guide looking to canyon walls of wood like these, no, "The trees is drinkin' it. That's what they live on mostly. When they git done breakfast you'll git warm enough."

For a time, the river seduces me from the forest. This season, before the glacier melt begins to pour from the Olympic peaks, the water of the Hoh is a painfully lovely slate blue, a moving blade of delicate gloss. The boulder-stropped, the fog-polished Hoh. Question: why must rivers have names? Tentative answer: for the same reason gods do. These Peninsula rivers, their names a tumbled poem of several tongues—Quinault, Quillayute, Hoh, Bogashiel, Soleduck, Elwha, Dungeness, Gray Wolf—are as holy to me as anything I know.

Forest again. For comparison's sake I veer from the trail to take a look at the largest Sitka spruce along this valley bottom. The Park Service has honored it with a sign, giving the tree's dimensions as sixteen feet four inches in diameter, one hundred eighty feet in height, but now the sign is propped against the prone body of the giant. Toppled, it lies like a huge extracted tunnel bore. Clambering onto its upper surface I find that the Sitka has burls, warts on the wood, bigger around than my body. For all that, I calculate that it is barely larger, if any, than the standard nineteenth-century target that Highpockets and his calendar crew are offhandedly devastating in my writing room.

Evening, and west to Kalaloch through portals of sawed-through windfalls, to the campground next to the ocean. In fewer than fifty miles, mountain and ocean, arteried by this pulsing valley.

DAY SEVENTY-FOUR

A night that sagged several nights long. Our aged tent, which has traveled as far as Nova Scotia and up and down the mountain west in all manner of weather, never was soggier, droopier. Rain hit the canvas all night in buckshot bursts. Seepage sprung in one corner and then around the doorway flap until by morning we were scrunched in our sleeping bag into the exact center of the tent, islanded away from the sopping edges like a pair of frogs on a lily pad.

Vehement as it was, the rain made the night's lesser threat. When the wind arrived off the ocean, the tent walloped and bellied, tried to lift us off into the fir trees somewhere. All in all as restful as trying to sleep inside the bag of a leaky balloon, and every hour or so Carol and I muttered inconclusively about the situation. It crossed my mind, and without doubt hers, that this might be a repeat of the big windstorm. Somehow it got decided that if this was so the weather would first define itself by swatting the tent down onto our heads and at that point we would face the issue.

More velocity did not arrive, we finished the night damp but stubbornly prone, and then began the drive home in coastal rain moving almost solidly through the air, as if walls of water were dissolving down over us as the car nudged them.

Swan's own overweathered site, the rainy perch atop Cape Knox, he concludes to leave on the morning of the seventeenth of August, even if it means abandoning the journey down the western coastline.

I told Edinso if he did not feel better I would return to Masset. He said if he went back it would be as bad as if he goes on and he thought my spruce salve had done his back good.

On they go.

11:30 A.M. . . . *we passed Salsthlung point and passed Natzun Bay into which three small streams empty, but there are no Indian settlements ancient or modern. Saw a school of whales rolling and blowing.*

2:20 P.M. . . . *we reached Kle-ta-koon point, near which there is a snug harbor inside the reef. On the shore is the summer residence of the otter hunters, a cluster of houses forming a little village called Tledso but at present unoccupied: a narrow rift . . . not over twenty feet wide, formed the dangerous and only passage for canoes and boats.*

Bouncing through the reef-cut—you can all but hear Swan praying to the cobbled bottom of the canoe to hold together— they came out *in a quiet little harbor as smooth as a mill pond.* A placid bayside site also notable for being almost empty of birds: *a solitary raven, two or three sparrows and a few sea gulls.* Swan, old combatant of crows, edgily jots that the quiet can only be too good to last. *As soon as a camp of Indian otter hunters comes here for a few weeks, the place will be alive with crows and other birds which seem to follow the abode of man, like nettles, sorrel and other noxious weeds.*

Storm returns the next day, *heavy surf, strong wind.*

Swan spends the time packing his *alcoholic specimens of fish* —they have been adding up steadily in the diaries, cuttlefish, sticklebacks, rock cod, buffalo sculpine, viviparous perch, young octopus—*in one large tin tank in a wooden box.*

The rain that night turns tremendous. *Fearful,* Swan records. The morning, the nineteenth of August, promises no better.

We are now 13 days from Masset and have advanced but fifty miles and at this rate we cannot reach Skidegate in three months and all our provisions will get exhausted.

The weather, the wild broth of the North Pacific, is proving too much.

Beside the campfire at Kle-ta-koon Swan must weigh risks one more time. Chance more of the whistling weather, more canoe peril, or cancel this bravura journey and any further exploration of the west shore of the Queen Charlottes.

He is a man who knows that life is no walk-through: that just now is his single try at this last frontier edge. But he knows too (veteran of all those tumbles by alcohol and that so-frequent slippage of his finances) that defeat will happen when it wants to.

Catch the moment with me, juggle its mood down through the typewriter to waiting paper, say with surety what you-as-Swan decide this rainswept night. Slippery item, surety.

Swan unpockets a diary and writes retreat.

Edinso's canoe is an old one and unsafe to proceed with so much weight in her, and prudence dictates a return as soon as the wind abates.... On consulting with Mr. Deans have decided

to return to Massett where I can leave some of my heavy articles
and proceed to Skidegate ... by the east side of the island.

DAY SEVENTY-FIVE

A warm rainy morning, a borrowing from April-to-come. The
rain makes fine, fine streaks, scarcely larger than spider's web,
against the evergreens. As I began today's brief visit to the
typewriter and diary pages, the day till now spent thinking of
Swan at his point of decision, of how it is when a dream at last
denies itself to you, a jay went past the window like a blue
spear.

One last spurt of—anguish? disgust?—in Swan's Queen Charlottes pages. *I can't understand this weather with the Barometer*
so well up.

Edinso announces his own baleful theory. *Our present ill luck*
is occasioned by Mr Deans stirring up the remains of the old
skaga or doctor back at Yakh nine days before.

DAY SEVENTY-SIX

Monday, the twentieth of August 1883. As Swan packed his tin
bins of fish for the retreat to Masset, *I heard the report of a gun,*
and ... an Indian named Kanow arrived. ... He has come to
hunt sea otter and will return to Masset as soon as he kills
any.

Double luck has just blown in.

Swan looks from his heavy fish tanks to the canoe of the
arrivee. If ... Amiably, Kanow agrees; he will cargo Swan's
load of specimens back to Masset with him.

Next the sky, which this morning has been gradually less
malevolent.

Swan waits, waits.

With one last northwest gust the wind and rain whirl away.

Swan sits under sunshine for the first time in a couple of hundred hours and begins to write the reversal of the Queen Charlottes' defeat of him.

This unexpected arrival and the relieving of our canoe of the weight of the case of specimens which weighs as much as a barrel of beef—nearly three hundred pounds, he noted elsewhere—*will make our canoe much lighter and as the Indians have been at work repairing her today, I hope we can make a start tomorrow early if the wind is fair. I have told Johnny to cook enough this evening so that we shall not have to go ashore tomorrow until we camp for the night.*

Broke camp and started at 5:20 AM, the twenty-first of August—south toward Skidegate Channel. If Swan's penciled entries in the pocket diary could take on the color of mood they should here go green with hope. The closest they can come is to speak in spurts, this day's journey a series of notations of shoreline points and rock formations zipped past, much seen but little investigated. Swan has his mind strictly on speed, and the mended and lightened canoe glides on and on until *at sundown we landed on Hippa Island.* By far the lengthiest day of advance, this stopless one: more than thirty miles, with about the same distance yet to go to reach the entrance of Skidegate Channel. Swan and Deans *after a hearty supper* plop to bed with the good-night assurance from Edinso that they are the first white men to sleep on Hippa.

Deans might have foregone the honor. Their tents had been pitched in a patch of cow parsnips and by morning the odor sickened him. *However a cup of strong coffee made him feel better* and Swan, not noticeably sympathetic to Deans's quimsy stomach, rapidly marshals everybody into the canoe again.

They have very nearly paddled to Skidegate Inlet in late morning when *mist shut down thick and the rain commenced*

. . . Edinso knowing of a camping ground at a place called Tchuwa, we pulled and paddled, now against wind and tide and finally made a landing at 1 P.M. on a pebbly beach composed of paving stones and shingle and so steep that one could hardly climb to the top which from the landing to the summit is at least a hundred feet.

Struggling to the top they find a tent site under large ever-greens, *a perfect ground in any Country but such a rainy one.*

Swan sought out a small dry cave, *sat down and wrote these notes.* . . . There was progress to report to himself: *did pretty well today.* . . . But that night, *a severe attack of neuralgia in my head which induced me to retire after taking my 9 o'clock meteorological readings.* . . .

He sleeps until seven the next morning, which approaches midafternoon in his traveling habits, and *arose refreshed and feeling unusually bright which I attributed to the healthful influence of the fragrant spruce boughs which formed the groundwork of my couch.*

Good health seems rampant: Deans is unnauseated and Edinso's back is better. Indeed, the chief arises so jovial that he *related many anecdotes and incidents of his early life.* His main tale of the day was of how he had discovered the gold—*white stones*—which set off the Gold Harbor rush on the west coast of Moresby Island in 1849. Swan, who as early as North Island noted of Edinso that *I find him rather inclined to romance, and listen to his stories cum grano salis,* later learns that this historic prospecting was performed by another Haida. *A Munchausenism,* he dutifully edits here into Edinso's fable.

The day's only woe is the weather, which grabs them again. *The rain beat through the tent in a fine mist like an umbrella under an eave gutter . . . while a small brooklet found its way under my bed.*

As the soggy canoe party sits out the hours around the campfire, a stone explodes in the blaze. Swan guesses the detonation *caused by water in a cavity of the stone which converted into steam.* Not so the Edinso version: *it was the Spirits who were angry and had made the recent bad weather. He then threw a quantity of grease and some tobacco in the fire as a sort of peace offering.*

Swan makes an offertory of his own by stenciling a marker *displaying the following legend.*

James G Swan   US National Museum & US Fish Commission Washington DC with James Deans   Indian Department   Victoria BC   Camped here Aug 23, 24. 25. 1883
Edinso chief of Massett Captain of canoe
Johnny Kit Elswa Skilla Tsatl Kundai Hanow SelaKootKung crew of canoe
I nailed this board to a tree where it will be a conspicuous object on landing, to any one who may be so unfortunate as to camp at this place hereafter.

Now only a matter of hours from Skidegate Channel if the weather and the canoe bottom both will hold, Swan and party push off to a late start the next morning, *7 oclock instead of 5 which we should have done. . . .* Luckily *we found the water smooth,* and the canoe slid easily.

Johnny had collected some spruce gum yesterday, and . . . all hands took a piece, and soon the jaws of the whole party were in motion. . . . We found the gum an excellent thing to chew before breakfast, cleaning the mouth, strengthening the stomach and aiding the appetite.

Chawing along in the improved weather, the paddlers idle more than Swan wants, and at one point stop to shoot at seals . . . *After a delay of three quarters of an hour without killing any we again started and lazily proceeded.* As the pace of paddling drops Swan's temper climbs. By now had come up *a light wind from the SW which was fair.*

I asked why sail was not set.

The reply was, "by and by," and the Indians stopped to light *their pipes.*

Swan erupts. Weeks of sopping weather, the dubious companionship of Deans, a doddery canoe with a fracture line down its center, Edinso's swings of mood, and now *by and by* and a casual cumulus of tobacco smoke. The ensuing scene in the diary pages is more terse than it possibly could have been: Swan ultimatuming Edinso *that I would not pay for any more time to be thrown away. . . . Finally the men took to their oars to their own accord, and having set two sails for the first time since leaving Massett, we began to advance. . . .*

Swan may have won the skirmish, but Edinso takes the day. The canoeists enter Skidegate Channel so late they are met by the ebb tide and must put to shore for the night. *Idled away too much time,* Swan grumps to his diary that evening.

The better news is that delay is all he has suffered. *I feel thankful that I am so near my journey, and in good health and that no accident has happened to us.*

Next day, the twenty-sixth of August, Swan determinedly sergeants everyone into the canoe before daybreak. Indeed, they barely have blinked into morning when, a few hours after their start, Swan is notating their arrival at the *Skidegate Oil Works ... very kindly received by Mr. William Sterling the superintendent, who at once ordered a nice breakfast for us . . . and Mr. Alexander McGregor his partner who offered me a room in his house to write in and to spread my bedding making me more comfortable than I have been at any time since leaving Masset.*

Swan as western venturer. Now that he is triumphantly at Skidegate, he puts me in mind of the history-bearer whom Bernard DeVoto once wrote of, the early frontiersman James Clyman. Clyman that uncanny accompanist to America's westward mood: born on George Washington's land in Virginia in 1792, westering with the fur trappers and explorers, battling Indians in the Black Hawk wàr in the same company as Abraham Lincoln, traveling the Oregon Trail in the 1844 emigration, rambling in California when gold was struck in 1848—ultimately settling to a ranch in the Napa Valley and living on until 1881, the presidency of Chester A. Arthur and almost to the time of this Queen Charlottes adventure of Swan's. In the way Clyman was, Swan too stands to me now as something of a template, an outlining human gauge: but of western possibilities rather than western past. Swan literally is a being of our continental edge, rimwalking its landscape and native cultures. If I could put questions to Swan across time I think they would try to reach toward invisible inward lines, those riggings of curiosity and gameness-for-damn-near-anything, hung deeper in him than anyone else I have encountered. Difficult to phrase, not say answer, but: what is the tidal pull of an earlier way of life, of the timescape of *first people* such as the Makahs and the vanished Haida villagers? What instruction does their West offer any of ours? And, since the diaries of the Queen Charlotte days say all but this: what, when reputation and thrill and all other incomplete reasons have been said, truly sends a man of sixty-five seeking along an unknown treacherous coast? What mightier impulses wade in the bloodstream? Questions which perhaps can never be fully met with words, and so keep me straining to hear beyond, into the deeps of a Swan.

Swan hurries a note of success to Baird at the Smithsonian . . . *20 days on the trip . . . head winds and rain all the time. . . . With the exception of the temperature being mild—54° the weather has been like the winter weather off Cape Flattery. . . .* His mood now after the watery three weeks of exploration and the complication of the cracked canoe is a rainbow of triumph and relief, *glad that I have ended this tedious and perilous journey from Masset to this place without accident. Old Edinso has purposely delayed our travel . . . but I felt safe with the old fellow as he is very skillful in handling a canoe.* In the mellowness of the moment Swan even allows Edinso to use his tent overnight and tells Johnny Kit Elswa to *give the Indians the balance of the rice which was enough for a good meal, a lot of biscuit, tea, sugar and some bacon.* By the time Edinso sets off up the coast to Masset in the cracked canoe a day or so later, however, Swan abruptly is inscribing him as *the biggest old fraud I ever have had dealings with.* . . . His fresh pique has been furnished by Johnny, who has had a thoughtful conversation with Edinso's canoe crew. *They say the old man's lame back was all sham.*

DAY SEVENTY-SEVEN

Warm breeze again today, nearly a chinook. Since morning I have changed shirts three times, each time to lighter material; now, at 2:30, it is sixty-four degrees. Winter is turning into winter/spring. Absolute proof: I have begun sneezing, an allergy has thawed. Captain John of the Makahs once explained to Swan why he and the other Neah Bay natives recited several sentences after sneezing: they were asking the Great Spirit to spare them. *If they did not utter this brief petition, the top of their heads would be blown off when they sneezed.* I may yet prove Captain John right.

With Edinso and the cracked canoe and the west shore weather all out of his system, Swan draws a deep breath and begins to calculate the brief remainder of his Queen Charlottes summer. The steamer *Princess Louise,* taking on a cargo of dogfish oil at the Skidegate refinery, will convey his mail to Victoria. His fish tanks delivered to Masset by the providential otter hunter will be shipped from there by the Hudson's Bay Company. A crew of Indians has been sent off for black cod, the final fish specimen. The summer's last task is to garner more art from the Haidas, along Skidegate Inlet and the eastern shore of Moresby Island where the tribal villages still were living places.

It is the morning of the twenty-eighth of August when *Rev. Mr. Robinson the Methodist Missionary came from Skidegate village with Ellswarsh and his wife, Sam his dumb boy and Ellen his youngest girl a child of about seven years. . . . Two years ago this family with an elder daughter Soodatl were in Port Townsend and occupied a room near my office where Ellswarsh worked making silver bracelets and other articles of jewelry. The chil-*

dren were very fond of me and came to my office every day and they had not forgotten the kind treatment they received from me.

Then the words Swan needs: *Ellswarsh invited me to go to his house at Skidegate village where he had some things to show me.*

After breakfast, the first morning of September, *Johnny rowed me to Skidegate village. The distance is about two miles. . . . As soon as our salutations were over, a mat was spread on the floor and two chairs placed, one for me and one for Johnny. Then clean water in a wash bowl with soap and a clean towel to wash our hands and faces. By the time we had finished, the Indians began to come in with things to sell . . .*

The pocket diary becomes a blizzard of buying: *carved spoon . . . scana mask . . . crow mask . . . Embroidered dance shirt of blue blanket, red figure, very fine . . . But as it was Saturday and I wanted to look around the village I concluded to defer other purchases till Monday.*

One matter Swan decides he has deferred long enough: his feelings toward James Deans. Now that Swan is finished sharing canoe and campfire with him several weeks of wrath are unloaded.

I find that Mr. James Deans who accompanied me from Masset and represented that he is in the employ of Dr. Powell has proved himself a great nuisance by interfering with my Indian trade and purchase of curiosities. He represented to parties here that he was in my employ and made bargains with Indians to take me about in canoes which I repudiated. He is filthy in his habits, and untruthful to a degree. I have not suffered him to go with me since I arrived here, and wish I never had seen the man.

This wish will be multiplied in a month or so when he discovers that Powell's Indian Department, considering Deans's assignment no longer valid when he missed the *Otter* and the first several weeks in the Queen Charlottes, will not reimburse Swan for any of the expenses of the free-lancing Deans.

Sunday, the second of September, the Indians dispatched for black cod return with twenty-five of the fish. Specimens the bodies may be, but *I had the tongues cut out and fried, and a chowder made of the heads, and roes and livers fried. They were all first rate....*

Monday, the third of September, brings a new bargain. *Ellswarsh to come tomorrow morning and take me in his large canoe to Skedanse village, Cumshewas, Laskeek and other places* of the eastern coast of the Queen Charlottes, the living shore of Haida culture.

DAYS SEVENTY-EIGHT, SEVENTY-NINE, EIGHTY

I noticed one of the great slimy slugs, so common on the North West coast, crawling on the floor near my bed, and on throwing it into the fire, Ellswarsh asked me if white men eat slugs. I said no, we do not.... He said that Indians did not eat them, but that chinamen do.... He was at Fort Essington last year, at the cannery at Skeena mouth. The chinamen who worked at the cannery made a soup of the slugs and crows which were boiled together in a big iron kettle. Those chinamen, said he, are different people from Indians, we dont eat slugs and crows, they would make us sick ... but the chinamen like em, they eat all the crows and slugs and all the soup, and scrape the kettle with their spoons, chinamen no good.

This is a new kind of a mess and I make note of it as slugs and crows may yet find a place on the bill of fare at the Driard House in Victoria, or Delmonico's in New York.

* * *

High good humor from Swan in this final chapter of his Queen Charlottes exploit. Slugs and soup and Chinamen, I almost expect cabbages and kings next on the triplicate pages. The collecting jaunt to the eastern shore has begun with Ellswarsh and three paddlers pulling in for Swan and Johnny Kit Elswa the morning of the fourth of September, and hard weather at their heels. The party canoes out of Skidegate Inlet and around the first point of coast southward, meets the full whap of storm, scuttles for shore. *Wind blew so violently that it was difficult to pitch my tent but having succeeded with the united aid of the whole party I found myself very comfortable, and I invited Ellswarsh to share my tent and table.* (And mentally invited the memory of Edinso to look on and howl?) Johnny Kit Elswa and the canoemen occupy a second tent and take their meals *in the open air by the camp fire.* Unluckily for Swan the first of those meals features *some red berries which they mixed with grease....* *They were sour and ... cleaned me out good.*

Freshly scoured from the inside out, Swan wakes the next morning to a fair wind. This rare chance to hoist a sail brings the canoeists early to the village of a chief named Skedance. *He gave us a hearty welcome and soon had a breakfast ready, composed of dried halibut and fish oil, fish eggs, boiled dried salmon, and boiled dried dulse mixed with fish eggs and red huckleberries.* So far off his feed from the previous night's experiment with berries-and-oil is Swan that he passes up this imaginative smorgasbord for bread and tea. His mood anyway is to bargain. After breakfast *Skedance showed me a fine chest or box elaborately carved, but did not name any price. He showed me some other things, and I bought of him two dancing hats, a bow and arrows made of copper, used as ornaments while dancing and a carving in wood resembling an eagles foot holding a salmon.*

Think of Swan by now as a person who has shopped through the supermarket and at the end of the last row begins to fill the basket as a reward to himself. In the next week at the villages of Skedans and Laskeek, Swan procures example after example of the Haida magic of knifestroke-onto-wood-or-stone. *I bought quite a lot,* he understates on his final day of bargaining, the tenth of September; his total trove to the Smithsonian, together with the fish specimens, was an eventual twenty-nine freight boxes' worth.

Swan's days, weeks, months of unveiling the Queen Charlottes have ended. He deserves to deliver his own last words. *I have had a rough time since I left Masset but have gained in health and knowledge and leave the islands with regret.* The refinery superintendent at Skidegate has told him the supply steamer departs for Victoria in a matter of days. *So I began to prepare to go on her as there will not be another steamer here till next spring and although I would like to remain all winter to see the medicine dances and masquarade performances I . . . must avail myself of this opportunity to return to civilization.*

DAY EIGHTY-ONE

Swan's first set of hours at sea for Victoria:

I dreamed last night that little Jangi, Jimmys boy, was in bed with me and told me that we should have a pleasant day and a fair wind, both of which we have had. In fact this has been one of the most delightful days I ever saw.

I found on waking, that I did not have Jangi but a wooden image of an Indian Skaga or doctor which I had put on the back side of my berth, which probably caused my dream.

DAYS EIGHTY-TWO, EIGHTY-THREE

Victoria, in almost-spring sun.

Not at all like the dry and dowdy little Queen whose name it wears, this capital of British Columbia. Rather, the city is in the manner of the youngest daughter of some Edwardian country-house family, attractive and passionately self-absorbed and more than a little silly.

Victoria imagines among other things that it is a sward of Olde England somehow rolled out like turf over Western Canadian bedrock. Consequently you can sip tea in the massive Empress Hotel while across the street, seaplanes yatter in and out of the Inner Harbor with shaggy civil servants from up-island or logging company men off to soon-to-be-deforested shores. A block away the Parliament building presides in grand daffy Empire style, a sprawl of gray stone beneath a central dome; the entirety of this castle of government outlined with lightbulbs so that at night it blazes like a profile in a fireworks display. I never look at it without expecting the dome to begin spewing up skyrockets.

Such preoccupation with glitter is not new. British troops and sailors stationed at Victoria in the last century would drill in such solemnly spectacular style that the watching Haidas went home and asked a missionary to teach them such fine maneuvers. To gauge from Swan's entries of his occasional visits to Victoria he noticed that the town was a bit high-faluting: *Had my hair cut. Paid 75¢   a Victoria swindle.* For its part Victoria likely found Swan a little too Americanly robust in his drinking and his opinions. (*Wrote to Dr Powell a letter of apology for my actions while in Victoria,* runs one diary entry of earlier years.) But according to the holdings of the Provincial Archives all seems forgiven on both sides when Swan arrived back from the Queen Charlottes in late September of 1883. The Victoria *Daily Colonist* pronounced that "Mr. Swan's researches have been conducted with assiduity and attended with success" and began running a series of articles written by him about his exploit. Better yet the British Columbia legislature invited Swan to speak, and he instructed the lawmakers for more than an hour about their little-known northern archipelago. Two notable features were his snub of Deans—*I had no occasion for the services of a white man, and consequently took none in any capacity*—and his runaway enthusiasm for black cod, which took up nearly half his address.

The British Columbians voted him their appreciation, and here I give him my ovation as well. Swan's west shore adventure defeated some of the North Pacific's most difficult weather. From the Haidas of the eastern shore villages he purchased—which is to say preserved, brought forward for posterity's study —a wealth of Haida craft and art. With his combination of pencil and pen and eventual typewriter he added to the lore known of the Haidas, at a time when it was not at all certain that the tribe itself would survive. Most of all he did his dare of himself: went off to one more West, lived according to the place's own terms, and came home to tell about it. I think of my last miles of walking out of the Rockies from the Marshall Wilderness and of hikes completed in the Olympic Mountains and along the Cape Alava shore, and believe I know some whisper of Swan's satisfaction.

The other journeyers of 1883, I turn elsewhere in the Provincial Archives to trace.

Deans died at Victoria in 1905. The lasting effects of his jaunt with Swan seem to have been some lame poetry ("On a Queen Charlotte Island Mountain Torrent": *Up in the mountains high/Springs a small river/Down through the forests high/Rushing for ever*) and an enthusiasm for Indian legends and artifacts. "He was always digging for Indian trophies. . . . He was looked upon, therefore, by many as a complete crank, an eccentric."

Edinso lived until 1897. His age was uncertain, but probably he was at least eighty-five when death at last caught him. A white settler at Masset remembered of Edinso's last years that "the old chief would wander around the village with an old blanket around him and a staff in his hand and an old stub clay pipe in his mouth. The old fellow would call on my mother at the Hudson's Bay house, come in the back door of the kitchen and sit on his haunches beside the stove and tell her yarns of the ancient glories of the Haidas." The *Colonist's* last word on Edinso was the declamation that "it is doubtless partly owing to his influence and example that the Haidas have taken so readily to civilized ways and become one of the most law abiding tribes on the Coast."

The famous man of the bunch is the carver, Charlie Edenshaw (as his name has come down in history). ". . . We now
know he was a prodigy among a race of artists," runs one en-
comium. Examples of his work in ivory and coal-black stone
called argyllite proudly grace the display cases of the Provincial
Museum, and in his name the Canadian government has erected
a memorial longhouse at Masset.

Of Johnny Kit Elswa there is a print of the studio photo
posed with Swan before they left Victoria for the north, and not
a trace more.

I decided to make one more delve, to the Ethnology Division
of the Provincial Museum to go through their collection of
photos taken in the Queen Charlottes in the nineteenth century.
A photographer made a stay at Masset and Skidegate the year
after Swan, and the village skylines of carved columns counted by
Swan rise vividly, the Masset carvings more fluid with images,
the Skidegate monuments more often topped with single great
bird figures. One bold Skidegate eagle seems ready to flap away
with the sixty-foot column in his claws.

As I flip the last of these hundred-faced horizons, ethnologist
Alan Hoover happens by from his office. "I've got something
to show you." He leads me to a back room shelved full of tribal
masks and baskets, reaches into a drawer, turns, grins, opens his
fist to me.

"Jesus," I breathe. "Jesus, Jesus. It's Jumbo."

Across the palm of Alan Hoover's hand the ivory elephant's
head lies like a meld of silver and gold. The trunk has been
carved and accented by Charlie Edenshaw so that it looks like
the downspout of a faucet; a glorious fat aqueduct of a snoot.
Jumbo's eyes are the large teardrop shape often seen in Haida
art, without iris or pupil, at once blank as blindness and seeing
all. His tusks curve up and across the trunk and like it are plump
and blunt. This is plainly an elephant of gaiety rather than ram-
page, and the carver put even more play to him by substituting
for flaplike ears a sweeping coiffure of elegant waves and tucks,

very much as if Jumbo had decided to wig up for an appearance at the court of Louis XIV.

What came into Swan's head when he first looked upon this suave beast of Charlie Edenshaw's at Masset ninety-six years ago I cannot know. But I find myself absurdly remembering a sardonic quote read somewhere: "'Every man for himself!' cried the elephant as he danced among the chickens." Or perhaps not absurd, for this is a wondrous ivory Haida Jumbo who can be imagined dancing with serene care, when he chooses, in any company whatsoever, capable as well of minuet and magical circling prance within a firelit longhouse.

DAY EIGHTY-FOUR

Swan to Baird:

I think that your attention has not been called to the fact that there is a balance due me of $1,147.82. . . . Those Englishmen in Victoria cannot understand why I could not have closed my accounts with them at the close of the year 1883. . . .

And Baird to Swan:

I notice what you say about coming east some time with your Haidah Indian, and overhauling the collections, and putting them properly in order. I have no doubt that it would be of great advantage to us, but the question is as to the means to compass it. . . .

Familiar shuttlecock, which the corresponding pair has been carrying on since Swan's completion of the Makah memoir two decades earlier. But Swan is arriving to the time of his life when the familiar begins to evaporate rapidly. Over the next few years he does a few dabs of local collecting for Baird and the Smithsonian, tries every so often to pry up some support there for another Queen Charlottes journey, then on the twentieth of August of 1887, the diary entry with a black box stroked around:

The news comes today of the death of Professor Baird who died yesterday at Woods Hole   Mass—I set my flags at half mast in token of my respect for his memory.

The Smithsonian itself passes from Swan next. By the end of 1889 he has written:

Professor Baird's death was a great blow to me from which I have not recovered. There is a new deal and no sympathy in Washington. A new king has arisen over Egypt who knows not Joseph.

These half-dozen years from the Queen Charlottes achievement to that disgusted sign-off of the Smithsonian emerge from the diary pages to me as written echoes. Line upon startling line the pen's *skritch skritch* now murmurs reprise of Swan's earlier Port Townsend life. Dolly Roberts has married a naval lieutenant and become Dolly Biondi, but Swan is drawn briefly to another well-made young lady: *Grand opening ball at Learneds Opera House. Took Harriet Appleton and danced for the first time in my life at a ball. Had a good time & got home at 2 AM.* He is back at the usual sheaf of paperwork jobs; his letterhead recites *Attorney at Law and Proctor in Admiralty   United States Commissioner   Commissioner of Oregon for the State of Washington   Notary Public   Hawaiian Consul* and there are constant matters in the ungirdled Port Townsend style: *Capt Moore of US Rev Cutter Wolcott came this morning to ask my advice about his Chinese steward who smuggled some opium on board when the cutter was last in Victoria, and yesterday he brought it ashore in the Captain's soiled linen and attempted to sell it to the steward of the Rush, now lying in port. There were 8 pounds of this opium which he seized & confiscated and now has the Chinaman in Irons. I told Capt Moore that I thought if he kept the Chinaman in irons for 10 days, it would be punishment enough as the loss of the opium worth $100 added to being 10 days in irons would be a sufficient vindication of the law and ... I did not think it necessary to put the Government to the expense of a trial.* He jaunts to Boston and family another time, goes to Matilda's grave, with more sentiment than scruple of fact plucks a geranium leaf as *a memento of my dear wife.* He occasionally visits Neah Bay, or Neah Bay will visit him: *Sch Lottie arrived from Neah this morning. All Jimmys family came up on the schooner. I took Jangi to Peysers store and gave him a complete outfit. He returned to the vessel as proud as an eagle.* Swan remains ready, at the nudge of a pen nib, to share with any correspondent his Indian lore: *Recd letter from Mrs Mary B Leary Seattle requesting me to give her an Indian word suited for the new City Cemetery—I suggested "Washelli" the Makah word for west wind, and quoted from "Hiawatha" to show that the west is the "region of the hereafter," and that "Washelli Cemetery" would mean the "Cemetery of the land of the here-after."* His palate is as enthusiastic as ever: *Capt Dalgardno called on me this evening and we celebrated New Years with a pitcher of punch stuffed olives and potted duck and felt much refreshed.* And so is his sporadic thirst for alcohol, for again, on the first of June of 1885, there is another court order adjudging and decreeing that "James G. Swan is an Habitual Drunkard...." As ever he keeps this hooded, like a falcon never allowed to flap up into view from his writing wrist: his page this day reports instead that *This morning I eat a hearty breakfast of salt cod and potatoes which caused a violent fit of indigestion.*

Yet something fresh does speak within the diary lines, and it is that Swan the pioneer is shading into Swan the Pioneer. I have watched this happen before, among the two Montana genera-tions older than mine: homesteaders or cowboys or sheepmen who endured decades enough that longevity began to intensify their outline, as a tree against an evening sky will become more and more darkly stroked, distincter than reality. Part of the process is simply to outlive the other figures from your time and Swan definitely has been doing so; his pages at times read like a visitation book as he makes calls on sinking Port Townsend acquaintances. Part of it as well is to have honed a skill sharper than those of your neighbors, and Swan has become rightly recognized for his knowledge of the coastal native cultures. As President Hayes had done in 1880, the famed anthropologist Franz Boas in July of 1889 pays his respects to Swan as a rare ambassador to the tribes. (Their introduction occurred in Victoria: *Met Dr Franz Boaz and went with him to see a lot of Haidas which had just arrived. They were all drunk but civil.*) And yet another part of the capping of the *P* of "pioneer" simply is—what else would it be in Swan's case?—literal: he joins and is an enthusiastic member of an old-timers' group called Washington Pioneers.

He amply qualifies. Washington Territory was not yet created when Swan sailed into Shoalwater Bay that late autumn of 1852, and now, the eighteenth of November of 1889 at Olympia:

This is the Inauguration day when we become a State.

The town is crowded to excess   The pioneers met at Columbia Hall and each one had a nice badge furnished....

At 10 AM we marched out and took our places in the grand procession. First the Tacoma Band, then the Pioneers headed by E C Ferguson   President, James G Swan   Vice President, Frank Henry   Secretary, & Geo A Barney   Treasurer. Then followed some 50 or 60 Pioneers, men & women   Then the Military, more bands   the Governors   members of the Legislature and citizens generally....

DAYS EIGHTY-FIVE, EIGHTY-SIX, EIGHTY-SEVEN

This has been a stormy cold disagreeable day, the first of February of 1893. *Snow falling all day. The worst day this winter. I have felt much depressed with the many deaths of friends since New Years. Felix Dobelli lies dead at the Undertaker and Capt Sampson died last Sunday and Mrs. Morrison is very low. My turn may come soon.*

The diaries of the 1890s. Common tan pocket notebooks for the decade's opening year. Not auspicious. But for 1891, an elongated Standard diary with maroon leather covers and gilt page edges. Notebooks again for 1892. Then beginning with

1893, five volumes in a row with *Excelsior Diary* in gilt script across a maroon cover. 1894 is longer and slimmer than the other Excelsiors, but the group is more uniform than any other of Swan's sets of years.

For Swan and his town, the decade itself is not at all so orderly, and red ink the more usual coloration than maroon. Port Townsend had boomed at the end of the 1880s; seven thousand population, streetcar lines, an electricity plant fed with slabwood; the big downtown buildings which still stand, three- and four-story dowagers of stone and brick, were built then. Naturally, railroad hopes had freshened. A line called the Port Townsend Southern, the first mile laid by the townspeople themselves, caught the attention of eastern railroad men—officials of the Union Pacific this time—and drew a promise of completion to Portland. The acreage Swan bought west of town twenty years earlier at last looked as if it would pay off; an offer of $100,000 had been made to him, he exulted to his daughter Ellen. Swan had bet as well by investing in a fish processing plant, and Franz Boas was salarying him to do some artifact collecting for the famous Columbian Exposition in Chicago.

Then with the depression of 1893, financial fizzle for both Port Townsend and Swan. Again no railroad, again no profit from the long-held land.

Whether the dull day, the eleventh of January, 1894, *or as a precursor of bad news I have felt remarkably dull and low spirited. The times are very dull, taxes are due and no money to pay them and I feel as if I have lost all.*

But there are thousands of people worse off, and I have good health. I have much to be thankful for, but I feel very despondent.

As when he explored the west shore of the Queen Charlottes, Swan now is going into territory where I, as a modern winterer, cannot follow. Just once have I experienced the dearth of money which plagues Swan now—sixteen years ago, when I arrived back to Montana out of the Air Force, stepping off the train at Ringling with two dollars, both of them borrowed—and mine was only a moment, tiniest fraction of his new chronic brokeness.

Stormy day, the twenty-sixth of December 1895, *remained at home and dyed my pilot jacket which had become faded and rusty   I used diamond navy blue dye and tomorrow I can tell how I have succeeded.* The next day: *Pressed out my navy jacket and it looks as good as new. The old pantaloons which I dyed and pressed a few days ago, and this fresh dyed jacket make my friends think I have just bought a new suit of clothes. I am much pleased as now I can renovate my old clothes with but small cost....*

Nor can I truly share the fact of age as it works now on Swan. I can watch his reports of decline in the diary pages of 1896 and 1897, how the wide days of Northwest summer seem to mean less to him now, and the days of coastal winter grow newly treacherous—*Snow showers this evening. I slipped down on the crossway and sprained my right thumb.* How he records as ever the letters sent and received, whom he has called on, met on the street, borrowed two dollars from, but all the while the incidents of his life becoming smaller and smaller, a walk around town chronicled as a canoe trip to Neah once had been.

I see, and am moved by, the way Swan begins to be cared for by his coastal friends. The women who were the Roberts sisters of Swan's smitten sentences of twenty years before, Dolly Biondi and Mary Webster, take turns with Sarah Willoughby, wife of the Makah Reservation agent during Swan's last trio of years at Neah Bay, in hearing again his stories, seating him to the table: *Dined at Mrs Websters on Stewed chicken, mushrooms and huckleberry pudding—delicious.* His landlord forgives him his office rent, the family of Jimmy Claplanhoo—Jimmy has fledged into *Capt James Claplanhoo* in the diary, owner and skipper of a schooner of his own—provides frequent visits from Cape Flattery and an occasional gift of a suit of clothes.

Study as I may, however, I know I do not grasp this process, silent as spiderspin, which is happening to Swan here and which is called age. My belief is that we cannot truly see ourselves as we will be when old; perhaps dare not; and so are unable to imagine very far into the oldness of others. All I can learn for certain from Swan, and it may be plenty, is that now some of his days are better than other of his days, but no day is easy.

Yet if such information must be secondhand until I encounter age myself, this would not be Swan's wordstream if it were not also clear as a diary pen can make it. On the first of April of 1898, Swan's eightieth year, he begins to use an old but unfilled pocket diary, a mustard-colored Standard published for 1890. Generally he remembers to add the tiny loop of ink atop the o of 1890 to transform the year, but when he doesn't, it is as if his entries ebb back and forth between the years the way—life imitates life—this winterbook has traveled between his time and mine.

The twenty-eighth of June: *Weighed myself on Joe Gates scales I weighed 143 pounds the lightest I have weighed in some time My long sickness pulled me down but I am getting better slowly.*

The twelfth of July: *Mr. Springs of Everett was here to day and talked against Port Townsend, said . . . if the rail road is completed it will do no good as vessels will all load at Seattle and a lot more such rot. I told him if the road is completed to here, that trains of cars can bring their grain direct to Port Townsend as well as to Seattle or Everett, but he would not admit that. . . .*
I told him he is an old fossil & he had better remain in Everett as it is an evidence of ignorance and bad taste to go into a town and run it down before its residents. He is a regular crank and is fit for such a place as Everett.

The second of August: *Have felt very much depressed all day. Think there is to be a change of weather.*

The seventh of August: *I did not go to church, as it seemed that everything was wrong about my clothes and I did not get ready to go out till 12 o'clock noon.*

The twenty-fourth of August: *A lot of Quilliute and Makah Indians arrived today and camped at Point Hudson　They are going to pick hops I went down to the beach to see them. They all knew me and were glad to see me. It looked like old times to see so many Indians on the beach.*

The eleventh of September: *Commenced a letter to my daughter Miss Ellen M Swan. The letter I received from her on the 7th I burned as it was a very disagreeable one.*

The fifteenth of September: *Mrs. Webster gave me a bagfull of doughnuts for bringing her mail from the Post Office to her however I took the doughnuts to Mrs Biondis and her sharp perceptive faculties soon found out the contents of the parcel and she soon had an impromptu course of hot coffee　cake and doughnuts　we enjoyed them.*

The tenth of October: *Dr Brooks O Baker examined me for vertigo which has troubled me at intervals since last January. He said it proceeds from heart weakness and gave me a prescription of his own preparing, of which strychnine forms one of the ingredients　Commenced taking Dr Bakers medicine this afternoon.*

The thirtieth of December: *Have had quite an attack of vertigo this evening.*

DAY EIGHTY-EIGHT

My first birth day in the new century, the eleventh of January 1900. *82 years old. May this new Era bring new prospect and may I live to see its so glorious promise unfold. . . . I have been reading evenings in my diaries and it seems singular to see half my life therein . . . 50 years ago I left Boston and 41 I began my daily journal but yet my early years at Neah Bay are fresh to my mind   Only when I recall the deaths of so many friends   Prof Baird   Maj Van Bokkelin   friend Webster   Bulkley & store-keeper Gerrish   my own dear son Charley last year, does the time seem so long as it is. And the Indians I formerly knew are gone   Swell   Duke of York   old Edinso   Capt John   only Peter alive . . . Ellens letters and the little sums she sends are all I have now to tide me over to improved times. My wish is that Pt Townsend will yet take its rightful place as the most magnificent city of the west and that my burden of debt will pass from me. As the Poet John G Whittier writes "for all sad words of tongue or pen   The saddest are these, it might have been!" But if it is ordained otherwise I have other remuneration in life   my collect-ing for the Smithsonian Institution   the Makah memoir   The Northwest Coast   my expedition to the Queen Charlottes Archipelago   the knowledge of Indian ways and language which otherwise would have been lost for future generations, I would not trade for more worldly wealth. For if I have not prospered greatly in my western life yet I am greatly prosperous in what I have done. . . .*

Swan did not write those words. I have written them for him, or rather, for both of us, this dusk of winter and of his life. The archival diaries end with 1898, the volumes of 1899 and 1900 held in a private collection, but the entries have been dwindling anyway, Swan lamenting to his daughter Ellen his failing grip: *My hand and wrist are still painful and I have to write slow. I don't think this is so much of a Rheumatic affection as it is the pen paralysis from over exertion writing. . . . But it is very annoying to me to have such continual pain in the cords of my hand when I attempt to write. I have been trying a little instru-ment called the "Electropoise" which my cousin Edward kindly sent from New York. It sends a gentle current of electricity to the part affected but it is too much bother for me to use it properly.* Swan hooked to an electrical rheumatism gizmo rather

than a pen is Swan become an old bewildered stranger to himself, I am afraid. From that eighty-second birthday of his, where
my imagination takes over the telling, he has four months and
a week to live.

But I discover an odd thing as this companion of my winter
begins to fade from life. There at the first days of this century
Swan comes into view to me in a strong new way: as if a white-
instead-of-tawny cat suddenly has padded into sight at the forest
edge. Swan stepping to the century-line which I crossed in his
direction almost three months ago now has endured into time
which touches my own. A little more than a year from that
eleventh morning of 1900, my father will be born at the homestead in Montana. The grandmother who will share in raising me
already is a seven-year-old farmgirl in Wisconsin. (In history's
less personal terms, put it this way: Swan was born when James
Monroe inhabited the White House and Napoleon was yet alive,
and now he is almost to Theodore Roosevelt's America, and
Einstein already is thinking the world into a nuclear future.)
Connection of lifespans is added to our shared places, our intermingled Wests.

So much of Swan I still do not know, even after studying him
through the fifteen thousand days and two and a half million
words of his diaries. In his lamplit times alone in the schoolhouse tower at Neah or the narrow office at Port Townsend, for
instance, what urges of the night worked in him, moving behind
his brow, under his thatch of beard, atop his thighs. Or why, like
me, he chose to invest his life at this edge of America over all
other—although I think it has most to do in both our cases with
a preference for gossamer possibilities, such as words, rather
than hard and fast obligations, such as terms of employment. Or
why he would admit into his pages whatever peeves he held, but
no hatreds; details of infatuation with a choirgirl, but none of the
fact of it; hints of whiskey, but never direct confession of too
many bottles. Unlearnable, those beneath-the-skin frontiers.
Even the outer ones leave questions, for I believe now that no
one winterbook—no book—can find nearly all that should be
said of the West, the Wests. Profundities of westering there

undoubtedly are, but do they count for more than a liking of mountains and of hearing a waitress say, *There you go* ... ?

What I do take from this time of musing in Swan's Wests is fresh realization that my own westernness is going to have to be a direction of the mind. Personal geography shifts restlessly in America, much as plates of bedrock are said to grind and jostle against one another far under the surface of the earth. My West, or Wests, inevitably are going to be smaller and a bit more skewed than Swan's and the more intensely held, felt, worried over, for that reason.

Yet any separations between Swan's territory and mine mysteriously close at some moments. Scenes of this winter and of Swan's own western-edged seasons do flow together, in the way that beings mingle in one of those magical carvings of the Haidas. ("They weren't bound by the silly feeling that it's impossible for two figures to occupy the same space at the same time.") Perhaps atoms merge out of the landscape into us. However it happens, the places are freshly in me. Whidbey Island, gulls balleting along the roofs of wind. Dungeness Spit, days there glossed with sea ducks and crowned with an eagle. The thrusting Capes, Flattery and Alava, their surfs bringing in perpetual cargoes of sound. This suburban valley, at its mouth the greater gray-blue water valley, Puget Sound. The cabin at Rainier, summing all these sites by being abode for a dweller rather than a citizen.

The patterns explore their way back and forth between centuries as well, and I see with less surprise than I would have three months ago that a torpedo test Swan watches in the Port Townsend harbor will become Trident nuclear submarines in Hood Canal. That his dream of railroad along one shore of Puget Sound must bend and become a transportation megalopolis along this opposite shore. That his introduction of the alphabet in the Neah Bay schoolhouse in 1863 has led to a federal grant for the preservation of the Makah language. That no more than Swan knew of such eventuating can I know what is ahead for my West.

And there, in that specific rill of realization, I suppose is the truest bond of pattern I have to you, Swan, old coastal nomad, remembrancer of so many diary pages, canoeist of yestertime. Winter brother.

DAY EIGHTY-NINE

Sometime in the morning of the eighteenth of May of 1900, Swan lies in his room and listens for footsteps. They are slow to come, time needed for it to dawn on one or another downtown citizen of Port Townsend that the old man has not been seen to emerge to the street as usual. Feet at last are heard and a knock questions through the door; then, silence all too much answer, the inquiring friend forces in to find Swan where the stroke has pinned him.

Life stays in Swan through that paralyzing day, but only half the night.

He is buried near the center of this graveyard west from Port Townsend's headland of houses, under a gray marble stone. Rust-orange lichens have crept down into the cut letters but they can be read: PIONEER-HISTORIAN   JAMES G. SWAN   BORN MEDFORD MASS. JAN. 11, 1818   DIED PORT TOWNSEND WASH. MAY 18, 1900. From here at the graveside my automatic line of sight is across the land Swan owned, to the dark hackled profile of Whidbey Island and beyond to the Cascade Mountains, but the view does have competition from the monuments all around, the urn-topped and pyramid-peaked markers of the merchants and ship's captains thrusting above his low box of stone.

The Port Townsend *Morning Leader* four days after Swan's death: "... The friends of the deceased were permitted to take a last look at the venerable pioneer, and just before the casket was closed a delegation of Indians from Neah Bay appeared and asked permission to take a last look a their oldtime friend and adviser. The Indians as they gazed upon the rigid features gave expressions of their grief in low moans and each affectionately patted the face of the dead man."

Swan's grandnephew in Massachusetts to the Port Townsend lawyer who notified him that debts would swallow Swan's scant belongings: "Of course the manuscripts & diaries can have no great money value . . . and I would hope they might be lodged in some library interested in the special subjects they relate to."

DAY NINETY

Winter's last dozen hours. *Today the Sun crosses the line and it is the first day of spring,* Swan wrote on this date, the twentieth of March, in his lustrous year of 1880 at Neah Bay, then stepped outside to admire his larkspurs and lilies.

As we approach Neah Bay, midmorning sun making shadowplay with the trees and sea boulders along the shore of the Strait, I calculate where we will be when spring arrives tonight at nine twenty-two: back aboard the big ferry, south from Port Townsend by about an hour; near Point No Point, its lighthouse the ushering beam from Admiralty Inlet into Puget Sound: almost home.

Two sites ahead of us before then. One is the rock tip at Cape Flattery where Carol and I will be by midday to watch for whales in northward migration, out past Tatoosh Island. From our watching times elsewhere on this coast, other springs, we know that first the spouts will be glimpsed, small here-and-gone geysers in the ocean, then sudden blades of dark in the water that are the gray whales. Only those ridges of their backs—the wet island of being which the Makah hunting canoes shadowed in on—rising in quick glistening view, until for an instant the great Y of a tail is seen to lift, then plunge.

But before the whales the stop at Neah Bay. Sometime amid this winter's constant scud of words the brief casual news: oh yes, *that* still exists, it's tricky to find but if you ask so-and-so at Neah Bay. . . .

Luck. We reach Neah at low tide and the rock deck of shore beneath the low coastal precipice lies open to us. A young woman who works for the Makah Tribal Council leads us beneath the cliff face, peering carefully. In a minute or so she says: "There it is. There." As she returns up the bluff to her construction work—the Makahs are building a greenhouse of translucent plastic to grow vegetable seedlings; progress I am glad to see from Swan's depot of potatoes—we are left with the bayline sheet of rock.

The sun's brightness stops a stride or so short of the cliff. Shadowed sandstone swells as high as my chest, bulges and rounds there and then recedes as a sudden ledge, angled at about thirty degrees. That afternoon in 1859 Swan stood atop something, likely a driftlog long since reclaimed by the Strait, to reach this beveled shelf. The deep-cut letters *J G S* are level with my eyes, and above them rides the stone swan.

Tail fluted high to a jaunty point.

Neck an elaborate curve gentle and extended as a suitor's caress.

Breast serenely parting the shadowed current of cliff.

As Carol inserts a roll of film into her camera I span my hand three times to measure the length of the bird, less than half that for its height. A bit more than two feet long, a bit less than a foot high, this swimmer of rock. Swan's diary entry for the afternoon of that long-past day is this project—*Worked carving a swan on a sandstone cliff with my initials under it*—and surely the stone embossment took the full set of hours. So clearly and intently did he sculpt that only the downthrust of the bird's head, where the beak and eyes would be, has faded with 120 years' erosion, the weathering-away providing a demure mask of time.

Otherwise Swan's swan, as I step back until it is just visible within the cliff-shadow, punctuates the flow of this coast as firmly for me as it did for him. The stone dot that puts period—and seed of the ellipsis for whatever continuation is on its way—to this winter.

ACKNOWLEDGMENTS

The first gratitude of anyone working with the diaries of James G. Swan must be to Lucile McDonald. Her articles in the Seattle *Times* of the early 1950s and her subsequent *Swan Among the Indians* (Binfords & Mort, 1972) are particularly valuable for background of the early—New England—portion of his life, which Swan himself tended to gloss over.

Throughout the time I spent with the Swan diaries in the Manuscripts Section of the University of Washington library, I enjoyed the unfailingly attentive talents of the staff there: University Archivist Richard Berner, Curator of Manuscripts Karyl Winn, Eve Lebow, Connie Pisano, Robert Mittelstadt and Christine Taylor. I was similarly fortunate in the skills and diligence of the staff of the library's Northwest Collection: Head of Special Collections Robert Monroe, Librarian Andrew Johnson, Dennis Andersen, Susan Cunningham, Sandy Kroupa and Glenda Pearson. And Georgia Kloostra of the library's Newspaper and Microcopy Center cheerfully helped me follow the most evanescent traces of Swan.

At Port Townsend, Helen Burns and Deborah McBride guided me through the Swan holdings of the Jefferson County Historical Society. In Victoria, the British Columbia Provincial Museum and the Provincial Archives were helpful to me in countless ways; I owe specific and special thanks to Alan Hoover of the museum's Ethnology Division. At the Smithsonian Institution, Deputy Archivist William A. Deiss and James R. Glenn, Archivist of the National Anthropological Archives, traced Swan correspondence for me.

My appreciation as well to the Makah Indian Nation for the hospitality of their Reservation; to anyone interested in the tribal past I recommend a visit to the Makah Cultural and Research Center at Neah Bay.

For their typing of the various drafts of this book, I'm grateful to Billee Lewis, Karen Murphy, Marilyn Ridge, and Merlyn Talbot.

Vernon Carstensen and David Hawke devoted an inspired evening to pondering the white tribe with me; Mark Wyman provided one quote I never would have unearthed, Susan Schrepfer provided another: double benefit in having historians for friends.

Finally, I'm indebted, on various grounds, to: Pat Armstrong, Gary Bettis, Eileen Bouniol, Richard Daugherty, Cliff Fiscus, Bill Holm, Pat Kelley, Robert Kelley, Amy d'Ernee Mates, Ann Nelson, Marshall Nelson, Myron Ogden, Jean Roden, John Roden and Victor Scheffer.

And Carol Doig.